RON WOLF AND THE GREEN BAY PACKERS

RON WOLF AND THE GREEN BAY PACKERS

Mike Holmgren, Brett Favre, Reggie White, and the Pack's Return to Glory in the 1990s

MICHAEL BAUMAN

SPORTS PUBLISHING

Sports Publishing books may be purchased in bulk at special discounts for sales promotion, corporate gifts, fund-raising, or educational purposes. Special editions can also be created to specifications. For details, contact the Special Sales Department, Sports Publishing, 307 West 36th Street, 11th Floor, New York, NY 10018 or sportspubbooks@skyhorsepublishing.com.

Sports Publishing® is a registered trademark of Skyhorse Publishing, Inc.®, a Delaware corporation.

Visit our website at www.sportspubbooks.com.

10 9 8 7 6 5 4 3

Library of Congress Cataloging-in-Publication Data is available on file.

Cover design by Tom Lau
Cover photo credits: Getty Images

ISBN: 978-1-68358-277-9
Ebook ISBN: 978-1-68358-278-6

Printed in the United States of America.

To all the Packer fans who waited—often for years,
often in the cold—for better days.

CONTENTS

FOREWORD

"DON'T GO THERE."

Those were the words Ron Wolf repeatedly heard when he told people he was contemplating an offer that would make him the general manager of the Green Bay Packers.

"You can't win there."

This was conventional wisdom in the National Football League in 1991. When the Packers were mentioned in the league at that time, it was often in the context of an angry coach telling a misbehaving and/or under-achieving player: "If you don't stop screwing up, I'm going to trade you to Green Bay."

It was the biggest threat to a player, short of a career-ending injury. Green Bay: Bitterly cold. Frozen tundra. Ice and snow for half of the year. And the town was small—oh, so small, by NFL standards—about 97,000 souls according to the 1990 census. This was no place for a professional sports career, unless you were a professional ice fisherman.

Yes, there had been greatness there before. There was the Vince Lombardi era when it was known as "Titletown, USA." Three NFL titles, and then two Super Bowl championships over seven years, and the "Ice Bowl" became not a joke about a truly difficult climate but a saga of man mastering the Arctic elements. And way before that, there were six NFL championships under the Packers founder and coach, Earl (Curly) Lambeau.

But in November 1991, as Wolf pondered the Green Bay situation, all anybody knew for sure about the Packers was that in the 24 years since Lombardi stepped down as head coach, the Packers had qualified for the playoffs only twice. And one of those came in a strike-shortened season.

They were 148–207–9 in those years. Worse still was the fact that each succeeding Packers head coach put up a record that was worse than his immediate predecessor.

The core problem was not actually the climate, or the size of the town, or even the frozen tundra. The most charming and singular fact of the Packers' existence, their public ownership, was also their curse.

Five times during their 100 years of existence, the Packers were in real need of money. So, they had a stock sale. The first time this happened, in 1923, the stock went for $5 per share. The most recent time it happened, in 2011, the stock went for $250 per share. But, from a fiscal standpoint, the stock was, and still is, worthless, never returning a nickel to the buyer. There is never a dividend. But it does make the stockholder a part-owner of the Packers, which at least drives up the emotional price of following the team. There are more than five million shares, in the hands of roughly 361,000 citizens.

Sitting atop the stockholders is a 45-person board of directors. Above that body is a seven-person executive committee. So far, this is a wonderful story about community involvement and grass-roots democracy. But there have been occasions when the people making football decisions were not necessarily actual football experts. As Bob Harlan, the team president and Packers CEO at the time of Wolf's hiring put it, it was like asking the guy who owned the hardware store to run a hospital.

This is what was happening in the post-Lombardi era. A Packers president would be elected, and then he would bring in his favorite Lombardi-era player to run the football operation. Bart Starr was unprepared when he got the job, but then grew into the coaching aspect of it. When he had become at least an adequate coach, Judge Robert Parins, team president, fired him, because this was a team president who wanted Forrest Gregg to take charge. Gregg could coach, but what he couldn't do was be a general manager. He didn't have that title in Green Bay, but unfortunately, he was given that sort of power with the Packers.

Just before Wolf was hired the Packers had a 50–50 power sharing relationship between the head coach and the general manager. In case of a tie, that's right, the president of the team had the tie-breaker. This is how, with the second pick of the 1989 draft, the Packers took tackle Tony Mandarich, who turned out to be largely a pharmaceutical creation, instead of Barry Sanders, who would become one of the all-time great running backs elsewhere.

The public was losing faith. And since the Packers are essentially a shared religious belief in Wisconsin, that's saying a lot. I'm not looking at this from afar. I was born in Green Bay, I grew up in northeastern Wisconsin, and I wrote extensively about the Packers as a sports columnist for the *Milwaukee Journal* and its successor the *Milwaukee Journal-Sentinel*, before and throughout Wolf's tenure. I was in the stands at the Ice Bowl, for the entire game, which demonstrated a serious, if not dangerous, level of interest.

By mid-1989, Harlan had risen to the Packers presidency. After a 6–10 season in 1990, and with 1991 headed in an even worse direction, he decided that an immediate restructuring was in order. He wanted a football man in charge of the football operation. This was a breakthrough of common sense. An extremely intelligent move would be needed next—having the right man in mind for this task. Fortunately, the man in Harlan's mind was Ron Wolf.

Wolf had put in a long and highly-successful apprenticeship with the Raiders as Al Davis's right-hand personnel man. Wolf then had a short shot with Tampa Bay, when he had the responsibilities of a general manager, but not the authority that the position demanded. That didn't work, but painful as that experience was, it was a football life lesson. Back Wolf went, first to the Raiders and more success, then a short stay with the New York Jets before Harlan called.

Wolf was nearing 53, and he had believed that it might be too late for him to be a GM. But Harlan's offer would give him everything he wanted in the job. And with the voices saying "Don't go there" and "You can't win there," he ran the offer by Al Davis. "It's like you're an owner," Davis told him. Davis would know, after all, because he was an owner. Ron Wolf knew, too, that this was his shot.

Presto. He should go there. He would win there.

Ron Wolf, in nine years as Packers general manager, had a record of 101–57, including the postseason. Even though he took over a 4–12 team, he never had a losing season as Packer GM, and only one .500 season. From oblivion's doorstep, the Packers in the Wolf years won three division titles, played in three conference championships, went to two Super Bowls, and won one of them. They won 25 straight games at Lambeau Field—29 counting the playoffs—from 1995 into 1998. They had once again become, as Wolf would put it, "The masters of the frozen tundra."

Wolf was elected to the Pro Football Hall of Fame in 2015, and deservedly so. What he did in Green Bay was not a miracle. But can we go as far as to call it a resurrection, or at least restoration, or a total revival of this franchise? The operation was, if not deceased, certainly on life support in late 1991. The Lombardi era was merely a memory.

The success that Wolf brought to the Packers lasted far beyond his years as GM. For the 25 years from 1992 through 2016, the Packers were 275–162–1. That was the best record in the National Football Conference over that period. In the AFC, the only team that was better was the Patriots. During the vast majority of this time, the Green Bay football operation was run by people and populated with people who had learned their lessons from Wolf—in scouting, evaluating and believing that working for the Green Bay Packers was not just a job, but a way of life.

Ted Thompson, who was hired by Wolf in 1992, was the Packers general manager from 2005 through 2017, during which time the Packers won six division titles, qualified for the postseason in eight consecutive years, played in three conference championship games, and won one Super Bowl. The Wolf influence in the scouting operation remained in place for years after Wolf left the Packers.

In fact, the Wolf influence has been felt throughout the league. Six men who grew up in pro football as Wolf disciples have become NFL general managers.

True, in the last two years, the Packers have had their first consecutive losing seasons since 1990–91, the last seasons of the pre-Wolf era. Thompson was shuttled into a senior advisor role after the 2017 season. Maybe his most recent drafts weren't up to his earlier standards. Maybe

Aaron Rodgers, the second-highest paid player in the NFL, has moved a few steps further from perfection. But after 24 years of stumbling around in the football wilderness, the 25 years of success still looked a lot like the Promised Land.

"Look at the success that Ron brought us," Harlan said. "The thing I'm always so proud of is after 24 years of being mired in mediocrity, we've had 25 years of being relevant. We've been blessed with having two Hall of Fame quarterbacks, I admit that. Thank you, Lord. It's like having a 20-game winner, 15 years in a row. But we not only had the turnaround, but it's been sustained. But it took somebody like Ron to come in and have the guts to do what he did."

What Wolf did starts with three names: Brett, Mike, and Reggie. There were all sorts of decisions that had to be made to turn 4–12 into a Super Bowl winner, but the quarterback, the head coach, and the dominant defensive end, represented the foundation for success. There were plenty of doubters for each of these decisions, but Wolf was supremely correct each time.

Although Wolf was extremely well-regarded for his work with the Raiders, it was in Green Bay, running his own shop and restoring a franchise to greatness, where he was able to lift his level from invaluable assistant to Hall of Fame general manager.

But don't get carried away with that Hall of Fame status. Ask Wolf about being in the Hall and he will respond: "Ronnie Wolf from New Freedom, Pennsylvania, tied with Shorty Ray for the least famous guy in the Pro Football Hall of Fame."

Hugh (Shorty) Ray, was the NFL's Supervisor of Officials from 1938 to 1952. By reputable accounts, he worked tirelessly to improve officiating techniques and to streamline rules. But Mr. Ray will not be mentioned again in this book. It is time now to relive the Green and Gold revival.

"If you're not getting better, you're getting worse," was one Wolf mantra, which was also a description of the Packers in the 24 years prior to his arrival. For the Packers, though, Wolf was a master at the "getting better" part.

1

Finding Favre

IT WAS LATE November and bleak on the day Ron Wolf took over as the general manager of the Green Bay Packers. His flight in from Chicago was delayed because, of course, it was snowing in Green Bay.

The status of the local football team was no more promising than the climate. Vince Lombardi had been gone for nearly a quarter century. The weather was cold, the town was small, the whole operation was barely even an outpost on the professional football map. The Packers were regressing to a 1950s, pre-Lombardi level of performance. Another small step or two backward and they would be in 1958 again; 1–10–1, including a 56–0 thrashing by the Baltimore Colts.

When Lombardi was here, this became Titletown, USA. In 1991, it was closer to what it had been just before Lombardi; the Siberia of the National Football League.

"I got up there and the snow was above my knees," Wolf recalled. "And it's November."

The snow started falling in what much of the world thought of as autumn. For the next four months, the snowbanks would just keep getting higher. This, though, was not at all the perspective of Wolf upon his arrival. He was not caught in the grip of cold negativity. He was looking for a way to turn a losing team into a winning team, a playoff team, and eventually a championship team, as quickly as possible.

Nearly three decades of experience in the NFL had pointed him toward this moment. He was ready to run a winning team. He was eager to start, but what he wasn't ready to do was to make a fashion statement. His 30 years of pro football personnel experience had not prepared him for this one particular aspect of his introductory press conference.

"I didn't have a suit," Wolf said. "One needs a suit for this. I had an old brown corduroy outfit; that was my suit. That probably went out with Pat Boone and white bucks. I even had a vest, but I didn't wear it."

His remarks were typically concise and to the point.

"I made the statement: 'I was brought here to win.' No shit, Dick Tracy," Wolf said, with a laugh at his own expense.

To revive this team, to revive this entire franchise, Wolf had one aspect of the process squarely in front of him. He had suffered through those two painful seasons in Tampa without a quarterback that approached his high standards. Here, he would be looking, in the first place, for the unique quarterback, the championship quarterback, the one quarterback who could make all the difference.

Wolf had a head start in this enterprise, so finding this rare and potentially franchise-turning quarterback did not take him all that long. Then again, he was a man in a hurry.

Wolf took over as general manager of the Packers in November of 1991. He was nearly 53 years and he was only 19 months removed from a heart attack. The combination of these factors, along with his own competitive, persistent nature, made him a man who would not simply take this opportunity but would seize it, keep it, one way or another, make it work.

"I wanted to speed the process up," Wolf said. "I wasn't sure how many ticks I had left, so I didn't have time to play games, if you will. Everything sped up, everything was done with a certain tempo, with the thought process in mind that we have to make this happen now, not next year or two years."

There were countless moves that Wolf made in his tenure that revived the Packers. But three of those moves stand out, for their intrinsic importance, for their brilliance, for their unmitigated success.

There was the hiring of Mike Holmgren as head coach. Holmgren turned out to be, in addition to a great offensive mind, a true leader of men. There was, in the National Football League's first year of free agency, 1993, the signing of dominant defensive end Reggie White, a powerful player and an equally powerful locker room presence. White gave the Packers instant credibility, not only for the moment, but for a generation of free agents to come.

But perhaps the single most important move was trading for the quarterback who made all the difference, Brett Favre. It was Favre who led the Packers to two Super Bowls, one Super Bowl championship, and perennial playoff contention. It was Favre who won three MVP awards and along the way set an NFL standard for indestructibility with 321 consecutive starts. And this was somebody who had spent the previous year, his rookie season, with the Atlanta Falcons, throwing only five passes, none of them a completion.

But Wolf knew potential greatness when he saw it. He basically bet his career on Favre, and he wagered very well. He gave Favre what turned out to be an incomparable opportunity. Favre knows this as well as anybody. With typical directness, he says: "Without Ron Wolf, there is no Brett Favre."

Wolf, on the other hand, directs the bulk of the overall credit to Favre. "First and foremost, he resurrected a dead franchise," Wolf says. "That's what he did. He breathed life into a dormant franchise. That's what he did. He brought respect back to the greatest place to play in the National Football League: Green Bay, Wisconsin. He did that. A lot of people want to take credit for what he did, but he did it. You know, the Yankees had a place they called 'the House that Ruth Built.' New Lambeau Field, that's 'the House that Favre Built.'"

This may be a chicken-egg sort of question. But the underlying point is that there is more than enough credit to go around. It starts, though, with Wolf's personnel judgment, spotting in Favre the greatness that could occur.

"It's about the right ingredients," Favre says. "And that takes the right GM, and that's the most important part. And the coach Ron hired, Mike Holmgren. Ron orchestrated maybe the greatest free agent acquisition in the history of the NFL in Reggie White. So, what a mastermind. He's not going to take that credit, but I did what he envisioned me doing. I didn't do anything that he didn't think I could do."

In 1990, Favre's senior year at the University of Southern Mississippi, Wolf was working as personnel director for the New York Jets. He was scouting, which is what he had primarily been doing since 1963. Wolf was in Hattiesburg, Mississippi, to see Favre, who led Southern Mississippi to stunning upset victories on the road over Alabama and Auburn that season.

Wolf was initially looking at film of the early portion of the 1990 season. "I went down there early, which was a mistake," Wolf said. "Brett had been in a serious automobile accident that summer, after which he lost 30 inches of his intestine. And he was trying to play and wasn't really that impressive. But he was still impressive. As I was leaving their film room, there was this old film guy, and he said: 'You should look at Favre as a junior.'"

Wolf did that. He was so impressed that he altered his schedule, staying in Hattiesburg for an extra day to study more film and marvel further at Favre's ability. "He was possessed of just an unreal arm," Wolf said. "I don't know how you couldn't see it. I mean, you could hear it. At that time, there were all these 'how-to' movies; how to play this, how to play that, how to play quarterback. The release, the feet, all the other stuff. Well, everything about Favre was perfect, how-to. It was just a matter of how to get it controlled. But when he released the ball, it was released the way it was supposed to be released.

"You don't walk into Auburn and Alabama and beat those teams. You don't do that. Pat Dye, who coached at Auburn, was asked who was the best player he ever coached against, and he said immediately: 'Brett Favre.'"

Wolf returned to the Jets offices and informed Dick Steinberg, the Jets general manager, that Favre would be the best player in the 1991 draft. Steinberg suggested that Wolf meant he was the best quarterback in the draft. No, Wolf said, Favre would be the best player in the entire draft.

Favre reinforced Wolf's case by starring in the East-West Shrine Game, which, at the time, was an ideal showcase for senior college talent. So, the Jets approached the 1991 draft with Favre and Raghib Ismail, star wide receiver and kick returner from Notre Dame, as their potential top choices. When Ismail signed with the Canadian Football

League, the Jets were all in on Favre. They had no first-round pick, because they had taken Rob Moore, a wide receiver from Syracuse, in a supplemental draft. In the second round, the Jets were picking third, behind the Cardinals and the Falcons.

"Dick Steinberg had worked a deal to move in front of Atlanta and we were going to take Favre with that pick," Wolf recalled. "But when it comes down to it, the Cardinals call and say they're not going to do it, the guy they want is there (Mike Jones, defensive end from North Carolina State). So, Atlanta takes Favre. And we pick Browning Nagle (quarterback from Louisville)." Nagle started 14 games in his professional career, and went 4–10, completing 48.7 percent of his pass attempts.

Favre's rookie season consisted primarily of watching. He was activated for only three games. He played in only two. But Wolf's judgment regarding Favre's vast potential had not wavered in the least. And on December 1, 1991, just five days after Wolf was named Packer general manager, the Packers were scheduled to play the Falcons in Atlanta. Wolf told Packers president and chief executive officer Bob Harlan that he had two scouting assignments to wrap up for the Jets, so he would meet him in Atlanta for the game.

It was Harlan who had made the necessary decision to completely revamp the Packers' football decision-making process by giving total authority and autonomy to a football man, in this case, Wolf. The Packers had been operating under a system in which authority on personnel matters was split between the head coach and the general manager, and final decisions rested with the team president. The Packers were essentially operated by a seven-man executive committee, which sat atop a 45-man board of directors. With Harlan's decision, with Wolf's newfound authority, the day of the well-meaning amateur had come to an end in Green Bay football.

"So, I'm sitting in the Atlanta press box Sunday morning," Harlan said. "Ron comes in, sets his briefcase down, and the first thing he says—well, I guess he did say hello—is: 'I'm going to go watch Atlanta's backup quarterback. If his arm is as strong now as it was coming out of college, we're going after him.'

"He left. So, I'm turning the flip card trying to figure out who in the heck this quarterback is. I thought when I turned over the flip card: 'Who's Fav-ray? I don't know who this guy is.'"

Wolf recalls that Ken Herock, Falcons vice president of player personnel, approached him in the press box and said: "If you want to see Brett Favre throw, you've got to go down there now, because once the team comes out, they won't let him take part in any team activities."

How did Herock know that Wolf wanted to see Favre throw? After the 1991 draft, Wolf had called Herock. "He had two Number 1s in that draft—Bruce Pickens, a cornerback from Nebraska and Mike Pritchard, a wide receiver from Colorado. I called him and told him: 'I would have traded both those guys you picked, plus a Number 2, for the guy you picked in the second round,' " Wolf said with a laugh. "So that's how he knew.

"So right away, I tell Bob I'm going to go down to the field and watch Brett Favre throw. But as I'm going down to the field, I'm surrounded by TV stations from Green Bay and Milwaukee, and they want to interview me. So, I never get down to the field. But I know now that I have an opportunity to get Brett Favre. So, I walk back up and tell this to Bob, that we have an opportunity to get this quarterback.

"Ron comes back to the press box," Harlan recalled, "and he says: 'We're going to make a trade for Brett Favre, are you okay with that?' And I said: 'Ron, I promised you last week that you've got total autonomy with no interference. The last thing I'm going to do is tell you, no, we can't do something like that.' He said: 'It's going to be costly.' I said: 'Fine, let's do it.'"

The trade with Atlanta came to fruition on February 10, 1992. The Packers got Favre, the Falcons received the 17th choice in the first round of the draft. They made a trade in which they swapped picks with Dallas, so they ultimately had the 19th pick. With that pick, the Falcons selected Tony Smith, a running back from, ironically enough, Southern Mississippi. He played three years, carrying the ball 87 times, before injuries ended his career. With the 17th pick, the Cowboys selected Kevin Smith, a cornerback from Texas A & M, who had a productive career, starting 93 games for Dallas.

"Atlanta traded that 17th pick to Dallas, who picked a corner who could play," Wolf said with a smile. "But a lot of people just attribute Tony Smith to that trade. I'll go with that."

Either way, it turned out to be a stroke of lasting genius. But there were moments when it didn't appear that way at all. Wolf was thrilled with his new acquisition, so thrilled that he neglected to include the standard language in the deal with Atlanta, making the trade dependent on the player in question passing his physical.

"I was so anxious to get a quarterback, but here, they're handing me the guy that I think, in 1991, is the best player in the draft," Wolf said. "And all it's going to cost me is a Number 1. I can't believe that. So, I'm in such a hurry that I don't put any specifications in the deal, such as 'player must report and pass his physical.' So, the deal is done. And invariably, what happens? He comes in and doesn't pass the physical."

Favre was diagnosed with a degenerative condition in his hip known as avascular necrosis, a lack of blood flow in the joint. It was a grim moment for Wolf. "They came up to my office and Domenic Gentile, our trainer, said: 'You've got to send him back,'" Wolf said. "I'm sitting there thinking: *Shit, I just bought a house. I'm going to be fired, for God's sake. Here it is, February, and my whole world has come tumbling down.*

"But I called Dr. (Patrick) McKenzie (an orthopedic surgeon and Packers team physician), because he had examined Favre when he was coming through the draft and I wanted to know why he hadn't been involved in this thing. And so, Pat explained all this stuff, which was like Greek to me. I didn't know what the hell he was talking about. So, I said to him: 'How long do you think he can play?' He said: 'Well, maybe four or five years.' Shit, that's all I had to hear. So, I went downstairs and said: 'We're passing him.' I think he played a little more than four or five years."

This episode taught Favre a few lessons. "I never was the sharpest knife in the drawer, but I learned a lot about avascular necrosis," Favre said. "Obviously, Bo Jackson made that known nationwide—everyone knew about that. And I was failed by several teams when I came out. Oakland, really was very interested, so was Seattle, so was Atlanta. Oakland and Seattle did take a quarterback in the first round. They passed on me because of my hip, I think. And the Raiders also wanted Todd Marinovich." (Marinovich was drafted by the then Los Angeles

Raiders in the first round of the 1991 draft. He lasted only two years in the NFL and was later plagued by substance abuse issues.)

"I think my hip deterred some people, the hip was just too much of an uncertainty for some teams," Favre said. "Had I not had the hip, maybe I do go in the first round. I don't know that for certain. Like I tell people all the time, they go: 'Atlanta made a big mistake.' I say: 'I'm very thankful for Atlanta in the way things played out. Because I would not have gotten to Green Bay had it not been for Atlanta.' So woulda, coulda, shoulda, it doesn't really matter, that the hip was looming. Would it deteriorate like they said or not? I was betting on the not. Fortunately, it worked out."

The other thing Favre learned was that Ron Wolf was willing to risk a considerable amount on behalf of giving his new quarterback a chance.

"I can't thank the guy enough for taking a shot on me and staying with me and seeing something in me that others didn't see," Favre said. "He deserves all the credit. Look, I just did what he expected me to do.

"But you know what? If I were a GM and I stick my neck out for a player, I expect him to give me everything he's got. I can't promise you that he'll play perfect week in and week out, I can't promise you that he won't get hurt. But what I would expect is, look, I'm sticking my neck out for you, you bust your ass, you do everything I ask you to do.' And I did that. I'm not saying that braggingly. I did what he expected me to do. I wasn't perfect, and it wasn't, 'I'm going to do this for Ron,' but I just did what he wanted me to do, what he paid me to do. And that's all you can ask for. When he says I deserve the credit, what did he pick me up for, what did he make the trade for? Because he knew in his mind that this kid was capable of great things. Ultimately, he was right."

Wolf essentially bet the remainder of his professional life on Brett Favre, questionable hip prognosis and all. Nobody knows that better or appreciates that more than the quarterback himself.

"He did that in a couple of ways," Favre said. "He did it by the trade and by over-riding the physical. Not only did he stick his neck out in that regard, but he stuck his neck out from a physical standpoint, and he's not a doctor."

What emerged over time was not simply a quarterback who was

capable of winning a championship, but a quarterback who became the first in NFL history to pass for more than 70,000 yards, with more than 6,000 completions and 500 touchdowns. Favre won three consecutive MVP Awards. And his durability would become the stuff of legend. Favre set an NFL record by making 297 consecutive starts; 321 counting the playoffs.

There are no expectations that reach that high for that sort of relentless refusal to take a day off.

"Even the great Ron Wolf can't say: 'I knew it all the time,'" Favre said. "I think he would have said what I would have said: 'Then they'll have to drag me off.' I think he would agree to that. Now, will they drag you off after 321 games, or after 100? That's not a question of how tough or not tough a person is. But I think you can meet someone and form a reasonable opinion of how tough they are, how knowledgeable they are. I think he gathered that, and he kind of said: 'Raw, I agree. Tough? Absolutely, no doubt whatsoever. If he's got a broken leg, he's got a broken leg, he can't play. I get that. But he's going to fight through things that maybe other guys wouldn't fight through. And that's what we need because you need someone who's going to be there week in and week out. And also, someone who's mentally tough enough, equally important, to physical toughness.'

"Maybe he saw that, maybe he saw that naïve toughness, if you will. I think he kind of calculated all of that stuff. I don't think he would have said 321 but I think he would have said: 'He will endure a lot more than most guys would.' And it's true, and it goes back to him sitting there brainstorming, thinking okay, the risk/reward thing is probably worth it.'"

There are countless examples of Favre overcoming injuries that would have kept lesser competitors off the field. The one that stands out in the minds of people who observed him closely occurred on November 12, 1995. The previous Sunday, in a loss to the Vikings in Minnesota, he had suffered a severely sprained left ankle that forced him out of the game in the third quarter.

In midweek, several reporters—myself included—were in the locker room at Lambeau Field when Favre hobbled in using a crutch. His ankle was swollen to a grotesque degree. Even more noticeable, was the fact that the swelling appeared to include all the colors of the rainbow. Favre had a gigantic, multi-hued ankle. It was more spectacle than body part.

After the quarterback had made his way, slowly and painfully, out of the locker room, we journalists on hand looked at each other, shook our heads and all agreed on this one notion: "He can't play Sunday."

But Brett Favre did play Sunday. He played against the Bears at Lambeau Field. He completed 25 of 33 passes for 336 yards. He threw five touchdown passes. The Packers needed every bit of his greatness in what became a 35–28 victory over the Bears.

The outlook for Favre during the week leading up to the Bears game didn't include anything resembling those sorts of feats.

"He didn't practice all week and Sunday came around," Mike Holmgren recalled. "The trainer Pepper (Burruss) said: 'Well, we can wrap it up.' I asked Brett: 'Can you play?' He said: 'Well, I can't run around.' I said: 'Can you drop back?' So, he did some of that stuff.

"I said: 'Okay, but if you're a sitting duck and they're banging on you too much, I'm taking you out. And don't give me any pushback on that. If I think you're too vulnerable, because you can't move, I'm going to take you out of the game.' He goes: 'Okay, fair enough.' And then he throws five touchdowns. That was remarkable."

For the coach, it was a lesson in what an immobile Favre could achieve if he stayed within the system and ditched "the goofy stuff," the improvisational gambits that he tried with some frequency. There was that, but this was also the triumph of the quarterback's mentality over adversity. This was one of the most obvious examples of Favre's ability to rise above injury, but it was far from the only one.

"His ankle was ugly," Burruss said. "The thing that I still quiver about with that injury, that ugly, ugly ankle, people under their breath think he took a bunch of Vicodin and played on it. And the coach (Dave Wannstedt of the Bears) said: 'They hoodwinked us. They said the ankle was bad and he'd never play, and he threw for five touchdowns.' But we had no idea that he would throw five passes, let alone five touchdowns. It just became part of revisionist history to say, 'We all knew, because he was a tough bastard.' Well, at that time we didn't know. He was writing his personal legacy at that time."

"If you go back through my career, every time I had a serious injury that was going to keep me out the next week, I played my best football," Favre says. "I can't point to exactly what that was. Maybe the focus was at an all-time high. Knowing the limitations and what needed to be done. Knowing you couldn't run around and they restricted you, made you focus. I don't know. Maybe it helped in regard to calling plays; 'we're not going to call movement plays, because he can't move.' Maybe a simplicity concept had something to do with it.

"The mental toughness was I was determined to play at a high level, week in and week out regardless of whether I was hurt or not. I also remembered that I got my job because the guy in front of me (Don Majkowski) got hurt. If it was an injury he could bounce back from the next week or not, it didn't matter, it was my opportunity.

"I always remembered that. And in the forefront of my mind, I don't care how good you are or what you've done you can be replaced at any point. So, if you're hurt and you think you can play, you better play and you better play well. My instinct was: 'They're going to have to drag me off because I'm not giving the next guy an opportunity, if I can help it.' Had I sat out some of these games with the ankle, or with a broken thumb, no one would have questioned it at all, but the next guy goes in, and plays lights out, you're replaceable. I always thought about that. I knew it was important to play because that's what I was paid to do, and I loved to do it. You have to play injured, week in and week out. I relished that. I loved proving that I could do it in the toughest of circumstances."

None of this could have been known in the winter of 1992, in the immediate wake of Wolf trading a Number 1 draft choice for a quarterback whose spot had primarily been at the end of the bench for the Falcons. Wolf received plenty of fan feedback that was less than friendly.

Mark Schiefelbein, an assistant director of public relations for the Packers at that time, and who later served the team in a variety of administrative positions, recalled one particular missive: "Ron got a greeting card from an attorney," Schiefelbein said. You open it up and there is a middle finger and the message: 'What the fuck are you doing?' Ron kept that all these years."

"Another attorney wrote me a seven-page letter, hand-written, about what an idiot I was," Wolf said. "I answered the letters. It was all like a form letter, but it was my signature, it wasn't somebody else's. I answered the letters, I did.

"I got some really pointed stuff," Wolf recalled with a smile. "They all thought I was Dan Devine, they thought it was the John Hadl deal again." (That was an infamous deal for the Green Bay franchise, made by Devine, then coach/general manager in 1974. Devine traded five draft choices—two first-rounders, two second and one third—to the Rams for Hadl, a proven quarterback, but also a 34-year-old quarterback. It turned out to be a dreadfully one-side deal, from which Devine and his team did not recover.)

The trade for Brett Favre was at the other end of the spectrum, for the player, for the general manager, and most important of all, for the Green Bay Packers.

Favre was excited by the trade. He said that he "kind of felt stuck" in Atlanta and "stuck" was an apt description. Chris Miller was performing reasonably well at quarterback. Jerry Glanville, coach of the Falcons at that time, had wanted the team to draft Browning Nagle rather than Favre. The trade, Favre knew immediately, was going to be a good thing. Even if he could not at that moment pinpoint Green Bay's location on a map, he had in his mind the name of every Lombardi-era player who made a difference.

"Growing up, the Cowboys were my favorite team, but I knew all about the Packers," Favre said. "I said this in my press conference early on, I wasn't real sure where Green Bay was, but I knew it was up north and I knew it was cold. But more importantly, I knew who Paul Hornung was and, Bart Starr, and Ray Nitschke, Willie Wood and Willie Davis, Herb Adderley, and the list goes on and on. I was familiar with those names. So, to be a part of it, I was really excited."

The core message Favre had in his initial public comments as a Packer was that if people were patient with him, they would eventually see that he would be worth that first-round draft choice. No matter how anybody else took that remark, Favre was being more honest than immodest.

"When I see old video clips of an interview or the way I played from the first couple of years in Green Bay, I sort of cringe, but in a smiling way because we know what the end result turned out to be," Favre said.

"But I'm like: 'You were such a knucklehead.' And I've said this, too, along the way, that I think one of my biggest assets at that time was being totally naïve to how hard and how great the odds were in favor of me failing rather than succeeding, especially succeeding the way it ultimately turned out.

"All those years, MVPs, a Super Bowl victory, my goodness. At one time, holding every passing record in the NFL for a guy who came from the wishbone—are you kidding me? So, I didn't realize that. I didn't think about it. I just thought: 'If they let me play, it's over. I'm going to succeed. Then it's my team.' When I watch those video clips, when I see those interviews, when I see those miked-up, I go: 'Aw, if you only knew. If you only knew.' And that was probably my biggest asset, because I didn't know. I was kind of oblivious, to whatever. Had a lot of confidence. I was really raw, and I would have said that then, but I didn't really realize how raw I was."

Favre had qualities that endeared him to teammates, apart from even the singular ability and the unique durability.

"I've told people that Brett was the best teammate I ever had," said LeRoy Butler, a cornerback when Favre arrived, who later became a perennial All-Pro strong safety. "The reason why, he went to all of these cultures in the locker room and introduced himself and started talking to people: 'Hey, how's it goin'? It was Don Majkowski's team, but Brett, he had all this raw talent and his personality was just unbelievable. Such a nice guy. People were saying: 'Quarterbacks don't act like this.' Normally, quarterbacks are divas, you know? They're like too high-class. But he was very good with everybody. People liked him and had a lot of confidence in him.

"We used to go against him in practice when he would do some of the opposing quarterback stuff. He threw a ball between (linebacker) Johnny Holland and (safety) Mark Murphy, hit (wide receiver) Perry Kemp. I said: 'There's a great quarterback. He's not too scared to make these throws.' Most quarterbacks would pull that down. Brett's, 'Nah, I can make that throw. I can make that throw.' That was awesome."

But with all that ability, all the personal accessibility, the rough edges could be rounded off at least to a workable extent. Wolf had picked an ideal individual, Holmgren, for that task, too. But the trade for Brett

Favre was a move that started the Packers on the long road from irrelevance to the top of the National Football League.

"Brett needed somebody to believe in him," Butler said. "When he got to Green Bay, people were saying: 'Why did we give up a first-round pick for a quarterback when we got Don Majkowski?' And lo and behold, Don Majkowski gets hurt. Ron foresaw all this stuff coming. I told him one year he was going to win the Nobel Prize for trading. He turned red. He said: 'Don't be saying that.' I said: 'No, man, you don't know what you done.' "

On the Tuesday after the Atlanta game, Wolf appeared before a meeting of the Packers executive committee to tell the committee members of his plan to trade for Favre. Favre, Wolf told the seven members of the committee, would be wearing jersey Number 4.

"I call on the legend of Number 4 that was Lou Gehrig," Wolf recalls. "I tell these gentlemen sitting in that room that, in my opinion, what Lou Gehrig was to the Yankees, Brett Favre will be to the Packers. There will be people walking around wearing his jersey number, he will be the stepping stone of greatness for the Packers.

"I'm sure that when I left the room, they must have been all over Bob Harlan. 'Bob, we've hired this fucking idiot? What in the hell?'" Wolf said with a laugh.

"But I was right about him. You saw people wearing his jersey and you saw a rebirth of the Green Bay Packers."

Between Ron Wolf's judgment and Brett Favre's will to succeed, what looked initially like a truly long-shot proposition turned into a success story. Wolf and Favre still form a two-man mutual admiration society. And why not?

"He was the best player that I've ever been around in my 38 years in the league," Wolf said of Favre. "And I've been around some really outstanding players. He was the kind of guy you wanted on your side."

"Without that trade, with that genius mind, seeing something that others didn't—including myself—all of this doesn't happen," Favre said. "I was confident, but I didn't have to stick my neck out there. Ron did. Both he and I feel very confident that without Ron Wolf there is no Brett Favre."

Now, in Green Bay, there was Ron Wolf. There was Brett Favre. The

Packers had yet to play a game that counted in this new era, but with Wolf and Favre the Packers' future would become immeasurably better than the recent past.

2

Wolf Finds the Right Head Coach

RON WOLF BELIEVED he had the right quarterback in mind when he took over the Green Bay Packers. The parallel task would be finding the right head coach.

On December 2, 1991, the day after the 1991 Packers played the Falcons in Atlanta, Wolf attended his first practice in Green Bay. He was not suitably impressed.

"We fly back from Atlanta Sunday night, Ron goes to practice on Monday," team president Bob Harlan recalls. "He comes into my office on Monday afternoon. He says: 'You've got a problem on your practice field. This team is 3–10 and they're walking around like they're 10–3.'"

Lindy Infante was then in his fourth season as the head coach of the Packers. From a 4–12 start in 1988, the team had moved forward to 10–6 in 1989, with some thrill-packed victories, leading to a sense that a corner had been turned. But the Packers had slipped to 6–10 in 1990. And they were slipping further, to 3–10, when Wolf observed them at practice in early December 1991.

Wolf would later say that the Packers he saw that day lacked, "a sense of urgency. So much of this business is a feel. You have a feel for a player, you have a perception of a team. And the feel wasn't right there. I knew this (current situation) wasn't going to work.

"I had no preconceived notion about Lindy Infante," Wolf said. "He had a tremendous reputation as an offensive genius. But when I got there they were 3–9 and after Atlanta they were 3–10.

"I remember sitting down with him—and this is going to be hard for me because Lindy Infante has passed away—but I remember sitting down with him and he wasn't very comfortable with me in there, obviously. And in the course of our conversation, he was telling me he had the third best offense in the NFC. That's what I remember. That stuck. You can take a statistic and make it do anything you want it to do, but to sit there and tell me that, that was number one.

"Number two, I wanted to bring some guys in to look at, and maybe replace some guys who were on the team. He didn't want to do that. So now, we had a conflict. It was just between us. I never said a word (publicly). He was telling me how important it was to have guys who knew the system. I had been through that before. I had been 0–26 in Tampa with guys that knew the system, but couldn't play the game and that was not going to happen again.

"So, what I found there was a bunch of hard-working guys. Those coaches worked late. They were in there working. But the player base wasn't that good. And the atmosphere wasn't that good. They were 3–10, but they were acting like they were 10–3."

Wolf was in Green Bay for a first-hand evaluation of the 1991 Packers because Harlan had made the unorthodox move of bringing in the new general manager 75 percent of the way through the season. Wolf had greatly impressed Harlan during a conversation they had four years earlier. Wolf had interviewed for the Packers GM job, but had withdrawn his name when it became clear that he would not have anything like total autonomy to make personnel decisions.

"Ron was my first choice," Harlan said. "In fact, the first time I called him, I said: 'You're number one on my list, and I want to talk to you until you say yes.'

"I went to the executive committee in November of 1991 and said: 'I want to totally change our football structure. The vote was 6–1 (to grant that power), one against it. One gentleman wanted to wait until the end of the year, go get a search firm, and do it that way. The others went along with it, so he said he would also go along with it to make it unanimous.

"Fortunately, we had a very good relationship with the New York Jets. Ron was player personnel director for them then. Steve Gutman was the president of the team at that time. I called Steve and I said: 'I know this is an unusual request, but we're going to change our football operation. We're going to give total autonomy to whoever we bring in. I want to hire Ron Wolf and I want to do it now. I want him to be here and tell me what's wrong.'

"Steve and I were close enough, he said: 'I'm fine with it, but I'll have to call Dick Steinberg, my general manager.' The next day, Dick calls me and says: 'I'll give you permission. This kind of opportunity doesn't come along that often.'

"I know I did it at a strange time, but here was my reasoning: You normally hire the general manager in January. He comes in during the offseason and looks at the team on tape, saying: 'This is good, this is bad, this is what we need to do prior to the draft.' I wanted to have Ron come in and have him live with the team, travel with it, be on the airplanes, be at the practices, be around the coaches, and then come and tell me what's wrong with the football team."

The change in structure was fundamental and dramatic for the Packers. Bob Harlan was putting the future of the franchise in the hands of one man. Mere hours into the new general manager's tenure, Harlan realized that he now had an exceptionally decisive individual running the Green Bay football operation. "Two days on the job and he had decided Brett Favre is going to be our quarterback and Lindy Infante is going to be out of here. Two days, a Sunday and a Monday and it happened that fast. I thought: 'Thank God we brought him in in November and didn't wait until January.'

"He was that decisive right from the start. He always did say to me: 'Are you okay with this?' And I always assured him that I was. As I look back on the nine years he was here, I'm sure I never told him 'no' to anything, because I had promised him that. It was important. If I was going to get somebody of his caliber, he had to know that he had that kind of authority."

The Packers finished 4–12, after defeating the Vikings in Minnesota in the final game of the season. Wolf appeared in the locker room after the game. LeRoy Butler, later a Pro Bowl safety, but a second-year cornerback at that time, recalls the appearance as being brief but very much to the point.

"Ron comes in. I'm just a young pup now, I don't know," Butler says. "He said: 'I'm going to make some changes. A lot of you guys may not be here as part of these changes. But I want to win a championship.' He didn't ask for any questions. He just turned around and left. He didn't have a smile on his face. You could see him thinking: 'I've got to find me a coach.'"

"Remember, I came from Florida State; we won 10, 11 games every year. So, it was hard the first two years in Green Bay. Lots of losing. It just seemed to me that we didn't have a direction for the franchise. There was some talent, but there wasn't enough to overcome the losing culture."

Infante was promptly dismissed. Next up, Ron Wolf would be looking for precisely the right head coach, the man who would play a central role in developing a new culture, a winning culture.

Mike Holmgren was front and center on NFL radar screens in the winter of 1991–92. He had never been a head coach at the professional level, but his work as an assistant appeared impeccable. He had learned offense from some of the brightest minds in the game: Bill Walsh at San Francisco, and before that, LaVell Edwards at Brigham Young University. The 49ers had won a Super Bowl with Holmgren as quarterbacks coach. They had won another with Holmgren as offensive coordinator.

True, Holmgren had been able to work with two quarterbacks who were on their way to the Hall of Fame—Joe Montana and Steve Young—but the closer you looked, the better Holmgren's performance proved to be.

"He did some things in San Francisco that were incredible," Wolf said. "One year (1986), Montana was hurt, and he had Mike Moroski and Jeff Kemp at quarterback and they went 10–5–1. In 1991, Steve Young was hurt, and they went 5–1 with Steve Bono at quarterback to finish 10–6. I was very impressed with that."

This was Wolf's one shot at getting exactly the right guy to coach his football team. He didn't miss. What was the thought process for Wolf on this absolutely essential hire? It changed, but eventually headed in the right direction. Wolf interviewed what he described as "hot-shot college coaches." But he determined that they could not fit his timetable.

"I wasn't interested in hiring a college coach," he said. "They have to learn. I had a heart attack, so I thought that I had limited time. And I did not want to waste time. I couldn't wait for somebody to come in and learn about the league. That's why I did a lot of what I did. I was impatient, in a lot of instances, to win. That's why a lot of things happened.

"Originally my thinking on hiring a head coach, after I determined there wasn't any way in the world I was going to keep Lindy Infante, I had to figure where I was going to go, who was the person I was going to hire," Wolf said. "When I was growing up in the business, defensive guys were the hot guys: You hired Don Shula, Chuck Noll, people of that ilk. So, I'm thinking: 'Who is a defensive guy that I can hire?' But then you stop and think: 'Who are the guys who are dominating the game right now? Joe Gibbs, offense. Bill Walsh, offense. Dan Reeves, offense.' Well, blub, blub, blub. Maybe I should look offense.

"I interviewed some defensive guys, guys that had the reputation. And some of those guys, I was just amazed at their lack of preparation. Just amazed. It's one of those things where you go into the interview—and I had never done this before, either—but I would at least expect a guy to come in and give me an idea of what he's going to do, who he's going to hire (as assistant coaches), what he's going to run, how he's going to do this. Some guys weren't prepared in that vein. 'Tell me a little bit about yourself.' I had little cards made up with questions to ask. But Holmgren aced all those things. He knew about the history of the Packers. He just sounded like he was ready, ready to be a head coach.

"Everything about Mike Holmgren was professional. It was how he carried himself. He carried himself like a winner. He was a winner. And he started going around on all these tours. He went to Tampa. He went to Indianapolis. I thought: 'What am I going to do? Where am I going to go if I don't get him?'

But from Holmgren's perspective, the Packers had a couple of advantages none of his other suitors had. One of those was Ron Wolf.

"I interviewed with six teams," Holmgren recalled. "But I knew this, as a kid growing up, and following the Packers, that way, the championships, Lombardi, Bart Starr, I was a quarterback, so even that way in San Francisco growing up the Packers were the Packers. Really, that was my thought.

"I interviewed with them first and Ron was kind enough to wait, because I went on a bunch of interviews after that. I will say this, though, in the old building in the lobby there, they had a collage of all that stuff, and it kind of struck me. I'm going: 'Man, this is the Green Bay Packers.' I knew they'd had a hard season, and I knew they'd been down for a while, but, these are the Green Bay Packers now. And that kind of struck me, that this is a special place in the NFL.

"I was a first-time head coach and it was important for me to align myself with the right man and that was Ron. I would say that's the main reason. I thought he and I connected right away. And when he said: 'Look, you go do this and I'll wait.' I thought: 'That's pretty special.'

"And then also, of all the teams, I think the year before I got there they were 4–12 and had struggled over the years. Somewhere in my DNA, the idea of fixing something and seeing it grow, that was an appealing thing for me. But the number one thing was Ron, it really was."

Harlan said he asked Holmgren: "'Mike, why did you pick Green Bay, with all these choices?' He says: 'Because of Ron Wolf. I knew he would find me players.'"

Holmgren was familiar with Wolf in part because of all the years Wolf had spent working across San Francisco Bay for the Oakland Raiders. "I didn't know him well, but you'd see him. He was kind of like the CIA," Holmgren said with a smile. "It was the Raiders and the 49ers, and the Raiders always had this thing and I'd see him at a number of things and you'd say hello. And he was actually kind of quiet. But I knew of his work, yeah."

Holmgren was prepared for his interview with Wolf because while he didn't have head coaching experience, he had experience interviewing for head coaching jobs.

"In '89 with the 49ers in the Super Bowl, we beat Denver, 55–10," Holmgren said. "And coming off the field people stuck things in my pockets and I thought: *What?* It was Arizona and the Jets. So, I had interviews with those two teams, and Mr. (Eddie) DeBartolo, who was the team owner then, said: 'Go do this, but just promise me that before you make a decision you come back and let me talk.' So. I said: 'Yeah.'

"So, I flew to New York and I flew down to Arizona and I went through the interview process in '89 and saw who that was. It was Dick Steinberg (Jets general manager), who was Ron's good friend. They were very thorough. They were very different types of interviews, but it kind of prepared me. I stayed, I didn't take either of those jobs, although I was offered both of them. It prepared me for the next time, I think. I kind of knew what the teams wanted, and you had to have your staff ready to go, you had to have certain things that you have to know, and you have to be sure when you go in for these things. I always want to be thorough."

In Green Bay, Holmgren would be a find-a-way coach. A 4–12 team in 1991 became a 9–7 team in 1992. Wolf was making roster changes at the speed of light, but Holmgren did his bit with an approach that made taking the easy way out extinct at Lambeau Field.

"That was one of the great things that I learned from Mike Holmgren," Wolf said. "They're going to play the game, there's nothing you can do about it, so don't whine and mope because you don't have this player or that player. You're being paid to do a job and the job is to put a team on the field that can win the game. If you don't have a wide receiver, then we go tight. If you don't have a running back, then we do something else. But don't come to me and tell me: 'Oh, my God, we don't have this guy, we don't have that guy. It's my job as head coach to get that team ready to play.' That's a wonderful, wonderful approach."

Holmgren as the Packers coach would have a commanding presence, which was only partially explained by the fact that at six feet, five inches, he was the tallest head coach in Packers history. He demanded, if not perfection, an attempt to reach perfection, and in the early seasons in Green Bay, he had plenty of opportunities to voice his displeasure when perfection was not remotely approached. One way or another, he had no problem holding the attention of his players. For Holmgren, this was a more nuanced skill than a ballistic show of temper.

"I didn't come in and bang the walls," he said. "I didn't think a lot about that. My height probably helps, in some areas. But what I've learned over the years was that you can't con people. Certainly not your players, and not the press. That's one man's opinion. Know what you want to say, say it, and be clear. What helped me was my teaching background, being in the classroom and preparing and getting young people to try to learn stuff. That helped."

While Holmgren was touring five other potential head coaching sites, another possibility arose for the Green Bay job. One of Wolf's closest friends over the previous two decades was Bill Parcells, who had left the Giants after leading them to two Super Bowl victories.

"Well, we talked about it," Parcells said. "We had a couple of discussions about the Green Bay job. But I had something wrong with me. I didn't know what it was, but I did know I had something wrong. The doctors were a little bit baffled themselves because I kept passing these stress tests, and yet, I was experiencing some things physically that I knew were not normal. My mind was not really ready to do anything because I was just not confident that, one, I was healthy enough to do it; and two, that under the circumstances, I could do it. I had bypass surgery eight months later. They thought that what was producing my reactions was adrenaline, but it was only as time progressed that we became a little more cognizant of what might be the problem."

"Bill came into the picture," Wolf said. "He's the only guy I ever saw who was able to do what he did. He kept taking these guys who, in my mind, were just very average players, he'd bring them with him and they'd win. New England, the Jets, Dallas, but they'd still win. I don't know how he did it, but he did it.

"So, I was prepared to give the job to Bill, but fortunately, he turned it down because he had to have a heart operation. And that kept our friendship because we would not have been able to co-exist. We were like oil and water. Whereas, with Mike Holmgren, I was able to exist."

That coexistence was essential to the success of both the general manager and the head coach. Shortly after this arrival in Green Bay, Holmgren learned what was essential to everybody else in northeastern Wisconsin.

"Early, early, this story happened," Holmgren said. "I'd been there two weeks, my wife, Kathy, wasn't there yet. I used to go the market on Ridge Road, it was pretty close to the stadium, get my lunch, bring it back. I've got my cart and a little old lady, it's like my grandma, she's coming at me, so I'm moving over here, she moves her cart, I'm moving over there, she moves her cart.

"Finally, I go: 'Excuse me.' She says: 'You're the new coach, aren't you?' I said I was and introduced myself. She says: 'You're from California?' I said, 'Yeah, I was born and raised in California.' She goes: 'Hey, California, I don't care if you win another game, you have got to beat the Bears. Do you understand that?' I said: 'I do, I do.' That happened. I called Kathy and I said: 'You won't believe what happened. My little grandma hit me with a cart.'"

Holmgren was 12–2 against the Bears during his tenure as head coach of the Packers, including winning the last 10 straight against the former Monsters of the Midway. When a street was renamed in his honor—"Holmgren Way"—winning the Super Bowl certainly helped the cause. But going 12–2 against the Bears would be at the heart of the matter for long-suffering fans of the Green and Gold.

Holmgren also brought in a first-class coaching staff, which included some of the best football minds in the game. Andy Reid went on to become head coach for the Philadelphia Eagles and the Kansas City Chiefs, but 1992 was his first season as a pro assistant coach. He came on board as an assistant offensive line coach and tight end coach, and later became quarterbacks coach. Holmgren made a lasting impression on him.

"Mike Holmgren is a Hall of Fame coach," Reid said. "I've done this for a lot of years and I said it when I was coaching for him—I didn't think anybody could do it better. He just had that feel and I feel the same way today. You mix that with a Hall of Fame general manager, and you've got what happened. They were able to turn that franchise around."

Beyond coexisting with the general manager and gaining firsthand knowledge about what Green Bay fans really wanted, the other essential relationship was between Holmgren and the new quarterback. In this regard, Holmgren was able to summon up the necessary blend of will and tolerance to make it work. Favre had immense potential and a singularly competitive nature. But he was raw, and he was headstrong. It was up to Holmgren to channel the entire Favre package into a winning

NFL quarterback. Holmgren went on to coach two Super Bowl teams in Green Bay, a Super Bowl champion in Green Bay, and another Super Bowl team in Seattle, but this might have been his central coaching achievement.

Holmgren had seen Favre at close range. "When I was with the 49ers, Brett was coming out of college," Holmgren recalled. "He played in the East-West Shrine Game out in California when it was a bigger deal. My job with the 49ers was to look at the top six quarterbacks in the country, so I went all over the place. One of them was Brett. So, I flew into New Orleans for his workout and in fact, conducted his workout. There were probably 15 other teams there.

"I ran him through his paces, I did the drills, I was on the field with him. The other guys are just watching. I did that and had a chance to visit with him after the workout. Then, of course, I wrote my report. The 49ers had Montana and Young, so we're not going to draft a quarterback, but I had to do my due diligence. I wrote my report up.

"So, fast-forward it, now I'm in Green Bay a couple years later. Atlanta had taken Brett. I get there, and we have two Number 1 draft choices. Pretty good deal, so I'm thinking: *This is good. With those picks, we'll get two starters hopefully Pro Bowl guys.* Then Ron come into my office one day and he goes: 'I'm thinking of trading the second draft choice for Favre.' I go: 'Oh.' Kind of caught me off guard. He goes: 'What do you think about that?' So, I somehow got the report that I'd written, and I'd said, something like: 'Great athlete, strong, likeable, little bit of a gunslinger, not sure if he can discipline himself to run the offense we want to run with the 49ers.' Because that was precision. 'But tremendous upside,' something like that. He said: 'Okay, let's look at it some more.'

Wolf was attempting to give Holmgren some ownership in the decision to trade for Favre. In retrospect, Holmgren saw that, appreciated that. "Here's the thing: Looking back, Ron had already made up his mind, I'm sure," Holmgren said. "But the beauty of our relationship—and it started right at the beginning—was that he involved me in that. And I think he valued my opinion. But he was my boss, so if he wanted to do that. . . . I suppose if I had said: 'I don't think so,' then he would have sat down and talked me into it, like he did with a couple of other players. But he said: 'Let's do this,' and he did, and the rest is history.

"You know better than anybody, those early years with Brett . . . . I'd still have more hair," Holmgren said with a laugh. "But, ah, man, to win in the National Football League, you need the quarterback. And we got one."

Favre started the 1992 season as the backup to Don Majkowski, who had been the "Majik Man" in 1989. Majkowski had flashed some serious improvisational ability in the 1989 season, but his arm was never in the same class as Favre's would be. Majkowski suffered a torn rotator cuff in the 1990 season and was never the same after that.

"Majkowski was the starting quarterback and Brett was the new guy learning stuff," Holmgren said. "Don had a decent first game against the Vikings. Then we go down to Tampa and he throws an interception, early, and so at halftime I made the switch. Majkowski was upset, which is understandable. But I said: 'The quarterback can't start the game that way. We can't do that.' So, Brett came in and played the second half and clearly wasn't ready to play. He hadn't studied or prepared. He'd call a play, and I didn't even recognize it, there was all this weird stuff. So, we lose, we get killed (31–3)." Majkowski completed 10 of 15 passes for 75 yards with one interception. Favre completed eight of 14 passes for 73 yards with one interception.

"So, we come back to play Cincinnati," Holmgren said, "and I have a meeting with those two, and I say: 'Okay, Don, you're back in starting, but you can't start the game that way. So, then Majkowski gets hurt (tearing an ankle ligament in the first quarter). Brett has to go in and play, and he wins it at the end with that remarkable play (a 35-yard touchdown pass to Kitrick Taylor with 13 seconds remaining). And then he plays for 17 years."

Holmgren smiles and shakes his head at the memories that return in waves on both sides of the argument.

"Oh, but he'd do remarkable things, and then he'd throw an interception, or he'd throw one off his knees, or do weird stuff, and it was just so different than Joe Montana or Steve Young, just so different," Holmgren said. "It was tough love. I blistered him. I was hard on him.

"We reached a point in 1993, when we had drafted Mark (Brunell). He was the other side of the coin, he was precise, he was controlled, and he was talented, he did great things. We had lost a game and Brett had done something and the staff was really (upset). I went around the room, asking them about the quarterback thing, how they felt. And quite honestly, other than (quarterbacks coach Steve) Mariucci, there was a lot of sentiment there to switch (to Brunell), there really was. It was thoughtful, it really was, I really had a good coaching staff and these guys were thoughtful. That evening I thought about it, and the next day I said: 'Nah.'

"I called Brett in, and I did say this to him, and I believe this, with Brett Favre or any other quarterback, the coach has to commit, and then, I've got to make him good. If he's got bad habits, I've got to break him of those habits. And I committed to him. I told him: 'Either way; we're going to wind up at the top of the mountain together, or we're going to wind up in the dumpster together, but we're going to be together.' I think that was the start of the trust and all that."

That was precisely the case, because for Favre it was a defining moment, not only in his relationship with Holmgren but in his quarterbacking career.

"I remember that vividly," Favre says. "That was such a relief and a confidence-builder. Now, hey, he could have been pulling my leg. But you know what? I think part of being a great coach is convincing your guys that you can win and beat anyone, being a motivator when guys seem to be unmotivated. Mike had a way of pushing those buttons, whether he was pulling my leg or not, it made a tremendous difference in that time. And ultimately that resulted in 20 great years."

"And then at the end of that season (1993), I had another exit interview with him, because we were 9–7 and then 9–7 again, but we got to the playoffs," Holmgren recalls. "I said: 'Okay, this is what I want you to think about in the offseason. We've got to eliminate some of the craziness, the wildness, the interceptions, blah, blah, blah.' And he goes: 'Mike, that's how I play.' And you can hear him saying that. "Mike, that's how I am.' I said: 'Okay, but do you want to be 9–7, or do you want to go the Super Bowl?'

"He said: 'I want to go to the Super Bowl.' I said: 'Okay, then we've got to work on this.' He goes: 'Okay.' And to his credit, it was another step. Every once in a while, he'd do something crazy, but he'd also do something remarkable. He was, little by little, becoming the quarterback

I thought he was capable of becoming. So, it was a series of things like that."

The "tough love" with which Holmgren approached his quarterback and prized pupil was, as Favre says, looking back, "necessary." But this did not mean that their relationship was characterized by anything resembling mutual dislike. Holmgren saw Favre's potential, and thus had a vision of how far it could carry his team. Favre understood that Holmgren was trying to rein him in, but that this effort came in a very good cause.

"I tell you, there were people saying there was bad blood between us," Favre says. "I don't know where that came from. He was extremely tough on me, extremely tough. But he was fair. I didn't always like getting my ass chewed, but first and foremost, no one ever chewed my ass as hard as my Dad did. (Irvin Favre was Brett's high school coach.) He was my coach; up until he died, he thought he was coaching me up until the last second.

"Mike was tough. But he taught me the game. My Dad didn't teach me the game. He taught me the toughness. And the thick skin. He didn't teach me how to read the curl in the flat. He didn't teach me the hot reads and stuff like that. He didn't teach me stuff like that. Mike taught me how to play the game, why we did drops a certain way, why it was important to throw the ball one foot in front of the numbers.

"Even though I might complete a pass, and I'd think: *Well, hell, it was completed.* There was a perfection about him, that, after he left I carried on with me and demanded of myself, but more importantly of my teammates—perfection. Not that we're going to be perfect, but we're going to try for perfection. That was Mike's motto: You expect the absolute best out of yourself in practice because that can dictate your performance on Sundays. Because anything less, is unacceptable. I totally agreed with him. He was a genius in that regard. My only regret was that we didn't have more time together."

An ability to adjust on a second's notice was required on both sides of this discussion. On December 18, 1994, the Packers played their last game in Milwaukee County Stadium. The Packers had been playing some home games in Milwaukee for 60 years. But with an enlarged Lambeau Field and a truly dedicated following of faithful ticket-buyers, it had become more practical and more profitable to play all eight home games in Green Bay, rather than five in Green Bay and three in Milwaukee.

The Packers, in particular Favre, provided a suitably memorable ending to their history in Milwaukee. In the dying seconds of the game, the Packers, trailing Atlanta, 17–14, took the ball to the Falcons' nine-yard line.

"We were down there, and I called our last timeout," Holmgren recalled. "I called Brett over. I said: 'We have two shots at the end zone. But you've got to drop back and throw, drop back and throw. Two shots. What you cannot do is run or take a sack. Those two things can't happen. You got it?' He says: 'Yeah.'

"He drops back, and he starts to run. And that's another one of those, 'No, no! Yes, yes!' And he makes it. And he comes over to the sideline and he's happy, we're all happy, we're all ecstatic. And I grab him, and I say: 'Did you hear me? I told you, you couldn't run.' He says: 'I knew I could make it. Well, he made it by that much," Holmgren says with a chuckle, holding his hands six inches apart.

Favre lunged into the end zone, just ahead of a tackler, with 14 seconds remaining in the game. The play stands out in Favre's memory, for what it represents not only about his ability and his approach, but for the whole coach/player relationship that is at the core of the game.

"I remember that vividly, too," Favre said. "I coached high school down here (in Mississippi) for two years and had a blast, looking at it from a coach's standpoint. You try to instill in these guys a certain style of play, but you can only do so much. You can't play for them. And then you have to allow them—which at times can be painful—to use their ability. Some of them think their ability is better than it is and that gets them in trouble.

"I was never the fastest, but I trusted my legs, I could buy a lot of time. I was well aware when I went into that huddle and called that play, of what I needed to do, and what I shouldn't do, and I think the instinct just over-rode that. I remember Mike telling me: 'Do not run. Throw it away. Whatever.' So, do not do what ultimately, I did, which was to go against what he said. I think sometimes you have to be willing to accept the trust of that player. Just like the coach is not always going to call the right play and sometimes you've got to bail the coach out. And that's one of those cases."

By the end of his third year with the Packers, Favre believed that he understood what his coach was attempting to do, and how he was attempting to do it. The coach and the QB had come, from different directions, to roughly the same place.

"About three years into it, I could almost tell you what Mike was going to call before he called it," Favre said. "I think the first couple of years he called plays that he had called when he had Joe Montana and Steve Young with the 49ers, and obviously they worked. And maybe they would have worked with us, but not the way he drew them up. I was all over the place.

"Being able to harness that, and calling plays that I hate to say I could read or relate to, Mike was so great at rather than saying: 'These are my plays, and this is the way it is going to work.' Sometimes it's like trying to pound sand up a flea's ass. It's like saying: 'We're going to be a power running team' when you don't have the offensive line or the backs. Or: 'We're going to throw the deep ball,' when you've got guys that run 4.9 40s. It just ain't gonna work. Some guys are like: 'My system is going to work.' Mike was not like that. He was, 'we're going to work with what we've got, to our advantage.' And he did that, and I learned that with each year, but about my third year, we were about on the same page."

"This was last thing that kind of sealed the deal," Holmgren says. "In the airplane coming home from a game, the seat next to me was always empty. You really didn't want to wind up in that seat. Normally, that was the hot seat. But I'm sitting there, and we'd won a game, and I'm half asleep and all of a sudden, here he (Favre) comes. Players are in the back, coaches are in the front, here he comes and sits down.

"I'm: 'What do you want?'" Holmgren says, with a frown for emphasis. "And he goes: 'I get it. I get it. It's slowed down for me. I understand.' So, I said: 'Good. We both worked very hard for you to get it. It's good.' So, after that, it was just a matter that I could ease up on the reins a little bit, little by little. He still, I thought, needed some guidance, and he was like the son I never had. When he was veering a little bit, I'd have to yank him. People thought we didn't get along. But when we got to this point, it was good, he was a pleasure to coach. I just had to grab him once in a while."

For the rest of the Packers, Holmgren was a taskmaster, demanding that the game be played the right way, the way he wanted it to be played. But he was also a sincere individual who cared about the well-being of his players, not just as athletes but as human beings.

LeRoy Butler was shifted from cornerback to strong safety by Holmgren's coaching staff in 1992, and Butler developed into a four-time first team All-Pro selection. But for Butler, what stood out about Holmgren was the human side.

"I used to tell the guys: 'He's too nice to be head coach,'" Butler said. "Because head coaches don't walk up to you and ask you how your family is doing. They could care less. But he's: 'How's your family? I want to meet your kids.' Okay. Or he'd be like: 'We're not doing pads today, because I want you guys to be fresh. Matter of fact, let's take a day off.' With Lindy Infante we were always two-a-days in pads, hitting all the time. Mike was like: 'We're just going to wear shorts and helmets and go through our stuff, and do some conditioning because we want to be in great shape. We want to run a lot of plays on offense, but not on defense.' Now guys really start buying in, because we were really a fresh team down the stretch. A lot of these teams were wearing down, but we were in great shape. I just will never forget that there was something different about him.

"Ron got a coach who was exactly what we needed. Players would run through a wall for Mike Holmgren. It's a blessing that Ron thought outside the box and gave him a chance. And Mike had the best staff. They were smart, and they were prepared. They were prepared for everything. I got a phone call from (defensive coordinator) Ray Rhodes. He said: 'We may take Terrell Buckley (Florida State cornerback) with the fifth pick (in the first round of the 1992 draft). I'm going to have to move you to safety.' I said: 'I'm only 189 pounds.' He said, 'no, no, the way I'm going to play you, you'll be a Pro Bowler.' I'll never forget that conversation.

"I owe a lot to Ray Rhodes and when he left, (to become head coach of the Philadelphia Eagles) I was torn up. But then I met Fritz Shurmur (Rhodes's successor as defensive coordinator). I think I was as close to him as you can get to a coach, without making it awkward. He was the first coach to ask me what I thought. 'Tell me what you think on this play. What would you do?' That's the best way of coaching. It's not a dictatorship. It's a democracy. Let's talk about it because we had this thing that if we were wrong we were wrong as a team, then no one individual takes all the blame. It was great psychology."

So, Ron Wolf had chosen particularly well in the matter of finding a head coach. Mike Holmgren was someone who could lead his team and develop his quarterback into everything that Brett Favre's magnificent ability could become. And the general manager and the coach shared responsibility and accountability.

"Ron said to me: 'If this doesn't work out, we can look in the mirror and know the reasons.'" Holmgren said. "I remember him saying that. He said, 'We get to set it up the way we want to set it up.' For a coach, that's great. I've been through some situations since, and you win games, but it's just like you're fighting battles. And it's hard enough to fight the battles on the field without this other nonsense. It even gave me a greater appreciation of our time there."

"Once we got to know each other, it was really simple, and I'll tell you what was really simple," Wolf said. "There were only two guys. If we fail, we can look in the mirror, we can see the reasons that we fail; the two of us. So, we've got to make this work."

They made it work. On his first two major decisions as the general manager of the Green Bay Packers Wolf was an emphatic two-for-two. He had the supremely tough and extraordinarily talented quarterback, and the right head coach not only for the new QB, but for a new era of Packers' achievement.

3

God, Wolf, and Holmgren Tell Reggie to Come to Green Bay

REGGIE WHITE SAID that God told him to come to Green Bay.

"Well, that and $17 million," Ron Wolf says with a smile. "Yes, he said: 'God told me to come to Green Bay.' But this is what won him: We paid him more money than anybody else: $17 million. Now, some people think that's chump change. But at the time, that was unheard of."

The time was the winter and early spring of 1993, which was the first season of free agency in the National Football League. The most prominent individual in the first free agent class was Reggie White, the most dominant defensive player in the game. In eight seasons with the Philadelphia Eagles, White, an astounding mixture of strength, athleticism, and a will to dominate the opposition, had 114 sacks. At age 31, he was still an imposing talent on the field. Everywhere else, he was still an imposing presence, a deeply devout man, who used his athletic prowess to promote the virtues of his fundamentalist Christian beliefs.

Wolf decided that the Packers should make an all-out effort to sign White. To those outside the Packers organization, this did not necessarily seem like a realistic possibility. When it came to White's free agency options, Green Bay did not appear to be even an afterthought. It was widely reported that the Washington Redskins, the Cleveland Browns and the San Francisco 49ers were in the lead for obtaining his services. It was also reported that White was being lavishly courted by his suitors, with his wife, Sara, receiving gifts that included a fur coat.

Wolf knew that an all-out effort to sign White also meant an all-out financial commitment to White. The general manager did not much care that the Packers were viewed as complete outsiders in the pursuit of football's most prestigious free agent.

"Ron comes into my office and says: 'We're going to make a run at Reggie White," said Bob Harlan, then Packers team president and CEO. "I thought we were out of our minds. I didn't think we had a prayer in the world. He said: 'It's going to cost a bundle.' Like always, I said; 'Do it.' I had such faith in the man.

"Ron was always so sure. Every time Ron made a decision, he'd show up at my door and I'd think: 'Oh, boy, here we go.'"

White was on tour, visiting potential employers, but the Packers were having difficulty just getting a visit from the leading free agent. "The thought was that we would be kind of used to bid the price up, and then he would go somewhere else," said Mike Reinfeldt, who, as the Packers Chief Financial Officer, would be in charge of negotiations with White.

The Packers would eventually sign White on April 6, 1993. But first, long odds or not, there had to be a courtship. The Packers were trying to get White and his agent, Jimmy Sexton, to adjust their schedule and fly from Detroit to Green Bay. There was, of course, snow in Green Bay and some commercial flights had been postponed or cancelled. But a viable flight option was quickly unveiled.

"My ex-wife was the step-daughter of Jim Kress, who was on the Packer board (of directors)," Reinfeldt said. "Jim Kress is the head of Green Bay Packaging (a firm that manufactures packing materials) and they have a jet. So, he lent his jet to go pick up Reggie. It's nice to know people with means, you know?" Reinfeldt said with a chuckle. "It was quick and easy, talking to my wife at the time, calling her stepfather, and 20 minutes later, we had the plane, which in times like that is what you have to be able to do."

Apart from divine intervention, and the financial considerations, there were other, essential centerpieces to the story of Reggie White's recruitment by the Packers. If God told Reggie to come to Green Bay, then there was a backup choir singing from the same hymn book in Titletown. There was Wolf, there was head coach Mike Holmgren, there was team president Bob Harlan, there was Reinfeldt, there were assistant coaches.

Wolf's advice to White centered on all the names of the greats whose fame lived on at Lambeau Field; players from the Lombardi era, players all the way back to the glory days of Curly Lambeau.

"I'll never forget, I was in that little cubbyhole in the back, little room, no windows," Wolf said. "Reggie comes in, this enormous man, and I told him: 'You're already a great football player. You come here, you'll be a legend.' That's what I told him. And he became a legend."

Part of the legend of landing Reggie was the recruitment meal. This was Green Bay. There would be no extensive wining and dining of the free agent. There would be no haute cuisine, no frills, no fancy trimmings. Reggie White and his agent were taken by Reinfeldt and defensive coordinator Ray Rhodes to a Red Lobster.

"There was a story that Cleveland had given him a mink stole. And now, we're taking him to Red Lobster," Reinfeldt said with a laugh.

Reggie's favorite food was catfish. You could get catfish at Red Lobster. Reggie liked his catfish filleted. The Red Lobster in Green Bay did not serve its catfish filleted. But White was assured that, if he signed with the Packers, he could have filleted catfish anytime he wanted at this Red Lobster.

And then there was the money, which wasn't finalized until later, but set an NFL precedent. The contract was, at that time, by far the largest ever awarded to a defensive player. For perspective, White's last contract in Philadelphia averaged $1.5 million per year. Here he would get an average of $4.25 million annually, with a front-loaded arrangement that maximized the impact of this deal.

"Seventeen million, yes, that was unheard of, but I think it was within our means," Reinfeldt said. "Salaries were increasing, but it wasn't like we had an All-Star laden team. The (salary) cap didn't hit until the next year. We felt we had ability to maneuver under the cap and make it work. We weren't going to do something that wasn't going to work.

"I think the other thing we did that was kind of unique, although now it's become almost commonplace, we might have been the first to do it. It was a four-year, $17 million deal, but he got paid nine million the first year. It was front-loaded, big time. Think of that. He was getting ($1.5 million a year) then all of a sudden, he's getting nine million. There's a $4.5 million signing bonus, $4.5 million salary, so he's being paid nine million, over half of his contract in the first year."

This would be the third major move of Wolf's tenure as Packers general manager, following the trade for Brett Favre and the selection of Mike Holmgren as head coach. Just a few years before, the idea that a player of White's ability and stature within the game would come to the Packers would have been a joke, but not a particularly humorous joke. If other motivational means failed with recalcitrant players, there was always the threat of a trade to Green Bay.

Signing White would not only make the Packers a better team, but it would change the image of this franchise. Hey, if Reggie signed there, it must be okay. His signing would open the door for a generation of free agents to look favorably upon the Packers. And not incidentally, it could also alter the image of Green Bay for African American players, at least some of whom had experienced this community as a lonely outpost.

Wolf had success in mind when the Packers went all in on their pursuit of White. He was in a hurry and the revival of this franchise required major moves, bold strokes. The Packers signing Reggie White may have seemed like an impossibility to the rest of the NFL, but to Wolf, it seemed like the next logical step.

"It was huge, for a lot of reasons," Holmgren said. "Free agency had just started and Reggie was the prize. And I remember, he was taking these tours of all these places and getting keys to the city, and leather coats and fur coats for his wife. So, when I heard that we were going to bring him in, I said: 'What are we going to do? Give him a block of cheese? How are we going to compete with this?"

The Packers competed in part by doing their due diligence on White, what amounted to scouting, as the recruitment went on. "In the meantime, we find out what kind of flower Mrs. White likes," Wolf said. "Every other day she got a dozen roses compliments of the Green Bay Packers, at their home."

And, Holmgren and Rhodes paid a personal visit to the Whites' home in Knoxville, Tenn.

"Ray Rhodes had a way about him with his players and they loved him," Holmgren said. "So, Ray and I were going to go to his home in Knoxville and surprise Reggie and try to talk him into (signing with the Packers). One of the things with Ray, was that he was a very colorful guy, in his language and everything. And Reggie was a devout Christian man. We go down there and I'm telling Ray: 'Now, look; understand that we have to talk to him a certain way. Don't get too wild and wooly on him.' He says: 'I got it. I got it.'

"So, we go there and we meet with Reggie and he had some friends there and his wife was there, so they invite us to lunch. So, we're going to start to have lunch and Ray says: 'Mike, Reggie, I'd like to bless the meal.' Right away, I'm thinking: 'I hope lightning doesn't strike the house.' Ray, in his own way, was very devout, too, but he did that and that got us off to the right start.

"We did click," Holmgren said. "Our Christianity—Reggie was a Christian, I'm a Christian—we could talk about those types of things. I knew that was important to him."

The personal-touch approach worked. "It was huge," Jimmy Sexton, White's agent said. "They were smart enough and perceptive enough to know that Reggie was a relationship guy. They sold him on the fact that it's like a big college atmosphere. He was coming out of a place where it wasn't fun for him the last couple of years."[1]

And then there was the once-in-a-lifetime blending of God and head coach. Shortly after that meeting with White, Holmgren left a message on White's phone. "I left the message on his phone: 'Reggie, this is God. You ought to go to Green Bay,'" Holmgren said, smiling at the memory.

---

1 *Milwaukee Journal*, April 7, 1993.

"I thought: *Either he's going to take this as it puts a smile on his face, because he's got a great sense of humor, and also understands how important I thought this was. Or he's not going to take it that way.* So, fortunately, he took it the right way. Now, Ron said: 'That's all well and good, because he came for the money.' And that's part of it, too. The contract we offered him, people thought we were nuts. The league thought we were nuts. You think about it in terms of today and it was peanuts. But it was a lot of money then. Especially because it was the Packers, who didn't have a storehouse full of money, or an owner with deep pockets and all that kind of stuff.

"But look—you had Reggie White, Brett Favre—defense, offense, leaders. Those were the pins you built everything around."

The story of Holmgren's phone message was a big hit with the players. "When we heard that, everybody in the meeting room started laughing," safety LeRoy Butler said. "We just laughed so hard it took 15 minutes for us to stop laughing. That's what made us love Coach Holmgren."

The rest of the world may not have thought much of the Packers' chances for landing the most single prominent free agent, but after face-to-face meetings with White and Sexton, Reinfeldt was convinced that the Packers were, in fact, in contention for gaining White's services.

"I'll never forget sitting down at Mike's house in the cellar," Wolf said, "and we're sitting down there and he said: 'This thing is coming to a head. We're going to get this guy.' I said: 'You're shitting me.'

"Back in the day you had a couple of whisper guys that would call you and tell you where you were. Will McDonough (of the *Boston Globe* and NBC) was a big whisper guy, he would call me and say: 'You're third.' And I wanted to yell and say: 'Noooooo! We got him!' But you couldn't do that."

Reinfeldt had considerable latitude in the negotiations due to the structure of the Packers organization. "I was not only the negotiator, but I was also the CFO (chief financial officer) of the Packers," he said. "So, I kind of knew how far we could go. There is a huge advantage there, when you're both the negotiator and the CFO. Mike and Ron would say: 'Could we afford that?' Then I've got to put my other hat on as the chief financial officer, you know?" Reinfeldt said with a chuckle. "I would say: 'Yeah, we can afford this.' And then you put your negotiator hat back on, and say: 'Well, let's do it then.' But it did give me great latitude. It also gave us the ability to act quickly.

"I had talked with Jimmy Sexton quite a bit already, so I had developed a pretty good rapport with Jimmy. In my gut, I thought we had a chance, just from the way Jimmy interacted, quite honestly. And then to see Reggie, we had a chance. We were the real deal. It wasn't a slam dunk, but we were in the game, you could tell that from Reggie."

It all came down to one final night of negotiations. The rest of the American sports audience was focused elsewhere but a monumental occurrence was on tap in Green Bay.

"Jimmy did the deal on the night of the NCAA championship, of the Final Four," Reinfeldt said. That was April 5, 1993. North Carolina defeated Michigan, 77–71 for the championship

"It went rather smoothly, it really did," Reinfeldt recalled. "We had two groups that really both wanted it to happen. We were fortunate. Some other teams, San Francisco in particular, were limited by what they could do in terms of some financial rules. We were motivated. We had Ron, we had Mike Holmgren, we had Ray Rhodes, we were geared up to make this work. We were going to turn and make Green Bay what it should be, return the Packers to the glory days. I think we were motivated to do that, and I think in Reggie, you had a player who was motivated, who kind of thought outside the box a little bit, and said: 'Why not?' because he could make a difference, with Favre and everything else. So that was a good combination."

In their meetings leading up to the final deal, White, Reinfeldt said, had been impressive.

"I think he was focused, he was engaging, he was in a good spot. He liked what he was doing, he kind of liked the limelight, he was the main plaintiff in the suit." (The National Football League Players Association sued under White's name, accusing the league of violating anti-trust law with its labor practices. The case was closed in 1993 with an agreement that led to a new labor contract.)

"He was kind of walking on clouds almost," Reinfeldt said. "You know, it was a good time in his life. He felt good about a lot of things.

He probably had to pinch himself because it had all kind of come together for him.

"I think he was also focused on going to a place and winning football games. That was important to him, too."

There was real shock value for the rest of the NFL when White opted to sign with the Green Bay Packers. People on the inside of the Packers operation were as shocked as anyone.

Mark Schiefelbein, a member of the Packers public relations department at that time, recalls that the PR staff was in Atlanta for league meetings.

"Reggie was larger than life at that time, "Schiefelbein said. "Mike Reinfeldt calls and says: 'We just signed Reggie White.' And I'm like: 'Get out of here, we did not.' Finally, Mike got frustrated with me, because he had worked through the night with Jimmy Sexton to get this thing done. He gave the phone to (team president) Bob Harlan and Bob says: 'Schief, we did sign Reggie White.' I remember going up to my hotel room, jumping up and down, saying: 'We signed Reggie White!'

"It was a turning point for the franchise. For those of us who grew up in Wisconsin, you wondered if that kind of success was ever going to happen again. I remember Ron saying: 'Hey, we don't have to take a back seat to anybody.' And right away, you started thinking: 'We *don't* have to take a back seat to anybody.' And then he gets Mike Holmgren, he makes the trade for Brett, he signs Reggie White. Now we've got these big-time people here, it's like, wow.

"Those three moves in a period of less than two years, I don't know that you could have a better string than Ron had right there."

White went on to play six years for the Packers. He was a force. Even in his final season with the Packers, during which he turned 37, he had 16 sacks. But he was more than his performance on the field. He was the "Minister of Defense," the term fitting him perfectly, since he was both an All-Pro defensive end and an evangelical minister.

White made his first major impression on Green Bay in the fifth game of the 1993 season. The Packers were 1–3 at that point, on a three-game losing streak that had most recently featured a 36–14 drubbing at Dallas. In Lambeau Field for the fifth game of the regular season, they were facing the Denver Broncos, who were 3–1 and who were led by the future Hall of Fame quarterback, John Elway.

The Packers built up a 30–7 halftime lead, but the situation was considerably less rosy late in the fourth quarter. The Broncos had closed the gap to 30–27, and with an interception, were set up with first down at the Green Bay 43, with two minutes, five seconds left in the game. The way this game was trending it appeared that the most the Packers could hope for was a tying Denver field goal and an overtime.

But then White, at the very moment that required him to lift his game and lift his entire team, became the pass rushing force of the Packers' most hopeful plans and dreams. He was simply an unstoppable force. On consecutive plays, he sacked Elway for losses of eight and 14 yards, ending Denver's possession, and, simultaneously, halting the Packers' losing streak.

For the game, White had three sacks. As the Packers left the field after running out the clock, the Lambeau Field crowd chanted: "Reggie! Reggie! Reggie!" well into the evening.

In the Packers locker room, White was asked what he thought with nearly 60,000 people chanting his name. In a voice that was both gravelly and powerful, White responded: "Praise God."

Those two sacks of John Elway represented his first opportunity to make certain that everyone knew that in his presence they had arrived at the intersection of the Green Bay Packers and his beliefs. For the uninitiated opposing tackles who had the misfortune to be matched against him, White would introduce himself before his first snap of the game with a question: "Have you accepted Jesus Christ as your Lord and Savior?" On a typical afternoon, White would then repeatedly outplay the tackle in question, thus illustrating the power of his own brand of Christianity.

Harris Barton, playing tackle for the San Francisco 49ers, lining up for the first time against White, got the introductory question: "Have you accepted Christ as your Lord and Savior?"

"Reggie, I'm Jewish," Barton responded. White did not say anything else to him for the remainder of the game.

One way or another White continually served as an inspiration to teammates. For the players, the signing of White provided a genuine boost to their hopes, their aspirations, and their collective self-esteem.

"I said: 'The losing culture is gone, because we've got Reggie,'" Butler said. "Getting Reggie was big because we had a leader. We all saw how good he was with Philly. Now we had an offensive leader with Brett and a defensive leader with him. Man, I still don't know how Ron did it; the smallest market in the league gets the biggest free agent."

That was precisely the effect Wolf was going for with the acquisition of White. "The fact was that he was an absolutely fabulous football player," Wolf said. "The fact that he cast his lot with us is a great credit to the great job that Ray Rhodes did in recruiting him and the great job Mike Reinfeldt did in the negotiating factor with his agent.

"But this was a case where I felt that we kind of turned the corner because now we had people working for the betterment of the Green Bay Packers. There was none of this 'I don't want to be the laughing stock.' No, it should always be about the Packers, the Packers, the Packers. It should always be that."

White had a view of the significance of his signing that went beyond the game of football. "It changed the stigma that was on this team, that black players couldn't have fun up here, that this town was racist. I think by me saying, 'I'm going to play for Green Bay' and then liking it here, it changed a lot of guys' attitudes, black and white. I think it made guys want to play here."[2]

The thing that was indisputable was that the acquisition of Reggie White had made Green Bay a more palatable, more viable, more hopeful football destination. And as the Green Bay portion of White's career unfolded, the legend of Reggie White expanded. Some of that was football-related. Some of it was faith-based. Some of it was a mixture of football and faith.

White suffered a severe sprain to the medial ligament in his left elbow against the Buffalo Bills on November 20, 1994. To that point in his career, he had been a model of durability. But the Packers were scheduled to play the Cowboys in Dallas on Thanksgiving Day, just four days after the injury. Two days after the Buffalo game and two days before the Dallas game, the Packers announced that White would not play against the Cowboys.

---

2 *Los Angeles Times*, January 26, 2011.

But he did play against Dallas. He did not start, but he played most of the game, registering six tackles, one sack, plus pressuring Cowboys quarterback Jason Garrett into an intentional grounding penalty. White, wearing a brace on his left elbow, was also seen lifting 325-pound Dallas offensive tackle Larry Allen off the ground with one arm. What happened? White described it as "a healing."

Perhaps an even more remarkable recovery occurred in 1995 when White suffered a torn left hamstring on December 3 in a victory over Cincinnati. The initial diagnosis indicated that the injury would require surgery and White's season would be over. The Packers made an announcement to this effect on December 13. That same night, White felt that the hamstring was markedly improved. White returned to practice the next day, and played in a victory over New Orleans two days after. He returned to the starting lineup for the final game of the regular season, and remained there for all three of the Packers' postseason games. The surgery never occurred. Another "healing" did.

A first-hand witness to these startling developments was Pepper Burruss, then head athletic trainer of the Packers, now director of sports medicine administration for the team. The memory of these miraculous recoveries is vivid for him.

"Reggie had hurt his elbow," Burress said. "He didn't dislocate it, but he severely sprained it. He wasn't going to practice. The one thing I remember about Reggie was that it was going to be touch and go. I was walking down to practice and I kind of liked the same spiritual music that Reggie did. He said in that gravelly voice: 'Pep, do you have 'Take Six,' which is an a cappella Christian group. It was a CD and he asked me to put it on for him. I did, and I went to practice. I came back, and Reggie was asleep. The CD was still playing on repeat or shuffle or something. And he literally got up—and I don't want to make this sound more dramatic than it is—he got up and he's flexing his elbow back and forth and he says: 'I think I'm healed. I think I can play. I think it was that music.'

"As with his hamstring, God did not put the muscle back together, but He certainly healed that ability to deal with the pain and dysfunction. Because I literally got a couple of hinges, for making braces, aluminum hinge, moldable plastic, made him a brace (for his elbow). That's what he played the next game on.

"I'll say that God healed his pain with his hamstring, or the fact that you don't know that it also happened with his elbow. And people will give you that look. The one that was more widely publicized was the hamstring, but the elbow was right there. Brett's ankle thing, wasn't a God thing, really, Brett was just being Brett, a tough guy. But Reggie was given praise for both of his somewhat miraculous recoveries.

"As far as I'm concerned, doctors have a superior, too. More often than I get asked about whatever injuries, people at the gas pump will recognize me and say: 'Hey, keep 'em healthy this year.' And I'll look over and say: 'Whoa, whoa, whoa. You're messing with God's work, pal, I'm just helping.' There's no competition there, but if you're an athletic trainer or a strength coach, if you're going to take credit for the good, you damn well better get ready to take credit for the bad.' I want no credit because we will have injuries, we will have surgeries, guys will get hurt. The question is who, when, how, and where. It's going to happen in this business. And that's why we have jobs because if no one got hurt we'd be out of work.

"Reggie's ability to overcome the pain with the hamstring was by far the most remarkable. There are still some cynical people who will say that we obviously misdiagnosed Reggie's hamstring and it wasn't as serious as we said it was. What's the miracle, what the big deal, *yada, yada, yada*.

"We had two MRIs that we brought to the (NFL scouting) combine the following year. I cut the name off and we asked the doctors in our combine group. The rather famous Russ Warren of the New York Giants was in there. He said: 'It's definitely torn.' We said: 'Think a guy could play with it?' I can't recall if he said exactly: 'Hell, no,' but it was something like that. We said: 'That's Reggie White and he played the next week. He said: 'What?' No, we did not blow the call. No, it was not a little 'owie' and we made a big deal out of it."

White aspired to what could be considered a religious life, but like the rest of humanity, he was not perfect. His impact on the field was immense, but when the field was the practice field, he occasionally had to be reminded to take it easy.

"He was genuine, but he was also a showman," Holmgren said. "It's 1995, here's (guard) Adam Timmerman. A rookie, gung-ho guy, trying to make the team. He'd go against Reggie in one-on-one pass protection, and Reggie would say: 'I'm old, take it easy.' But Adam doesn't let up. Reggie proceeds to just knock the stuffing out of him, embarrasses him, which he could do if he chose to.

"The players always said, anybody who went against him: 'Don't get him riled, just be nice to him; you know, 'good rush, Reggie.' But if you ever got him upset, oh, golly. So, I go 'stop!' and call the team up. I say: 'This team, we've got Pro Bowl players, we've got All-Pro players, we've got rookies, and when I see, maybe our best defensive player trying to humiliate a rookie, it bothers me. I said: 'Knock that shit off.' I pointed to Reggie and I said: 'Don't do that anymore.' That goes for everybody. Everybody is trying to make the football team. Compete, but let's understand what we're doing.

"So, we finish practice. I call the team in like I always did and then they go, except for Reggie, who is standing right there. 'Hey, Mike.' I go: 'What do you want?' He says: 'I don't like it when you curse at me.' I said: 'Okay, I apologize. I don't like it when I have to curse at you, either. You understand why I was upset, though, because of Adam?' I said: 'He's trying to make the team. You're Reggie White. He's a rookie. As long as you understand why I did it, I'm sorry, and I won't do that again. You promise me now, you understand what I'm saying.' He says: 'Okay.' And runs inside."

White's fundamentalist beliefs led him to make some highly public and derogatory remarks about gays and lesbians. He believed that homosexuality was simply a bad decision and that it could be "cured" by a regimen of Christian conversion therapy. He denounced gays and lesbians in a speech before the Wisconsin State Assembly in March 1998 and was subsequently, and justifiably, criticized widely.

"I was at the Competition Committee or something when I heard about it," Holmgren said. "I called him and said: 'What in the world . . .?' He said: 'Well, I didn't think . . .' I said: 'Stop right there, that's right, you didn't think.' "

When the Packers next gathered for team workouts, Holmgren said that White, who was not accustomed to being a target of media criticism, told the coach that he needed to have a press conference to voice his side of the story. This idea struck Holmgren as having a huge potential for distraction. The coach said no. A compromise was reached in which White could have two interviews with reporters of his choosing.

I was one of the two reporters. When we met for the interview, I thanked White for choosing me, and he responded: "I know you disagree with me on these issues, but you'll be fair." That was the best thing he could have said to somebody in my position. I said that this was his chance to say whatever else he wanted to say. He responded with a detailed argument that the media were inaccurately trying to portray him as a Republican, in order to cut him off from the African American community. "I have strong family values," White said, "but I'm not a Republican."

I went out to the afternoon practice to inform my colleagues what I would be writing. Holmgren spotted me and jogged over.

"All right, what kind of disaster do I have on my hands now?" Holmgren inquired. I reported that Reggie believed that the media were portraying him as a Republican in order to cut him off from the African American community.

"Thank God!" Holmgren said with a smile. That seemed to be a completely fitting response.

For people who knew White, the entire controversy was something of an aberration. White was respected, and admired, and simply liked by the vast majority of his teammates, including those who argued with him regarding his views on the LGBTQ community.

"Reggie was larger than life," Holmgren said. "But he was such a goofball in the locker room, he was funny and likable. So, he didn't act like a superstar, most of the time. You know what a good-hearted soul he was."

For his part, White found some attractions in the Green Bay franchise that no other NFL locale could have possibly offered. For one, there was the singular focus on football.

"One of the most intriguing things about Green Bay is there's hardly anything to do here," he said. "You've got to concentrate on what Vince Lombardi said: 'God, family, and the Green Bay Packers.'[3]

Also, there was the Packers' status as the only publicly-owned major professional sports franchise in North America to consider. Throughout

---

3 *Chicago Tribune*, July 19, 1993.

the history of the franchise, whenever the Packers needed money, they had a stock offering. The shares never return a nickel to the purchasers of the stock, but the stockholders are, for all intents and purposes, part owners of the Green Bay Packers. They are represented by the board of directors and the seven-person Executive committee.

"That was a big attraction," White said. "I never knew Green Bay was owned by the community. To know you don't have to fight with a single person was a big factor. People who have stock here are fans and they want to see everything possible for this team to win. And these are some of the nicest people I ever met in my life."[4]

White died in 2004 at age 43, due to cardiac arrhythmia. His status as a legend had already been established in the previous century.

His signing with the Packers had worked in all directions: for Reggie White himself, for the Packers, and for their devoted followers. With White's acquisition, Ron Wolf had put the third basic piece of the foundation for success in place. He had the right quarterback, the right head coach, and now, the right dominant defensive player. A previously hopeless situation had been transformed into a winning situation.

"He found the quarterback," Holmgren said. "And then when he signed Reggie, he had the building blocks for both sides of the ball. The other people to fill in, to make your team good, when you have somebody like Ron, he's going to do that, once you have the lead dogs in there."

"Reggie said: 'God told me to come to Green Bay,'" LeRoy Butler said with a smile. "Ever since then I've been looking up: 'Thank you, God. I appreciate that.'"

---

4 Ibid.

4

From New Freedom, Pennsylvania, to a Long NFL Journey

WHENEVER RON WOLF is in a humble mood—and this occurs with considerable regularity—he will refer to himself as "Ronnie Wolf, from New Freedom, Pennsylvania."

This phrasing nicely conveys the image of a small-town lad, even if the lad has risen to the very top of his profession. To understand who Wolf is, we have to start in New Freedom, which means a rural beginning. There will be plenty of twists and turns—Berlin during the Cold War, Al Davis, an ultimately urban character, a rare experience of failure that happened in Florida, a successful second marriage—all interspersed with a man spending much of his life in darkened rooms watching football players on film.

But the beginning was in Wolf's hometown of New Freedom, a place that, in his boyhood, could have defined the term off-the-beaten-path.

New Freedom is located east of Gettysburg, just north of the Mason-Dixon Line, in the picturesque, wooded, rolling countryside of southern Pennsylvania. Wolf was born there on December 30, 1938. The town now has a population of about 4,500 and is primarily a bedroom community for the nearest major city, Baltimore. But during Wolf's boyhood, according to census data, the population of New Freedom was about 1,200. Before the advent of nearby Interstate 83, which runs from Baltimore to Harrisburg, was completed in 1959, this was a truly rural, remote setting.

The journey that Ron Wolf made, from New Freedom to a place of real prominence in the National Football League and then to the Pro Football Hall of Fame in Canton, Ohio, was truly a significant trek.

"I think one of the most amazing things about Ron is where he came from and where he ended up," his wife, Edie, says. "I mean, you've seen where he started out, New Freedom. He comes from this little, teeny, tiny farming community where everybody basically knows everybody, most everybody stays, if not in the town, then somewhere around there, and somehow, he gets it into his head that he's going to do something different. And what he did was really different from what his classmates ended up doing. Even wanting to make the military his career, which was his first goal, is different than everyone else. I look at that and I think it speaks to his iron will and his drive, that he always kept pushing for something different than what he'd grown up with."

What was it like growing up in New Freedom? There were small-town virtues, but the career options were largely limited to an insulator factory, a Superfine Canning operation, and farming.

"My mother (Marie) was a housewife, my Dad (Guy) was a plastics engineer, he worked at the insulator factory," Wolf said. "He had six brothers, four of whom were farmers. He had a sister. She married a farmer. His oldest brother was a concert pianist and he would travel to Europe with a guy named Jose Iturbi (renowned conductor, pianist and harpsichordist). He died young, my Uncle John.

"But my Dad was a plastics engineer. He stayed in New Freedom, so that his sons could graduate from the same high school there. I have a brother (Guy) four years younger. My Dad later went to work for Leviton Manufacturing Company, Inc., in Warwick, Rhode Island, the largest privately held manufacturer of electrical wiring equipment in North America. He ran that company.

"You don't realize this because you're kind of isolated in a way, but it's a small town. There was a narrow focus. Growing up, you could work at the canning company, plastics factory, or you could drive a bread truck. But by the time I got to high school, the baking company was no more, so that was scratched. Those were your options and most everybody stayed in the area when they got out of high school. I was one of the few people to leave.

"I worked at the canning company in the summer time. I was very adept at loading peas and lima beans into the trucks," Wolf said with a smile. "I was really good at that. That was probably the best thing I did.

"I was at one time a paper boy. The York paper in the morning, the Baltimore paper in the afternoon. That was kind of it. I started at age 12 picking potatoes. You could get five cents a bag, which was two bushel baskets in a bag. You could make maybe 60 or 70 cents a day. Not bad for 12 years old. Get you an RC and a Moon Pie. I swear, that's what I'd get.

"I was also a Blue Gooser for a while. A Blue Gooser is, I worked in a peach orchard. At night, paste the label on, slap the label on Blue Goose peaches.

"I was a real country kid. I grew up in a town of 1,200 people; no traffic lights, everybody knew what everybody did. A farming community, the two big things were an insulator corporation that did plastics and a cannery. When you graduated from high school you went to work in the factory, you went to work in the cannery, or you went to work in Baltimore. That was it, or you worked on a farm.

"But we. . . We would go out and raise hell on Friday, go drink beer and all that stuff. That's kind of like Brett Favre. He was a country guy. Now we're talking about a little bit different kind of money. The most money I ever made was $83 a week working in the cannery," Wolf said with a smile.

"Played baseball and football. Played receiver; actually it was called end in those days because you never went out. Everything was tight, split-T. They discovered I could catch the ball, and they let me spread out a little bit. I was a much better baseball player than a football player. Shortstop in college, but in high school, a left-fielder and a first baseman."

Wolf has publicly gone a considerable distance to portray himself as less than a stellar student. In his Pro Football Hall of Fame induction speech in 2015, Wolf said that he had "graduated 101st in a class of 83 at Susquehannock High School."

There is a chance Wolf's academic performance was at least slightly better than that. "I don't have a good recollection of what he did academically, except I don't recall him being elected to the National Honor Society," said a Neil Harvey, a boyhood friend of Wolf's. "I think he excelled in some of these sports that he was interested in and did okay academically."

In fact, outside the classroom, Wolf was already exhibiting the kind of comprehensive grasp of details that would characterize his career in football. Harvey, who became a superintendent of schools in York County, recalls that "He [Wolf] had a penchant for facts. He could remember different areas of baseball or football as we talked. And then in adult life, I can recall being in Florida, being in a car with Bill Parcells and Ron and they were challenging each other with questions going way back into the '60s; who graduated from what college, and so on. So, it continued that he would have a penchant for details that other people normally would not. This is without a computer."

The boys in New Freedom would be boys. Larry Krebs, another boyhood friend of Wolf, recalls: "About in 11th grade, Ron got mixed up with some rowdies in the school, but that didn't last long. I think the principal gave him a couple licks across the desk with his belt.

"We would drive up to Hanover, there was a club up there, and we'd occasionally drink a beer, when we weren't supposed to, you know what I mean? But we kept our noses pretty clean. At Halloween, we'd take fodder that was on the fields and pull it toward the road, tie up half the road, that's the kind of mischief we got into."

Krebs, who went on to own a successful office beverage company, has maintained a friendship with Wolf. "I liked him from the start," Krebs said. "He was such a likeable guy. What a gentleman. What a person. Whatever I would say good about him, it still wouldn't be enough."

"He is not overstated in conversation, but he has a droll sense of humor," Harvey said. "He's quiet, and unassuming, but all of a sudden, he'll come out with a "Well, that's a hell of a thing.' He didn't say it at first. Or, 'that guy needs to have his head examined if that's what he's thinking.' And he would say it almost to no one. 'What was that, Ron?' 'I shouldn't say.'

"As a young fellow, I thought that he was rather quiet. I just thought that the two of us seemed to connect, with his quiet, unassuming way. And then sometimes he'd get that twinkle in his eye and then we go do something not that terrible. But you could have that kind of fun with him also. We simply had the interests of sports as we grew up and talked. And he had the quality of one who would stay true with his friends. We didn't have the incidents, where, 'you said this, I said that, and now you go your way and I'll go mine.' We just had the continual likeness and the freedom to express to each other what our thoughts were. And we didn't always agree, but he was there for me and I hope I was there for him."

Fortunately for Wolf, an important part of his formative years consisted of his father taking him to professional and college football games. This made what turned out to be a lifelong impression on the younger Wolf.

"My father was a Chicago Bears fan," Wolf recalled. "He was a Chicago Bears fan because in 1940, in New Freedom, he drove down to Washington and watched that championship game where the Bears won, 73–0. The first professional football game I ever saw was in 1948, the Chicago Bears in Baltimore, which was really interesting because (Bears owner George) Halas and (Redskins owner) George Preston Marshall were coming into an All-American Football Conference city to play an exhibition. That's unheard of. The Bears had (Sid) Luckman, (Johnny) Lujack, and (Bobby) Layne; those were the three quarterbacks. George Connor was a rookie, Bulldog Turner, Bill Osmanski, I mean, they're all there. Sammy Baugh (Redskins quarterback) they were all there. But we were on the Bears side. That started it.

"My Dad and I would go watch the Colts play… . He was a sports fan. He was not like his brothers. He was a Yankees and Bears fan. We would go down and watch the Yankees play the Senators. I want to tell you, that was a long drive in those days, single lane roads, going from New Freedom to Washington, DC. But I really became a football fan and in 1953 the Colts come back into professional football. And my Dad buys season tickets.

"Six games, $5 apiece. You can figure out what those season tickets cost—60 bucks. We went to every game, every Sunday. We grew up with those Colts. And one of those guys was (defensive end) Gino Marchetti, who was as good a football player as anybody I've ever seen. And of course, (defensive tackle) Art Donovan. Then, finally, in 1955, they got a quarterback, a bonus pick by the name of George Shaw. I mean, finally, this is our savior, George Shaw. In 1956 he gets hurt and they run this guy in there named Unitas. I'll never forget, 1957, I come home on leave from Fort Bragg, I go down to Westminster, Maryland, where they trained. And I was down in a hollow. And it's hot and sticky. And you hear this guy call the cadence and it's like 'Wow, who is that guy?' And it's Johnny Unitas. They were training Jim Parker to play offensive tackle. Training him. And what Marchetti did to him that day was incredible.

"You think of the best left tackles ever to play the game. He's not the best, but as (former NFL head coach) Bum Phillips once said: 'It don't take long to call the roll,'" Wolf said with a laugh.

"I have to say I was very fortunate because of my Dad. My Dad didn't make much money, but he was a sports fan and a football fan. I had an opportunity to go to games and I could appreciate the thrill of that."

After high school, Wolf thought he would pursue a career in the military, so he enlisted. He realized days into his Army career that he might have been mistaken.

"This is not the way I envisioned this," Wolf said. "Guy's got eight years in, he's a corporal. Maybe he's making $112 a month, you know?"

But the way it subsequently went worked for Wolf. "I was not an outstanding student," he said. "When I went into the military, I was very fortunate. I had taken typing in high school and I could type like the dickens, I could type fast. So, in the military, they go through all this stuff, they find out that you can type and they put you in a headquarters company. So, I was in a headquarters company, Eighteenth Airborne Corps, Fort Bragg, North Carolina. That's in Fayetteville, North Carolina, one of the garden spots of the world. Chiggers and sand fleas. So being at headquarters company, and you room with guys and they're getting assignments all the time. Finally, I said: 'If you come up with a good one, get me out of here.' So, they came up with a chance to go to Berlin. So, I go up to Fort Dix (in New Jersey) to fly to Berlin, to fly to Frankfurt, actually, and then to Berlin.

"They test me in Fort Dix and they assign me to the office of USCOB, US Commander of Berlin. There's 32 of us, one of whom was a major general, Barksdale Hamlett, the US commander of Berlin. There was a general's cook, and a general's driver, but most of them were officers. But what a unique group. I was assigned to the intelligence office of the US Commander of Berlin, Col. Robert Lawlor, a graduate of West Point. He was a survivor of the Bataan Death March. And because of that, that was the thinking in those days that you would never be a general because you had been captured. The Navy didn't do that, but the Army did that."

The standard line about Army intelligence being a contradiction in terms was not applicable in this case. Wolf was sincerely impressed by the caliber of the personnel in his unit.

"I was around really sharp people," he said, "and I realized: 'Wow,' I've got to make something of myself.' So, I decided I would try to go to college when I got out. I had debated whether to stay in three more years. They were going to promote me to E-6 and we lived well there. We got money to eat, premium money, per diem money. We got money to go across to the PX and eat. It was a heck of a deal . . Having an opportunity to be there, being around really intelligent people, made me appreciate the need for a college education. I was a typist."

In the meantime, here is a young fellow from a small town in Pennsylvania, and he is in the midst of the Cold War, with East Berlin and the cutting edge of the Soviet bloc as next-door neighbors.

"You drive down Clay Alley, and over there you can see where the other guys have their tanks parked and pointed this way; right down the street and that was the Soviet sector," Wolf said. "That was a time when you could go into East Berlin, this was before the Berlin Wall, so you could go into East Berlin. But if you went into East Germany, you got captured and then you were dishonorably discharged.

"This guy I roomed with had a little British car about the size of this table," Wolf said, gesturing toward a standard size coffee table, and we would drive over there. And one night we got lost over there and oh, shit. Fortunately, we found a kid on a bike and he took us back to the Brandenburg Gate and we went through. That was exciting," Wolf said with a smile. "How did we get there?

"Fifteen months, 28 days in Berlin. You talk about turning a light on. Wow. I really wasted a tremendous opportunity, it made me realize that."

Wolf did not re-up. He came home and reviewed his options. "Now, the problem is I'm in Pennsylvania and the only place that would take me was Maryville College in Tennessee, right outside of Knoxville," Wolf said. "And they took me on a trial basis because I was a veteran."

Wolf returned to playing baseball, as a shortstop in college. "I'd missed five years, so it was hard as the dickens to hit that thing," Wolf said. "We played against Carson-Newman (University), against a guy named Clyde Wright who was a left-handed pitcher. And you know what? He threw me six pitches and I still haven't seen them."

Wolf could be forgiven for that shortcoming. Wright had a 10-year big league career, peaking with the 1970 season in which we went 22–12 with a 2.83 earned run average for the California Angels.

In any case, Wolf's interest in football had hardly waned with the passage of some years.

"I had this fascination. I wanted to work for the Baltimore Colts, that's who I wanted to work for," Wolf said. "I would send these letters to the 12 teams. Half of them sent these questionnaires back, player questionnaires. I don't want to be a player; I was willing to do anything in the world that I could possibly do. And in 1959, the American Football League has formed.

"My Dad had now moved to Providence (Rhode Island). I am in college, Maryville. We go to Providence. I get all dressed up in my Baltimore Robert Hall seersucker suit. And I go to Boston. I'm going to go up to 1776 Commonwealth Ave. to get a job with the Boston Patriots. I don't know anything about Boston. I ride the train from Providence, get off in Boston, and walk from the train station. I've got blisters and everything else. I walk in there and say: 'I'd like to have a job.' They say: 'We don't have anything.' I turn around and walk out," Wolf concludes, chuckling ruefully at the memory of his younger self.

After two years at Maryville, Wolf transferred to Oklahoma. "Everything works out," he said. "When I went to Oklahoma, I became a history major. The name Buchanan is a famous name at Maryville College. And it just so happened that the head of Asian Studies at Oklahoma was a guy named Percy Buchanan, who I think graduated from Maryville College, or had an affiliation with Maryville College. His parents were missionaries in Japan, so he knew Japanese; he was involved in breaking the Japanese code in World War II.

"I wanted to go into the CIA. And he's the CIA recruiter. He has this connection to Maryville College and I'm going to all his classes. But I had always had this desire to work in professional football. I just never thought I was going to get into professional football.

"Anyway, I kept peppering letters, and in 1962, they started a newspaper called *Pro Football Illustrated* in Chicago. I was a student at the University of Oklahoma and I would read the newspaper. I started a correspondence with the editor, whose name was Ted Elbert, correcting some things he had wrong in there. They hired me. They asked me if I would come up there. I lasted up there, maybe a half a year, because it went under. But in that half a year, I was introduced to all the powers in the National Football League; everything was done out of Chicago, because of George Halas. All the league meetings, the draft, everything was done there.

"Ted Elbert (who later became an Emmy Award-winning producer for NBC-TV News) happens to be, in the spring of 1963, in San Francisco; his sister is getting married. And the Raiders hire a fellow by the name of Al Davis as head coach and general manager. And Ted can write it off, so he goes over and interviews him. And in the course of the interview, Al says he's looking for somebody in his talent department, who knew names. So, Ted recommended me. I had just taken my last final at the University of Oklahoma. The phone rings and it's Al Davis. He says: 'Would you like to come out for a trial basis with the Oakland Raiders?' Well, I knew the name, but I didn't know him. I'm trying to picture their coaching staff and I got him confused with Joe Madro. But anyway, that's how it got started."

As it turned out, the majority of Ron Wolf's time in the National Football League would be spent learning and applying his trade under the guidance of Al Davis. This was at times a mixed blessing, given Davis's mercurial nature. But there was an exceptional football education to be had and Wolf was the most eager of students.

"I go out there in May," he said. "What Al Davis would do, since he was head coach and general manager, with four assistant coaches, every night I would make the run to a place to get sandwiches, come back, and for three hours we would grade, by position, each team in the American Football League. I mean, all the left tackles. And that's how I learned, sitting in the room with those guys, watching them so you could see that the left tackle at San Diego is better than the left tackle at Boston. So that's pretty much how you do it. You could see what the strengths were, what the weaknesses were. That's how you learn. 'A picture is worth a thousand words.' That was kind of his approach.

"So, you understood what it took to play each position. The whole time, he would harp: 'Height, weight, speed.' He had four assistant coaches. Now, they've got 24 assistant coaches. It makes no sense. It's a waste of money.

"So then he decides to hire me full time, puts me in the talent department. I am the talent department, they don't have anybody else, because the guy he had hired, he fired. In those days, the draft was in November. So what happened was, you did the bulk of the work in the springtime. And you would go to the colleges. Also in those days they would really practice football. But you're pretty much at the end of the spring, you knew pretty much who the players were and where you had to go in the fall. You just hoped in the fall that guys were well when you were drafting them. Spring practice was the determining factor."

So, Wolf hit the road, which was how he would spend most of his time for years; in the spring at spring practice, and in the autumn, again watching practice, and looking, somewhere between relentlessly and endlessly, at film.

"One of the great things that happened to me was, in spring practice, I used to travel the same territory as a guy name of Chuck Noll. At this time, he was coaching in Baltimore as secondary coach. For some reason, we kind of hit if off; here's a young guy trying to learn. I would go out to eat with him, and just gobble up (Noll's knowledge). That was really a great education. I also met a guy named Joe Thomas, who built the Vikings and then built that thing in Miami that (Don) Shula gets credit for, but really, Joe Thomas did it. Another great opportunity. It's kind of like that thing: 'When E. F. Hutton talks, everybody listens.' That's kind of like Joe Thomas.

"Like: 'Why would you draft Larry Csonka?' 'Well, you dumb ass, because he can play football.' Because it was height, weight, speed and his speed was poor. But he could play football. It was about football. Boy, he was a knowledgeable guy. Learned a lot from him, and obviously learned a lot from Chuck Noll and Al Davis.

"So that's how I got to Oakland. And in 1966 Al is named commissioner of the American Football League and he takes me with him to New York, which was really an honor. Then we had the merger, which he did. He brought about the merger because the Giants signed (placekicker) Pete Gogolak. And that was a big mistake. All of a sudden, Mike Ditka, Roman Gabriel, and John Brodie, several players from the National Football League have signed future contracts with the American Football League. And unfortunately, the Giants didn't have any players worth a shit to sign, so the Raiders send a guy named Willie Williams, who wasn't any good, but he was a Pro Bowl player for the Giants. Corner. Slow.

"So, they have the merger, we go back to Oakland and make the trade for (Daryle) Lamonica and take off. Get (George) Blanda. Wow. We take off. Hell of a football team, 13–1 we were that year (1967). Go play the Packers in the Super Bowl and get clobbered (33–14). Roger Bird dropped a punt, or we would have gone in (to halftime) 13–7. Instead, we went in 16–7 and never got it right after that."

Wolf was Davis's right-hand man as player personnel director during a period of consistent success for the Raiders. In the 23 years Wolf was with the Raiders, they had 17 winning seasons, won 10 division titles, played in eight championship games, and three Super Bowls, winning two of them. Davis was obviously in charge, but Wolf, tirelessly researching and evaluating players, was a key component to the Raiders' success.

"Obviously, Al was involved in the selection of players, he's the boss," Wolf said. "But it's up to me to funnel all that information to him. I can go anywhere I wanted to, whenever I wanted to. I'd spend two weeks on the road, come home for a week, and then spend another two on the road. I had to because I had to know who the players were. We were stretched thin. It was a different time. There's no combine, there's no this, no that. He didn't micro-manage in that era. Now, we get ready for the draft, I'd better know my stuff, or I'd be canned.

"It was a tremendous experience. In '80, we had not that good of a football team, but we won the Super Bowl. Great credit to (head coach) Tom Flores and his staff. And in '83, we kicked the living crap out of the Washington Redskins, who were favored by 18 or 20 points. That wasn't even close (38–9) but we had a real football team. And in 1985, we probably had a better football team, and we lost to the Patriots in LA.

"So, in that period there, Al Davis kind of changed a little bit. It became not about the Raiders, it became about Al Davis. We go to LA, suddenly he's on the floor at the Lakers games. He's out at Spago (a noted Beverley Hills restaurant). It's about Al Davis.

"It was hard for me, because suddenly it became a tougher job. It was about finding the sleeper, the unknown player. He liked that, all of a sudden. 'Al Davis found this guy.' It became harder to do."

Wolf spent 25 years with Al Davis. That longevity with the Raiders says that Davis, at his peak one of the best talent evaluators in the game, respected Wolf's judgment. But what was it like working for Al Davis?

Davis had a signature outburst when he thought that Wolf had erred in some basic way: "Ronnie, you're fuckin' with my life."

But Wolf's work was typically well above that level. He and Davis formed a winning combination in Oakland and later, Los Angeles. "I think it was probably pretty good," Wolf said. "He taught me. The way he did things I would never do them. But in the end, I think he was really proud of me. I'm the only one of his that ever came out and amounted to a hill of beans.

"Look at the record he had. Dominated the game in the '60s, '70s, '80s and '90s. I mean four decades. I remember sitting with him, we're in LA, and he's having this (feud) with Marcus Allen. And in my time with the Raiders—25 drafts, 24 seasons, Marcus Allen was the best player to ever play with the Raiders during the time I was there and there were some great players. But he was the best. So, I'm sitting with Al, he's having his dinner. I said: 'You know something, Al, that's really interesting?' He said: 'What's that?' I said: 'You know, in the '40s, '50s, and '60s, Paul Brown dominated football. In the later '60s, '70s, and '80s—the '80s is where we are now—you've dominated pro football. There's one unique thing about both of you guys.' He said: 'What's that.' I said: 'Well, you couldn't get along with your star players.' My God. Oh, did he come apart. 'You can't compare him to that, that guy (Jim Brown) is the greatest guy ever to play!'

"But we got along okay. First of all, he was very bright. His IQ was 181 or something like that. He knew every facet of the business of professional football, as well as coaching. He was a coach, he understood personnel very well. He made some of the greatest trades in the history of football to build that Raiders team up to '67; went 15–1, won the (AFL) title and then played the Packers (in the Super Bowl). Had a good year in '63; '64, '65, '65, '66, just stumbled and then just hit. A tremendous football mind and a tremendous work ethic. A lot of people in the game of football really respected him. You'd be surprised at the number of people who would call to ask his opinion. One was Weeb Ewbank, and he was coaching the Jets. That was constant. People like that would call and ask him questions.

"To work for him, really at the beginning it was great. It was all about the Raiders. It was only the Raiders, that's all we're concerned with, which is a pretty good mindset. Then it started rolling and really rolling well. Then I left and went to Tampa and then came back and things had changed a little bit, although in '80 and '83, we won the Super Bowl. It became a little different. Before it was like we were all united for one thing. Then suddenly it became about Al Davis. That didn't mean he didn't work hard. He still worked hard. Suddenly, the edge was off, and by the edge I mean the trades he made or the picks he made, some of those players couldn't play. He was going to make them play, that type of thing.

"He had a temper, but he also let you alone, he let you run your department. He didn't want you running somebody else's department, however. We used to have a grease board. You'd have the grease board and you'd rate the players, here are the wide receivers, here are the players you'd put in the first round, so on and so forth. So, we'd come in. Al was color-blind. Everything on the board would be written in black;

suddenly we'd come in the next day here's a red or a green. Hmmm," Wolf said with a chuckle.

"He taught me the business. I learned an awful lot from him, but what I think I also took from him was how not to do things, if that makes sense. He was commissioner of the league at one time, for God's sake. He was a brilliant man, but at one point in there he allowed the sycophants that he surrounded himself with to tell him how great he was. That kind of diminished things. Suddenly he liked that. And at the end, it didn't work.

"But when you think of the Raiders, who do you think of? Al Davis, and that's as it should be. He was tough to work for, because he let you do your job, but during the draft if somebody drafted a player that nobody knew anything about, he would get ballistic almost. The one guy I can remember is Bill Lueck. I think he was drafted here, by the Green Bay Packers. We didn't have him as a live player for our draft, so we didn't discuss him. Here Al's going: "Vince Lombardi just got him. You'd better know what you're doing."

Wolf laughs again. He helped to make the Raiders great, and earned the opportunity to steer his own ship. There came a time when he would deal with Davis as an equal.

"I was looking at this book," Wolf said, pointing to a Packers media guide. "This book has more information than it needs to have. But it has guys we lost in free agency. We lost Desmond Howard to the Oakland Raiders, which is something really interesting."

Howard was a premier return man, who was voted MVP in the Packers victory over New England in Super Bowl XXXI. Subsequently, Howard wanted to play wide receiver on a regular basis and wanted the money that went with a position upgrade. Wolf had determined that, as terrific as Howard was as a returner, he was not an NFL-caliber wideout.

"We weren't going to sign Desmond Howard because he couldn't play a position," Wolf said. "Al and I had a gentlemen's agreement. He called me and said: 'I won't mess with any of your players, if you agree not to mess with any of mine.' I said: 'Well, fine. I won't mess with any of your players.'

"Well, he takes Desmond Howard. So, I call him. I said: 'Al, I thought we had this agreement.' He said: 'Aw, I'm not letting that guy go to Denver.' I said: 'You should have called me, because there's no place he can play.' He said: 'Aw, I don't agree with that.' But that's Al Davis. 'I'll make a deal with you.' That's why I never made a deal with him.

"But Howard couldn't play a position, not in Packers football, and obviously, he couldn't play a position in Raiders football, either."

Throughout his career, even when he became general manager of the Packers, Wolf went on the road, essentially working as a scout of college players. It was the only viable way he knew to find the talent, to grade the talent, to discover the answer to the essential question about each player he saw: Was this guy a football player, who could play at the highest level?

"Just think about the life it is," Wolf says. "You get into the school at 7:30 in the morning. You sit there and watch film or tape; film earlier, tape later. You get there early, because there will be other people who want to use the room. You get the tape, you watch, if you had the opportunity, you buy a sandwich from one of those lunch trucks. You eat the sandwich, then you go to practice, jump in your car, go to the airport, fly to your next school. Get into the next airport, pick up your car, drive to the hotel, have dinner, hopefully you can get a pretty good place to eat, but usually it's a McDonald's or something like that. Then you're up until 12 typing your reports or writing your reports. And the next day you're up at 5:30 because I have to do a half-hour walk because of the heart attack. And then the whole thing starts over again.

"When you look back at it, it's an interesting life. But there is a certain dedication involved in that. The only thing that changes is, one day you're at Alabama, the next day you're at Mississippi State, so on and so forth. And you're very fortunate if you're at some place for two days. It's wonderful if you're at a place for two days. I was at Hattiesburg, Mississippi for two days and look what happened," Wolf says with a smile. "Maybe I should have done everything for two days."

And this is no place to let the frustrations of life on the road, or the difficulties of travel that even the best of scouts cannot control, interfere with your judgment. Wolf, who is his own most severe critic, and will speak at great length about the mistakes he has made, vividly recalls one of those instances.

"A lot of what happens on the road influences how you look at a player," Wolf says. "I'll never forget going to Arkansas State. They had a guy down there by the name of Bill Bergey." Bergey was a linebacker drafted in 1969, in the second round. He played a total of 12 years, for the Bengals and Eagles, and was five times named as a Pro Bowler.

"I'm coming from the University of Tennessee at Martin, so I'm trying to get across the Mississippi into Arkansas. So, I go to this place and the ferry is out. So, I've got to go all the way down to Memphis, and then I go back up to Jonesboro.

"Now, this is not a good day. I mean, this guy could have walked on water and he wouldn't have been good enough to play," Wolf said with a rueful smile. "And that's what happened. By the time I got there, I walk in the room at Arkansas State University, Bennie Ellender is the head football coach. In the middle of the room there's a pot-bellied stove and it's colder than hell. And that's their offices back in the day.

"So, I often relate to that. I didn't like Bergey and I was obviously wrong. But all the things that went into it, did not speak well of Bill Bergey," Wolf said with another small smile. "And that wakes you up. You talk about missing a player. I thought, 'I can't ever let this happen to me again.' So, as you grow and as you learn, things get better.

"But it's a lonely existence, if you do it right. Some guys just rely on what the (scouting) combine puts out. I obviously couldn't do that."

For Wolf, there was no substitute for seeing the player in action, even in practice. It beat taking someone else's word for what the player was, who he was, how he was.

"Being that I was on the road a lot, you go to the University of Georgia and you say to yourself: *I wonder what that Herschel Walker looks like?* "Wolf said. "You go to practice and you don't have to wonder. You got him. Or you go to Auburn. *I wonder what that Bo Jackson looks like?* Go to practice. Oh, my goodness. You go to Oklahoma State. Barry Sanders? You can't find him, he could run underneath this table. But what a talented individual."

The height-weight-speed mantra that Wolf learned from Al Davis would be waived in this one instance. Sanders was only 5 feet, 8 inches tall. But the incomparable talent was more than enough compensation.

"Running back, you either are or you are not," Wolf said. "My first exposure to that guy was a game against Texas A&M, where he scored five touchdowns; punt return, kick return, run, pass, I don't how else you can score touchdowns, but he did it. And he did it against a really good football team, Texas A&M. That's one where you go: 'Ooh, my goodness, what have we here?'"

Wolf left the Raiders in 1975 to take what he thought was an opportunity—what looked like a general manager job with the Tampa Bay Buccaneers—but in reality, turned out to be a hard-earned lesson in football life. Wolf had the responsibility of a GM but not the authority. He did put together the 1979 Bucs team that advanced to the NFC championship game. But he was gone by then.

There were problems with the team's owner, Hugh Culverhouse, and with the team's head coach, John McKay. Ron Wolf heeds an admonition that dates back to ancient Greece: "Do not speak ill of the dead." He has no interest in ripping either Culverhouse or McKay. He looks at the Tampa Bay experience as a painful, but eventually useful, experience.

"We lost 26 straight games and then won two (in 1976–77)," Wolf says. "We were 2–26 and then I got fired. It was the only expansion team in the history of the National Football League at that time that in four years was playing in a conference championship game (1979). Sixteen of the 22 starters were my guys. I'm really proud of that. Our defense in '77—I sound like Lindy Infante here—was on the field over 60 percent of the time, finished third in the league. It was a really good defense and the majority of those guys were on the '79 team all played in that game; the whole secondary, all the linebackers, and Lee Roy Selmon, the best guy I ever drafted—235 pounds and he could lift this house. A really good person to go along with it. His brother, Dewey, on the other hand, played linebacker. If Lee Roy had had Dewey's meanness, *woo*. No telling, he could have been the greatest player ever to play.

"But my whole time there I couldn't find a quarterback. I tried like the dickens. Thought we had one in a guy named Parnell Dickinson, who was from Mississippi Valley State. Unheard of to have a black quarterback, and you can imagine what Tampa is like.

"Culverhouse was going to show people how you really make money on professional football. But that didn't really happen until Jerry Jones came in. And Jerry Jones showed everybody how you really made money.

"But what happened was, (Culverhouse) and McKay were contemporaries. They were both in the Air Force in World War II. They both played golf. I didn't play golf. I thought you worked hard. This was my first exposure to an experience of being in a place where people were working for themselves, not working for the Buccaneers, if you get what I mean. I had never been in that type of environment under Al Davis. We were all working for the betterment of the Raiders. I had a couple guys who were trying to get my job. I didn't realize that until afterward. I was very naïve. I was very cocky and very naïve. I found out that I really didn't know as much as I thought I knew. . . . I learned a basic tenet for me. If I ever got that opportunity again, there was going to be one person in charge. I didn't want to have to go through the chain of command. When Bob Harlan offered that to me, it was what I was looking for.

"The one good thing that happened out of all that was that I met my wife, Edie, my best friend and the love of my life. I met her in Tampa. That's the plus factor."

Ron and Edie, who was a clinical psychologist, were both going through divorces at the time that they met. Wolf had three daughters from a previous marriage.

"We lived in an apartment complex that was mostly singles, young adult singles," Edie said. "It was in Florida, so it was built around a pool. And everyone was at the pool on the weekends, and he was the only person there that ever had a book. So, my very first impression of him was, "Well, you know, here's someone who's a little different.' I'm an avid reader, so I always have a book."

Wolf recalls that the book in question was John le Carre's *Tinker, Tailor, Soldier, Spy*, a commendable reading choice in any circumstance, but particularly impressive considering the significance of this meeting.

Ron and Edie were married in 1978. Ron Wolf frequently refers to his marriage to Edie as the key to his success. But before that success, he had to endure some serious losing in the Sunshine State.

"They can say all that they want about losing," Wolf said, "but it's a terrible thing to go through that. I have no empathy whatsoever when people start losing. They want people to feel sorry for them. Hey, I've been there. This is a standard that will never be broken. As the man said:

I have been to the mountain top. I have seen the other side. No one else is going to experience that, no one.

"I can recall going to All-Star Games. People don't want to be around you, because you're a loser. People don't want to go out to eat with you, because you're a loser. People don't want to have anything to do with you, because that stink might blow off on them.

"I had a chance to do it (run his own shop), yeah, but they didn't give me the title general manager. It was like a general manager. The owner said: 'I can't give you the title general manager because you're not like Don Klosterman, who's a real general manager.' But as far as football was concerned, I did that.

"McKay hired poor coaches. He bad-mouthed the National Football League and those guys paid him back. I think what happened was that McKay wanted to get his own guy in there and he got his own guy in there.

"You have to remember, I was incredibly naïve. I worked hard in there. I spent my time in there. It was a different thing to me. I knew what our problem was, we didn't have a quarterback. But we also didn't have other pieces, either. The offense was awful.

"It was a very unhealthy situation and I didn't realize that. I've got people in that office sticking knives in my back, and I'm thinking we're all in this together. I didn't realize until after I got canned, all the stuff that was going on there. You can say: 'Well, you should have known that.' I wasn't there. I was out on the road or in my little room, watching film, doing what I thought I was supposed to do.'

"Made some really good trades, I thought. Got a guy named Mike Washington (defensive back, who became a regular), from Baltimore, he became a corner, stayed to play a corner. Jeris White—the other corner—got him from Miami. Got a guy named Cedric Brown, a safety from Oakland. We had a hell of a secondary. Mark Cotney, got him in the expansion draft, he was a white guy. Drafted Selmon, David Lewis, traded for Richard Wood, 'Batman' from USC. Everybody thinks McKay did that, but I did. Signed a guy (Cecil) Johnson, outside backer. Hired Tom Bass as my director of pro personnel. When the defense fell apart, McKay took him and made him defensive coordinator and he did a hell of a job.

"Those are not fond memories, but I grew up considerably there. It confirmed my belief. Everybody in the game has a belief in how you put together a team roster and all that. My belief is, you start with the quarterback. You start with that right out of the get-go. If you don't have a quarterback, you don't have a chance. My two years there I could never get that guy. I thought, made a trade with San Francisco to get Steve Spurrier. I knew pretty much what Steve Spurrier was, but I thought that because he was Mr. Florida, that it would give me some time. Unfortunately, he's not handed anybody when he comes there. I'm talking about (Lee) McGriff and (John) McKay are his receivers. And I think you can look this up, I think McGriff never caught a pass in the NFL and he started seven games." (In fact, it is worse than that. McGriff played in six games, starting three.)

"Those are the handicaps that he had. Plus, he got the shit kicked out of him. And the interesting thing is, he weathered a storm that first year. I just finished reading his book. What happened was, somewhere, Hugh Culverhouse went to Spurrier after the season was over and asked him what he thought of John McKay. And if you know Steve Spurrier, he told him. And then we had to cut Steve Spurrier. We had this tripartite agreement—you know, McKay, Culverhouse, Wolf—well, it was always 2–1. This time, it was 2–1, he was gone. We had to let him go. He couldn't really play, anyway."

"But he's the best college coach I've ever seen, Steve Spurrier. I know this. I tried to hire him for the Packers. He said; 'You know, I get in my car and drive for 50 minutes and I'm at the beach.' I said: 'I can top that. You can get in your car here and in 10 minutes you can be at the beach.' He didn't want any part of that."

Ron Wolf tried something else in Tampa Bay. Due to factors largely out of his control, it didn't work. Fortunately, the door was still open for a return to the Raiders, although Wolf also had an offer from the Lions. Going to any football function in Detroit in those days was a two-part operation. There was the flight to Detroit, then there was the trip from the Detroit airport, which was considerably west of the city, to the Pontiac Silverdome, which was considerably north of the city. The ride often seemed longer than the flight.

"I was able to go back to the Raiders," Wolf said. "The interesting thing was, Detroit wanted me. Monte Clark called me. So, I'm in Tampa and I don't think anything about it. They're out in Pontiac. I don't know where that is. Get on an airplane, go up to Detroit, we ride from that airport up to Pontiac, I'm looking out the window at all those snow drifts. That ride did it. I made up my mind."

Wolf returned to the Raiders. But he would eventually move on to a place where he could, in fact, have both the necessary responsibility and authority to create a championship team. He would end up in the one pro football locale that was, by NFL standards, very small and completely out of the way. In that regard, it would be something like New Freedom.

5

The Packers Find Ron Wolf

A 1987 DINNER at a Denny's just down the street from Lambeau Field may have been the turning point in the history of the Green Bay Packers franchise. But at the time, a trip to Green Bay looked to Ron Wolf like a waste of time.

Wolf was accustomed to success. During the time he spent with the Raiders, teams that he helped Al Davis assemble played in four Super Bowls, winning three and reached the postseason 16 times. From 1965 through 1990, the Raiders had a grand total of three losing seasons. "Ron was an unsung star among stars, one of our greatest contributors," Davis said after Wolf had taken the job as general manager of the Packers. "He's as good as there's been as director of player personnel."[1]

But Wolf was less fulfilled by the job after the Raiders moved to Los Angeles in 1982. Wolf felt that Davis's focus changed from a purely team perspective to a personal one. "When it started, it was about the Oakland Raiders," Wolf said. "Suddenly, it became about Al Davis, not about the Raiders."

---

1 Quoted in the *Milwaukee Journal Sentinel*, August 7, 2015.

So, Wolf was open to other opportunities, one of which occurred in 1987, when the Packers were looking for a general manager.

"I happened to be in Honolulu at the time at the Hula Bowl," Wolf recalls. "Forrest Gregg was the coach and I can recall people running around asking me if I had talked to 'the Judge' (Robert Parins, then president of the Packers). I didn't know who 'the Judge' was. That's how this all got started.

"I fly from Honolulu to LA—we were in LA at that time, the Raiders—and then I fly to Green Bay. That was my first real exposure to the Packers of the '70s and '80s. And being in the American Football Conference, I knew nothing, absolutely nothing about the Green Bay Packers. I stopped over in LA and our offices were in El Segundo, I hopped over there, watched four or five games so I had an opinion of who the players were. And then caught the flight to Green Bay and didn't take the job.

"I vividly remember at the time that the two best players were (wide receiver James) Lofton and (tackle Ken) Ruettgers. And this was a time when Lofton had gotten into trouble and was no longer going to be on the team.

"What happened was, I'm moving time zones, so I'm a little tired. I fly to Chicago, and we have a three-hour delay because of snow. So, I don't get to Green Bay until (very late), where Bob Harlan, bless his soul, met me at the airport and I had dinner and we talked. And we talked a long time. I did not know Bob, but he was a gentleman throughout the entire process."

Harlan, who became president and chief executive officer of the Packers in 1989, was corporate assistant to the president at the time of Wolf's initial interview. As it turns out, the snow-delayed flight and an ensuing dinner at Denny's, conveniently located just south of Lambeau Field, turned out to be an epic occasion. Harlan was so impressed with Wolf that, when Harlan rose to the top of the Packers organization, he absolutely knew who should be running the football operation: Ron Wolf.

"Ron was in town, to talk about the job that eventually went to Tom Braatz," Harlan said. "In '87, Judge Parins was still the team president, and one of the jobs he gave me was when he wanted somebody brought in I would go the airport and pick them up, and then later, take them back to the airport.

"I knew Ron for a number of years. Anybody who worked for Al Davis had to be two things: He had to be very intelligent football-wise, and a heck of a hard worker. I'd seen Al at league meetings, I knew how he operated. So, Ron flies in, he gets in about 9:30 or 10 o'clock on a Sunday night. The first thing he says to me is, 'Bob, can we go and get some dinner, I haven't had anything to eat.' Well, there's not a lot of options in Green Bay at 10 o'clock on Sunday night.

"So, I took him to the best place I could find—I took him to a Denny's, which is still down here on Oneida Street," Harlan said with a smile.

"And we just sat there and had a hamburger and talked about nothing but football. He was very interested in the 45-person board of directors and the executive committee, he wanted me to tell him about all of those situations. He wanted to know about the facilities. He had a lot of questions. And I, at the same time, talked to him about how he would put a scouting staff together, how would you find a coach, things like that.

"I was just very impressed with how direct he was; there was no hemming and hawing. He knew what he wanted to do and how he wanted to do it. And I felt, 'boy, he's going to be good.'"

"We talked about football," Wolf said. "We talked about how things are put together. I was very impressed that this gentleman took the time to sit there with me, because obviously he had waited for hours at the airport when the airport, for all intents and purposes, was closed down."

To Harlan's recollection that Wolf had asked a number of penetrating questions, Wolf responded: "Really? I probably would, because I had been through a very interesting experience in Tampa."

Impressed by Harlan's empathy and understanding, Wolf proceeded on the following morning to the job interview: "So, I got up the next morning, went in for the interview, and quite frankly, I remember it being a cold place, the Packers' offices," Wolf said. "There wasn't a warmth there. Don't get me wrong. I worked for the Raiders for 24 years, 25 seasons, that isn't a warm place either. But this was not a warm place, and I'm not talking about temperature.

"When I went through the interview process, I just wanted to know one thing and the one thing was: Who is in charge? I had been through an experience in Tampa, so I wanted to know who was in charge here. Who calls what? So, I started out, I asked a few questions, meaningless questions that didn't mean anything. And I didn't get the answers that I wanted.

"I don't think they had any kind of deal. I'm talking about the Judge here. They would tell you one thing but you could tell it was going to go the other way. I mean, you ask a little question: 'Can I fly first class?' just to see what the answer is. The answer was 'No.' 'Do I get a company car?' 'No.' So, now they had two strikes against them, because I had those things as a peon with the Raiders. Why in hell am I going to come here?" Wolf said with a smile. "Those were just little things, but little things become big things."

"I think what happened the next day, at the interview, is he found out that it was a 50–50 split (between the general manager and the head coach), that he did not have total authority," Harlan said. "The plan was to give half the power to (the head coach) and half the power to whoever got the (GM) job. So, Ron has his interview and he comes back into my office and I say: 'Do you want to go get a bite to eat?' And he says: 'No. Let's go to the airport.' He was finished. I said: 'You're sure?' And he said: 'Yeah, yeah, let's go.' You know, typical Ron. We drove to the airport, I said: 'Interview was okay?' He said: 'Okay.' Very non-committal to me. Next morning, he withdrew his name."

"I knew that this wasn't for me," Wolf said. "So, I called Bob, I didn't call the Judge, from the airport in Green Bay and told him to remove my name that very day."

So, Wolf returned to the Raiders, but he would not be with them indefinitely. The heart attack that he suffered on April 10, 1990, changed his perspective and his employment.

"If I told you the reason I left (the Raiders) you would say: 'You're an idiot,'" Wolf said. "But it's always the small things, it's never the big things. I'm lying in the hospital and Edie comes in and says they want me to return the company car. Here I am in the hospital, we got the draft coming up, and they want the car.

"I can't drive, so Edie is driving me to work. We were in a school in

El Segundo. The football office was on one side, and the football players, and the football complex, was on the other. And we would conduct the draft out of the football portion, so I was always over there in the other building. So now the draft is over, and Edie is driving me in and there sits the car; three, four weeks later, and there it is. It's such an important thing to have the car and there it is, still sitting there. And that was it.

"I was very fortunate that Dick Steinberg had just been named general manager of the Jets and we worked out a deal. Went back there, one of the best year-and-a-half of my life. I learned so much from that guy, how to do things, how to prepare for the draft. We took the stuff that he had, when we went to Green Bay, and got rid of a lot of busy work, and tried to incorporate stuff into a better way of evaluation. That year-and-a-half with him, I learned, wow, I learned so much."

What did Wolf learn from Steinberg that he had not learned from Al Davis?

"I would say specifically how to adequately treat people, all around," Wolf said. "That, in essence, people are really good, but you're going to find all sorts. People that are confident, people that are not confident. Dick was an information-gatherer. If we're going to study this guy, he'd like to have 50 reports on (him). I said to him one day: 'Let me ask you a question: You've got this file on this guy. You can't possibly read all the shit that's in here. What do you do?' He said: 'I look up the guy that I know.' So, he's looking at one report. But you can say: 'Look at all the paper we got. You want paper, we've got paper.'

"He was a stickler for detail, but when it came down to it, they had this system, it was the Cowboys' system under Gil Brandt (longtime vice president of player personnel for Dallas). Tex Schramm (longtime general manager of the Cowboys) brought that with him to the Cowboys and Gil Brandt took advantage of that system.

"They had letters: A, B, C, D. Nobody could be an A. Jesus Christ couldn't be an A. C was a little player, and everybody else was a D. D could only go to 69. If you had a C—that's Tony Dorsett or Barry Sanders, small players that could play—they were superstars. If you got a B, holy smokes. Brett Favre was a B. They had all these little specifics that had numbers and the numbers had to add up, so you couldn't cheat. You were what you were. Unless the numbers didn't come out, in which case Dick would sit in there and change the numbers so they did come out. These are things I learned," Wolf said with a laugh. "If you're a good player, you're a good player, so why go through all this other stuff? Those are the things that we eliminated.

"But it was so interesting to watch how he did everything. He loved scouting. He believed that you had to go out on the road, you had to attend games. . . . Those were the things I learned there, just how to treat people. He was a really good person."

Now, we come to 1991. Bob Harlan is in a position of real authority in Green Bay, but he sees bad turning to worse with the on-field product. And he hears the complaints. In the 24 years since Vince Lombardi's departure, the Packers had five winning seasons and two playoff appearances. Five head coaches had been hired, and each had a lower winning percentage than his predecessor.

"We were just on a stairway going down," Harlan said. "It was in my mind that we had to do something different. Now the first year I was president things went very well. (Don) Majkowski had his breakout season, we played very well, and I thought: *Maybe we've finally got the quarterback that we need.* Then when we started falling off in '90 and started off playing poorly again in '91, I thought: *This is ridiculous.* And it really was. I mean, fans were calling me and they were saying, 'the league has passed us by,' or 'we're too small now for the NFL,' or 'we'll never win again,' or 'the Lombardi years were the last great era.' They were losing hope, they really were.

"Green Bay was the black eye of the league and that had to change. There were so many things we had to change by bringing in Ron. Let's get our respect back. To have our fans say to me: 'You know Bob, the league's passed us by, it's over,' that's a terrible feeling.

"I decided in the offseason going into the '91 year, if things keep going like this, where can we go, what can we do to change it? My first thought was, the executive committee, which had been selecting the head coaches for years, they're very smart businessmen, very intelligent and highly loyal, but they're not football people, you know? We simply need a football person to make football decisions."

This was to be a radical departure from the way the Packers had operated in the post-Lombardi years. Harlan not only recognized the need for a fundamental restructuring of the franchise, he also selected the ideal individual to run this operation in Ron Wolf.

Harlan received the approval of the executive committee for the organizational restructuring. He knew, from Ron Wolf's work and from a dinner at Denny's, who he wanted as the lead "football person."

"Ron was my first choice," Harlan said. "In fact, the first time I called him, I said: 'You're number one on my list, and I want to talk until you say yes.'

"It sounds stupid to say that it all goes back to that night at Denny's, but that helped me tremendously. I had such a feel for him after that. I mean, I knew who he was for years, but you had to sit down and talk to him and hear his questions. He was very inquisitive about the organization."

And Harlan also knew, from that 1987 experience, what it would take to get Wolf to accept this job.

"So now, four years later, I knew what Ron Wolf wanted to hear before he was going to come here and take the general managership," Harlan said. "He wanted to hear his title, his salary, the length of the contract and what duties he had. I knew number one: he had to have the responsibility to hire and fire the (head) coach.

"So, after I talked to Dick Steinberg (to obtain the Jets' permission to talk with Wolf), I called Ron. We visited for a little bit, I told him what I had in mind. There would be total autonomy. I said: 'I can promise you right now, there will be no interference from the executive committee or the board of directors. It's your operation to run.'

"On a Friday I faxed a contract to him at a hotel. On Saturday he called me and said: 'Bob, I think we have a deal.' He told me that he didn't have an agent, but he said, he had an advisor and he wanted to run it by him. I think it was a five-year deal, the salary didn't approach the millions of dollars that people are making today."

The salary was reported to be about $400,000 per year.[2]

"We didn't debate the salary," Harlan said. "I remember I put the

2 *Milwaukee Journal*, November 28, 1991.

number one point on there, 'authority to hire and fire the head coach,' I knew he had to have that.

"So, we reached a deal very quickly. He signed the contract and we took him downstairs for his press conference."

Harlan's initial decisions—to restructure the organization and then to put Ron Wolf in total command of the football operation—opened a path to success.

Bud Selig was the owner of the Milwaukee Brewers at that time. He would serve as Commissioner of Baseball for 22 years, and subsequently be elected to baseball's Hall of Fame. In 1990, he was named as a member of the Packers board of directors. He was in a position to know what worked and what did not in the world of sports. He saw the transition from the amateur-led Packers to the Ron Wolf era and he knew what it meant.

"I'll tell you who I give a lot of credit to," Selig said. "It's Bob Harlan, because Bob hired Ron and gave him free reign. After that I got to know Ron, through many board meetings. The more I saw of him, you know, I've been in sports a long time, I really liked him. He was a really interesting guy, devoted, dedicated; oh boy, was he ever. There was something about him, he was a no-nonsense type of guy. He was in Green Bay and he was there to do a job, as you well know. But I got to see it up close, at board meetings and other things. I really liked him a lot."

Pepper Burruss, who would become the Packers head athletic trainer and became director of sports medicine administration before retiring in 2019, sees the crucial role that Harlan played in the Packers' revival.

"As much as Ron Wolf deserves Interstate 43 to be renamed after him, I give huge kudos to Bob Harlan for finally getting frustrated to the point of convincing the executive committee that they're going to bring a guy in here and give him an iron fist," Burruss said. "Really, really, the guy who deserves more credit than he gets is Bob Harlan."

So, the era of non-football people making football decisions was over in Green Bay. This was the opportunity Ron Wolf had been waiting a professional lifetime for—28 years into that career—and it would be structured exactly the way he wanted it to be structured.

"Who was in charge of what was very, very important to me," Wolf said. "Bob was very gracious because he put me in charge of the whole football operation. It was time for me to shit or get off the pot, so to speak.

"When I got there, they had this long run of losing. With each coach it got worse and worse and worse. And I think the guys who were on the executive committee were probably gun-shy. Because you can't go out in that community (when the Packers are losing). You going to go to Oneida Country Club? They don't want to go out. At least when Bob presented that opportunity to me, I had to meet once a month with the executive committee. I would talk to them for maybe 20 minutes, answer whatever questions they had, and then move on. I got out, somebody else came in. But if I had anything to do with football, I didn't have to go to them. I went to Bob Harlan. There's the difference. You had one guy in charge and that was Bob Harlan.

"You need to go somewhere with someone who understands what we're going through here."

Harlan had seen the downside of previous structure of the Packers and he knew that the organization had to go in a better direction. So, Wolf was going to have his authority, his autonomy, and his chance.

"If we were going to change the way we were doing business, then you don't start saying, 'No, no our executive committee doesn't like it,'" Harlan said. "I never went to the executive committee and asked. I just said: 'This is what Ron wants to do.' I also told the board: 'I don't want any interference with Ron. I don't want anybody giving him any suggestions whatever.' And they agreed.

"Before I was president we had people on the executive committee talking, and I'm not trying to put them down, because when you think about it, that was their role to monitor the football operation, but they were very strongly opinionated. There were a lot of arguments and things. It's like asking a man who runs a hardware store to go down the street and run a hospital for you. We didn't have anybody who had that kind of football knowledge. We just had to change. We were falling too far behind people.

"It is intimidating to look at it from the outside. I remember years ago, people screaming about 'we've got to change this!' I remember one time they brought in Bart Starr (then head coach) to meet with the board (of directors) on a Saturday morning. It was ugly, the way these people on the board of directors were screaming at Bart. I thought: *We've got to get rid of this. It's got to go.*

"People on that board were angry, and they just stood up and screamed at him. It was ugly. I thought: *We're never going to have that again.* And fortunately, we never did."

Instead, Ron Wolf was at last being handed a job with all the tools he believed he needed to succeed.

"That felt good," Wolf said. "I didn't tell anybody. In fact, I flew to Chicago and then to Green Bay for the announcement (on November 27, 1991). And I was again stranded in Chicago because of snow in Green Bay," Wolf said with a smile.

"While I'm in Chicago I call Al Davis and tell him what's going on. And his words to me were: 'You're just like an owner.' And how could you turn that down? First of all, you're talking about a person; I thought I was a director of player personnel for life. I'm 52 years old. They never hire anybody my age to be a general manager any more. But then fortunately George Young got his foot in the door with the Giants. And then Dick Steinberg, who was older than I was, even though he looked 10 years younger, got his foot in the door.

"So, if somebody gave me the opportunity, I'm jumping at it. There were only two places I wouldn't go. That was Arizona and Indianapolis (because of issues with the ownership). I would have gone anywhere else.

"What he handed me, in essence, was what Al Davis says: 'You're like an owner.' The great thing was it was all in my hands. I remember telling this to Holmgren. I sat down with him after he took the job. I said: 'There are two people who when we wake up every morning we're either going to succeed or fail. And the only two people we can blame is each other. I mean, they gave it to us: 'Here, you do it.'

The Packers of the recent past had made every mistake in the book. In the 1989 draft, for instance, they passed on Barry Sanders, who became one of the greatest running backs in the history of the game and took instead offensive tackle Tony Mandarich, who had been a legendary college player at Michigan State. Mandarich turned out to be largely a creation of steroids and was no big deal in the NFL.

"I know Lindy (Infante, head coach when Wolf arrived) told me when I came in there that he wanted Barry Sanders, not Tony Mandarich. Obviously, had they taken Barry Sanders, I never would have been there," Wolf said with a laugh.

"With the 50–50 arrangement (between the head coach and general manager), if one guy wants to take a quarterback in the draft and another guy wants to take a defensive tackle, who makes the decision?" Harlan said. "The president. And we're not in a position to make that kind of decision. We shouldn't be. Changing the way we did business was the key and getting the Board out of it. And thank God for the 25 years of success; the Board has stayed out of it."

Wolf did receive some early instructions from a member of the executive committee.

"When I first came to Green Bay and had a meeting with the executive committee, Tony Canadeo was one of the seven members on that committee. (Canadeo was a Pro Football Hall of Fame running back, who played for the Packers in the 1940s and early 1950s. Before that he was known in college as "The Gray Ghost of Gonzaga".)

"Tony Canadeo's statement to me was: 'I really don't care what you do, just beat them Bars.' And I didn't get that at that time. But then, having had an opportunity to witness what that game meant, on both sides of the ball, was something that makes the NFL what it is. This is really a true rivalry."

Against the Bars, who are more commonly known as the Chicago Bears, the Packers went 15–3 during Wolf's nine-year tenure. "It was wonderful," Wolf said. "That was really, to me, one of the crowning achievements. Plus, we went eight consecutive years and broke a record. Lombardi never did this, Lambeau never did this, Halas never did this—winning the games in Chicago, eight consecutive years. Really, really proud of that."

To put that performance in perspective, in the nine years before Wolf took over in Green Bay, the Packers were 4–14 against the Monsters of the Midway. There was considerable work to be done in this area and Wolf's Packers did it.

But in November 1991, Wolf had no victories in hand. What he did have was a plan, a very sound plan as it turned out. He knew what kind of an organization he needed to build in Green Bay. He had been waiting a long time for exactly this sort of opportunity. To other people in the game, Green Bay didn't look like an opportunity. It looked like a ticket to failure.

"At that time," Wolf said, "I had people call me and tell me: 'Why would you go up there? You won't have a chance up there.' And all I wanted was a chance. You could have offered me anything and I would have come here.

"I had an idea. I wanted to win 100 games in 10 years. We did that in nine years, 101 wins. A lot of the other things just evolved. Like I came up with the idea of the honorary captaincy program, to bring back these players, these great players, have them talk to our players, tell them what it was like to be here, to be part of a winning tradition. And if I had any problems getting ahold of somebody, I'd talk to (Hall of Fame linebacker Ray) Nitschke, and they came in."

Part of Wolf's concept of improvement was that the Packers needed a facilities upgrade. Winters were brutal in Green Bay. Green Bay winters started in November. The snow that fell in November was still on the ground in March. Everybody hoped that a thaw would set in before Easter. The Packers' situation required, no, demanded, an indoor practice facility. The Don Hutson Center, named after the legendary Hall of Fame wide receiver from the 1930s and 1940s, opened in 1994, and gave the Packers shelter from the ice, the snow, the frigid temperatures.

"What I wanted was professional football as it should be; nice, clean, neat facilities," Wolf said. "Hence the Hutson Center. When I first got here, Lindy Infante was the head coach and they're practicing outside. You can't practice with that stuff, with snow and ice on the grounds, guys are slipping and sliding. So, I'm thinking: *What the heck is the advantage to this?* Of course, there is no advantage to it. But the object of what I wanted to do is win. And we were fortunate enough to win. You know, winning cures a lot of ills now."

The Ron Wolf that the Packers were getting was a man on a mission, a man in a hurry, a man whose heart attack in April 1990 had not slowed him down. It had, instead, given him an added impulse to take matters into his own hands, and to do it in a hurry.

Mike Reinfeldt was the Packers' chief financial officer and vice president of administration during the Wolf era. He had worked as the Raiders' CFO during Wolf's time with that organization.

"I knew Ron, I was at USC (as associate athletic director) and he was still working with the Raiders (at the time of Wolf's heart attack.) "I remember going to visit him in the hospital. I think he changed somewhat, because in the past, during my time with him with the Raiders, he was more willing to be part of a team, kind of be an equal and he was sometimes a leader and sometimes a follower.

"After he went to the Packers he embraced that role as a leader. I'm sure you've seen that thing where people do that part of the time, but when he came to the Packers, that was part of the mantle that he was going to give the Packers, not only focus but the willingness and the wanting to be the leader and move the group in the direction that he was going to lead. That was a big change that I saw."

The Packers under Wolf would eventually become a mirror of what he believed that the game—and the special circumstances of Green Bay—demanded. They would be a big, physical team, ideally suited to playing in the cold weather, bitterly cold weather, if they could play on into January. And they would handle the wintry surface of late-season Lambeau Field much better than any visiting team could.

There would be one other, less tangible element. The Packers would not be about their recent failures. The point of reference would be the glory days, not only of Lombardi, but of Lambeau. The focus would not be on failure, but on the 11 championships, more than any other NFL team had won. Playing for the Packers, working for the Packers, would not be a job. It would be a calling. It would mean being a part of the revival of a franchise with a storied tradition.

Ron Wolf would insist on that approach, and it would be much different than the recent past in Green Bay. And the winning would be much different, as well. The Packers, thanks to Bob Harlan's decision to restructure the organization, had found the right man and the right path.

6

Ron Wolf Finds the Packers

RON WOLF'S VIEW of the Green Bay Packers in late 1991 was not at all rosy. But that may have been part of the appeal for the new Packers general manager.

"Nobody wanted to go there," Wolf said. "But I wanted to go there and prove I could do it."

Wolf will acknowledge that he was not completely aware of just how far from hopeful the Packers' situation was when he arrived in Green Bay. But that was probably a good thing. The franchise had no recent familiarity with winning. For recent coaches and general managers, employment by the Packers had been a ticket to failure.

To objective eyes, Wolf was not inheriting a very promising situation. Ted Thompson, who had a 10-year career as an NFL player, would work his way up through the personnel ranks with the Packers under Wolf's tutelage, and would later become the general manager whose Packers teams won a Super Bowl and qualified for the postseason in eight straight seasons. He attended the Packers last home game of the 1991 season, with Mike Reinfeldt, who had been his roommate with the Houston Oilers, and was now the Packers' chief financial officer. The atmosphere was not conducive to any sort of celebration.

"I was good friends with Mike Reinfeldt, and he invited me to come up to Green Bay for their last home game of 1991," Thompson recalled. "And obviously, they weren't going to the playoffs and they lost to Detroit, handily. It was never really much of a game and I remember Mike and I were just trying to get out of the old building without running into any people, because, you know, when you lose a game it's like the end of the world. It didn't take an expert to see that it wasn't a good team at that particular time."

Against these circumstances was Ron Wolf, along with his knowledge, his resolve, and his judgment. And in familiarizing Wolf with the history of his new northeastern Wisconsin circumstances, fortunately for Wolf, the human repository for all aspects of Packer lore was employed right there in the offices at Lambeau Field. Lee Remmel had worked as a reporter and columnist for the *Green Bay Press-Gazette* for nearly 30 years, and had been in the Packers front office for 20 years. He was the executive director of public relations when Wolf took over the team. Remmel was a fountain of knowledge. He once described the Bears/Packers rivalry in his weekly game notes as "antediluvian." It turns out, that means "before the flood." And that's how far back Remmel appeared to go with his storehouse of Packer lore.

"I wasn't aware of how bad it was," Wolf said. "Fortunately, we had a walking Packers dictionary there, by the name of Lee Remmel. Having the opportunity to be around a man like Lee, who was a walking fact book of Green Bay Packers history, was a tremendous experience for me. What a remarkable employee he was. I think he actually peed green and gold.

"I was blessed because when I got there I asked Lee Remmel: 'How can I find out more about the Green Bay Packers?' He said: 'You need to see a documentary called: *The Grandstand Franchise*. It was done by PBS. Two hours, it was narrated by Ray Scott (television play-by-play man for Packers games during the Lombardi era).

"I sat and watched that, and it really struck home what it meant to be a member of the Green Bay Packers group. It was an honor, not the other way around. To witness what (Curly) Lambeau achieved in that city, what he did was incredible. How he convinced these great players to come in and play for a buck-fifty a game, I don't know how he did that. And to my way of thinking, other than to have the stadium named after him, he didn't get enough credit for what he did, because it's all about Lombardi, although what Lombardi did is in itself incredible.

"Watching that film, I suddenly thought: *We can make this a positive, not a negative, to come here and play.* Citing those names, those names that surround that field. Bring them in here, let them talk, let our players hear what it meant to be a member of the Green Bay Packers. I guarantee you 90 percent of those guys on that 1992 team had no idea who Lombardi was. Yet every day they drove down Lombardi Avenue on the way to work. There was no clicking there. They thought it was the name of a trophy.

"The guy that helped me the most was a guy named Ray Nitschke, bringing the honorary captaincy back. And what that cost me was a parking pass," Wolf said with a smile. "It was a heck of a deal. Let's take advantage of those 11 titles."

To people who could do their jobs, Wolf's high standards were a cause for celebration. And so was his whole-hearted embrace of what the Packers meant, and thus, what working for them meant.

"I learned so many things from Ron, and one of them was an appreciation for the history of the Packers," said Mark Schiefelbein, then a member of the Packers public relations staff. "And he always talked about that. Always do what's best for the Packers. He said: 'Always remember those who came before us.'

"It was, I think, 1993, Ron was the one who started the honorary captain program. There was a lot of talk that previous regimes didn't want the older guys around, that they wanted to distance themselves from the Packers of the '60s. Ron got in there and said: 'Hey, we need to embrace this. This history and tradition is second to none.' He had come from the Raiders and they were big on their history. Ron would select the guys and I would call them on behalf of Ron and the Packers. We'd invite them in for the weekend, they'd be introduced, and Ron always wanted to meet them personally and thank them for their contributions. Every year we'd talk about the players and who we wanted to bring in. And he was like a little kid with that. He loved that part.

"He knew the guys from earlier eras, whether it was a Tony Canadeo or a Billy Grimes or a Billy Howton, he knew everything about these guys. It was just fascinating to listen to him. If it was a quieter time of the year, you'd go into his office and Ron would be watching old films of the Packers from the '40s, the '50s. He was an historian.

"Those alumni really appreciated that. You bring them back and it's their day in the sun, if you will. I can remember calling guys on behalf of Ron. (Running back) John Brockington comes to mind. I remember calling him, saying: 'I'm calling on behalf of Ron Wolf and the Packers, and we'd like you to come back as an honorary captain.' There's a pause and then John said: 'Hey, I'm going to get booed. My last year there, I didn't play very well.' I told that to Ron and he said: 'He's not going to get booed.' And he got a standing ovation. Not only did that bridge the gap, but it brought a lot of players back into the fold who hadn't been there for a while, maybe didn't leave on the best terms. It was nice that they could come back and the fans still loved them. To this day, John Brockington still comes back all the time."

The Packer players of the 1990s would not be pampered under the Wolf administration, but they would be treated as human beings. The new leadership recognized that the culture had to be adjusted. As Mike Holmgren said: "It had been hard to be African American in Green Bay."

"Let's make this a place that people want to come to play," Wolf said. "So, we brought food in for our players. It's called soul food, from Milwaukee. We brought in a barber for our players from Milwaukee. We did little things like that."

The little things felt more like big things to some of the African American players, who previously would have to drive two hours to Milwaukee just to get a haircut.

"Ron made things so positive for us that we had no doubts," safety LeRoy Butler said. "Everything from getting guys haircuts and having soul food shipped in from Milwaukee. That was huge. There was this stigma that guys couldn't get what they wanted to live, and so they might not want to come to Green Bay. When Ron heard we were going two hours for haircuts and the team was probably 60 per cent African-American, they fixed that. Man, I was in hog heaven. I said: 'This is the way you treat somebody.' And we started winning. We weren't going to win until we started coming together. And then you see it just building and building."

"We built that indoor facility (the Don Hutson Center)," Wolf said, "which was a magnificent facility and is still good today, for which I'm deeply indebted to the executive committee for doing that, so we could practice football. It's important, because you can't practice outdoors there in November and December. That's one thing Lindy was doing, they were out there in snow, trying to stand up. You can't stand up.

"Remmel told me stuff that went on with Lambeau and Lombardi," Wolf said. "Plus, I had three guys I inherited on the scouting staff who worked for or played for Lombardi: Ray Wietecha, John (Red) Cochran, and Dave Hanner. Hanner wouldn't say anything bad about anybody unless you asked him. That was beneficial for the young guys in that room, like Ted Thompson and John Schneider. I would say Red, tell these guys about Charlie Trippi. Or who was the best player of Lombardi's era? They all said Paul Hornung. He could do everything and he was tough."

And Wolf determined that he would assemble an all-star supporting cast. Gordon "Red" Batty was brought in from the Houston Oilers as equipment manager. Pepper Burruss, with whom Wolf had worked with at the Jets, was brought in as head athletic trainer.

"I had a lot of help, a lot of good people," Wolf said. "Red Batty, Pepper Burruss, they were true professionals. Red Batty changed the core down there in the locker room. We became a professional football team. We became more than a professional football team with the structure of how he handled everything."

For someone on the outside looking in, the Packers of the early 1990s had no visible mystique. Asked if he originally thought of working for the Packers as a privilege, Burruss responded:

"No, no, no, Number I had no idea what I had joined. When I went up to talk with the late Phil Pionek (executive assistant to the president of the Packers), we had no HR department, maybe it was about insurance or something. I said the classic missed line that everybody says around here: 'Tell me, does the city own the team?' And he said 'No, it's publicly held stock.' He said: 'Would you like a share?' My ears perked up and I said: 'Of course, I would.' 'Well, I'll put you on a list.'

"I did not grasp the small-town aspect of this. In 16 years with the Jets I was recognized out of character twice. . . . In Green Bay, I would be pumping gas, minding my own business and from the other side of the pump, there would be: 'Hey, how's Favre's ankle?' I had no idea what I had gotten myself into.

"So, no, I didn't know anything about nobility. And I'll stick my foot in my mouth and would have to say with some degree of confidence, as an outsider I knew the Packers to be backwards, cheap, stuck in the past, on and on."

Considering Wolf's offer of a job, Burruss visited the Lambeau Field training facilities.

"Visited with guys in the training room," Burress said. "Everybody revered (then Packers trainer) Domenic Gentile, just as a human being. I've always, always said that I did not come here to replace the late Domenic Gentile. I came here to fill in for him. I walked away thinking that I could do some good here, meaning that I saw nothing against the late Domenic Gentile, but I sensed from Ron that there was going to be a culture change.

"There were no computers in the training room. It was vintage mid-to-late '70s, and this was 1992. My first visit to the training room on the north side of Lambeau Field. I went home and told my wife, 'I'm not sure, hon. I'm just not sure.'"

Wolf became the general manager equivalent of a evangelist, touting the history, tradition, and virtues of the Green Bay Packers to employees, would-be employees, and anybody who might be able to lend a hand.

"First of all, to have an opportunity to work there is a once-in-a-lifetime opportunity if your career is in professional football," he said. "I really have great respect for those people who came before me, the pioneers, if you will, of the game. And I did not fully appreciate what I was getting into when I went to Green Bay, Wisconsin. But let's face it, it's a walking history book. Every time you turned around that building, you bumped into the legends of the game, the people who made this the best spectator sport in the United States of America. They're all right there, and to be blessed to have that opportunity to be a part of that, to someone like myself, it's just incredible. It's incredible. You pinch yourself every once in a while.

"I used to say that when I walked onto Lambeau Field, I got a chill and some wag once said: 'Well, hell, it's 15 degrees out there,'" Wolf said with a laugh. "But I did, every time I went out there. And I was not one of those guys who went around shaking everybody's hand (on the other team) because I wanted to kick their ass. There was a purpose there. I wanted to win the game. I didn't want to shake somebody's hand, but when I went down there, most of the time it was in the preseason, and to walk through that tunnel and to realize, *this is where they walked*, not really because I know that they walked on the other side, because I was there in '62 when there wasn't anything in the end zones.

"It was kind of like when I retired and Peter King (then of *Sports Illustrated*) knew I was a baseball fan and invited me to go to New York for a Yankees game. And I happened to know Stevie Donahue, the trainer for the Yankees who was a very close friend of Pepper Burress, the trainer for the Packers. So, we go down into the bowels of Yankee Stadium. This is where Ruth walked, Gehrig walked, DiMaggio. I mean, this is the real deal here. Wow. But that is the same feeling that I had with the Packers. There was this hall where they had all the banners. It wasn't a very big hall, but you walk down there, suddenly you knew who Cal Hubbard was, Mike Michalske (linemen from the late 1920s and '30s).

"One of my first visits, Lee had me go to downtown Green Bay to talk to a gentlemen's club; that was something that everybody did. And at the end of the talk, a couple of these old guys came up to me and said: 'Now young fella, I want to tell you something.' Now, hell, I'm 52 years old. 'The two best guards ever to play for the Green Bay Packers are Mike Michalske and Gale Gillingham and don't you forget it.'

"I mean that was, in itself an education. I mean, hell, I never heard of Mike Michalske.

"So, I became a true believer. And we were going to use that. We were going to play on it. It's a great tradition. How can you not play on that great tradition? The Lombardi era. Curly Lambeau. How can you not play on that? And we did, and our guys got indoctrinated. And they liked to hear that, liked to hear these guys come in and talk to them. I guess Nitschke kind of rubbed some of them the wrong way, because I guess he called some of them out, which would be his style. But it meant something to those guys because it meant you could have a life here."

Wolf fired people who did not meet his exacting standards, or failed to approach working for the Packers as a noble calling, a true privilege, an honor. Popular players or civilian employees, nobody was exempted. Some of the employees were long-term, well-known, popular figures. That sort of thing would not change any part of Wolf's approach.

"I had to let some people go," he said. "Now, I'll never forget Mike Reinfeldt (Packers chief financial officer and vice president of administration) coming into me one day, saying: 'You can't keep firing all these people. You can't keep doing it because it's ruining morale.'

"I looked at him and said: 'What about my morale? Don't I count here?'"

"I remember that," Reinfeldt said with a chuckle. "That's 100 percent right on. That's classic. But he was right: His morale, the morale of the Green Bay Packers, how we look at what the organization is trying to accomplish."

Wolf's underlying theme never varied. "If they can't do the job, I don't want them around here," he said. "This is not a right to work for the Green Bay Packers. It's a privilege.

"I think people thought I was a hard-ass. To my way of thinking, I'm not a hard-ass. But if you're going to mess around with the Green Bay Packers . . . I always looked at it like this: If I ever made a mistake, and I made several, Al Davis would look at me and he would say: 'Ronnie, you're fuckin' with my life.' I never fully understood what that meant until I sat in that chair. And I got it. And that's kind of how to look at it.

Mark Schiefelbein recalled saying to Wolf: "'Ron, people are afraid of you.' He goes: 'Get out.' I said: 'You're intimidating to people.' He said: 'No, I'm not.'"

Years later, Wolf, reminded of that conversation, said: "I would never think I was tough. I think I was decisive. I hope I was decisive."

There is no question that, from a distance, Wolf appeared to be, as he put it bluntly "a hard-ass." But people who knew him better believed that he acted not out of some personal need to dominate the scene on Lombardi Ave. They shared the perspective that whatever he did, it was for the greater good of the Green Bay Packers.

"He wanted excellence," Schiefelbein said. "Absolutely. When I think of Ron, I think of accountability. He held himself accountable, and he wanted you to be accountable. If you weren't, he didn't have much time for you. He wanted people who worked hard, were accountable, always did what was best for the Packers.

"One time I asked him, because before that, I don't think the Packers had fired a lot of people. Now Ron came in and made some moves right away, and I don't think it was easy for him to do. So, I asked him, was that hard to do? He said: 'Personally it is. But professionally, there's a goal here that we have as the Green Bay Packers. Anybody who gets between us and that goal, for us to reach that goal, then I have to make that move.' You could get the impression that he was a cold and calculating person because he did those things, but that was the furthest thing from the truth. He was a very kind-hearted person, I thought, but he also knew what he had to do."

Wolf's enthusiasm for the Packers was demonstrated more by deeds than by words. He made his point with anyone who was paying attention when he traded a Number 1 draft choice for Brett Favre, who had been riding the bench the previous season in Atlanta. He was a no-nonsense, goal-driven individual.

"It's the understatement of the day to say that Ron never was a rah-rah guy," Burress said. "I had a behind-the-door relationship with Ron and another one in public with Ron. I think most people were kind of 'afraid' of Ron."

There were some adjustments to be made for the new personnel.

"I got ripped in a letter by the daughter of (a former member of the Packers training staff)," Burruss said. "There was an article about the trainer and the image of trainers. In the article, I said: 'The trainers are no longer the image of the fat guy with a cigar and a bucket and a ladle.' And I got this really angry letter that I was singling out somebody. And it was somebody I didn't even know.

"I took the letter immediately and kind of went running upstairs to Bob Harlan. Bob read it and said: 'Well, you pretty much described him to the tee.' I said: 'Bob, that wasn't my intention.' Bob talked me off the ledge, but it was really just in the cliché sense that athletic training and now equipment rooms really had to now embrace technology and it was no fault of theirs. But I kind of said that I needed to bring it from the '70s when I got there, to the '90s. And I think that's what Ron wanted. He wanted it in the equipment room, too, and he had to find this guy and he found Red (Batty) and on and on and on."

"He made an adjustment bringing in a fulltime security guy with Jerry Parins. Al Treml was rather cutting edge with video equipment and the like. Then the push for the Hutson Center. There was a palatable excitement about progression and it was all good. I think Ron was steering the ship and it was going the way he wanted it to go.

"Interacting with Ron, he had so much passion and focus for his job, it was kind of an all-encompassing thing for him," said Reinfeldt. "It was 24 hours a day: *How do I get the Raiders better, how do I get the Packers better?* He was totally consumed by the job that he had, and loved it. It was fun and invigorating to be around him.

"He was totally focused on being better. It wasn't about his ego. It wasn't about power. It was about creating the best football team possible. That was his total focus. And I think in both places it was contagious—contagious for the Raiders and contagious for the Packers."

There wasn't going to be any lack of movement with the playing personnel, either. Wolf wanted "roster churn," and why not? He was taking over a team that had just gone 4–12 and had won one postseason game in the last quarter-century. The applicable Ron Wolf adage was this: "If you're not getting better, you're getting worse."

"Ron talked to me about that," Mike Holmgren said of the roster changes. "When we'd been with each other for a while, I realized that was just how he did things. I just trusted him so much. He's really good and he was my boss so I knew that if he wanted to come in and say: 'I'm bringing this guy in,' he could do that. But he never did it that way. He'd always come in and we'd talk about stuff. 'How do you feel about this? Are you okay with this?' And he always included me in that and in my development, again as a first-time head coach.

"There would be guys that come in—Bill Maas, Steve McMichael—we'd bring in these veteran guys, that really, their best days were behind them, but I think that on a young, developing team there was a presence there. Even Jim McMahon (as a backup quarterback). The quarterbacks and the offensive guys I had more (input with), but with the defensive guys, he liked to do that, he liked to do that. Just see. Once I knew that was what he was going to do, my job was to put it together and not complain about it. That happens too much now. You get those two guys (head coach and general manager) banging heads, you're going to fail. I trusted him, and how he did it, as far as I was concerned, he was very generous with me."

The coaching staff's acceptance of the roster churn was a major plus for Wolf. Lindy Infante's reluctance to go in that direction had been a major factor in his departure after the 1991 season.

"I want to say this," Wolf said. "Look at the job that (the coaching staff) did in '92 and '93, because we had a revolving door there. I told Mike: 'We're going to churn this roster up as much as we can.' In those days, you had a roster of 53 and you could only activate 45, so that bottom eight, if they're not good enough to get the suits, we're going to keep changing. And he bought into that, the assistant coaches bought into that, as a result we got some players out of that. (Defensive tackle) Gilbert Brown, (punter) Craig Hentrich, to name a few. It didn't work quite like I had hoped, but at least we got some really good guys.

"If this guy's not good enough to dress, let's bring in that guy and maybe he's good enough to dress. They bought into that and did a marvelous job taking that collection of players.

"I think we did a pretty good job of cleaning out the locker room, getting rid of those guys who it was just a job for them. It wasn't just a job. That's one of the things I had a hard time with when I first got there. Even the people within the operation, it was a job. No, no, no, we're working for the Packers. The *Packers*. This is a Packers' thing."

Complacency became a thing of the past on the Packers roster. The players could not help but notice that there was a daily parade of people coming into Green Bay, auditioning to take their jobs.

"You always saw a new guy at every practice," safety LeRoy Butler said. "Ron would have like a first-class (scouting) combine. Every two weeks you'd see what seemed like hundreds of guys working out. He wanted not to sign all these guys, but he wanted people to know: 'I can always replace you.'"

Butler chuckled at the memory. "He'd leave the door open, and we'd see all these guys. We'd talk about it. 'Man, you'd better get your act together. He's got all these guys in here.' It was very remarkable."

Now it was time for Ron Wolf to take the last three decades of his experience in the game and apply all that knowledge to his first draft as general manager of the Green Bay Packers. He would operate with a very basic premise in mind.

"I was raised by Al Davis and with Al Davis, it was "height, weight, speed"—that was preached all the time," Wolf said. "Obviously, you need size to play this game. That was stressed. Every moment, that was stressed as we prepared for the draft. Height, weight, speed, and the only time that failed was when we deviated from height. We never deviated from speed, but little players, I was determined that you need big people to play the game. We're going to eliminate little guys."

One thing you learn about Ron Wolf is that he will spend much, much more time discussing his mistakes than he will discussing his achievements. The achievements far, far outweigh the mistakes. But he will give you chapter and verse about the mistakes. That notion speaks to his first draft choice, Terrell Buckley, cornerback from Florida State. "Height, weight, and speed?" Buckley could run, all right, but he was listed at 5 feet, 10 inches tall and 180 pounds. Looking at him standing at his locker, it was clear that 5–10 was at least a mild exaggeration.

"This is a very interesting story," Wolf says. "This is the story of Terrell Buckley. My first draft in Green Bay, and I'm trying to understand the offensive players the 49ers have. We're preparing for the draft and it comes out that the best offensive player, in the opinion of our offensive staff, is a fellow by the name of Desmond Howard (wide receiver and Heisman Trophy winner from Michigan, listed at 5–10 and 185). The best player on defense is Terrell Buckley; that's from the defensive staff. Neither one of those fit height, weight, speed.

"And Desmond Howard didn't fit what the 49ers were playing with. They were playing with (Jerry) Rice and (John) Taylor (at wide receiver). But hell, they were the team. Fortunately, the Redskins jump in front of us and take Howard. So, we take Buckley. (Washington picked fourth in the 1992 first round, Green Bay fifth). And I remember (Bill) Parcells saying: 'He's the antithesis of everything you believe in.' And he's right," Wolf said with a hearty laugh.

Parcells, who had already coached the New York Giants to two Super Bowl championships by that time and would go on to be elected to the Pro Football Hall of Fame, was a friend and a confidant for Wolf.

Parcells also had a chuckle at the memory of Wolf picking Buckley. "We had talked about what we were looking for at corner. I said: 'What are you doing?'"

Buckley would be a classic example of what Parcells held as a fundamental football truth. If you started making exceptions to your standards for what a player should be, soon enough you would be stuck with "a team of exceptions."

In the case of this exception, Buckley had intercepted 12 passes for Florida State in 1991, and had also been a successful return man. The alternative for the Packers was Troy Vincent, also a cornerback and a return man, who was 6–1 and 200 pounds. He was a solid performer, if less spectacular than Buckley, and he was the right size. Vincent had only intercepted two passes in 1991, but there was a very good reason for that. Playing for an undistinguished (5–6) Wisconsin team, there was no reason for the opposition to throw at Vincent when much less challenging options existed elsewhere on the defense.

Buckley's career in Green Bay was, put charitably, undistinguished. He made occasional plays, but his size was never going to stop being a problem. After one game in which Buckley had considerable difficulties, Wolf appeared in the Packers locker room. To reporters' persistent questions regarding Buckley's shortcomings, Wolf at one point responded: "You guys think that Terrell Buckley is a piece of shit. He is not a piece of shit."

"T-Buck" lasted only three seasons with the Packers, but he did go on to have some success with the Miami Dolphins. He started 131 games over the course of his pro career and finished his career with 50 interceptions.

Vincent, conversely, started 200 games in his pro career, primarily for Miami and the Philadelphia Eagles, and was named All-Pro in three seasons. He had 47 career interceptions. He subsequently went on to win numerous awards for his involvement in charitable and community betterment activities, including the Walter Payton Man of the Year Award in 2002 and the Bart Starr Man of the Year Award in 2004. In 2017, he won the NCAA Silver Anniversary Award for his achievements not only in football, but also in community service. In 2014, he was named the NFL's head of Football Operations.

In preparing for the draft, the Packers had a psychological test on which Buckley fared better than Vincent. They subsequently dropped that psychological test. In any case, Wolf relearned a lesson that he had learned much earlier.

"After having that experience, and watching what happens in Wisconsin in November and December, you realize you need a different type of player," Wolf said. "You can't have those little, scrawny-assed guys. You need big players. You need Big Ten players, bigger players to play in that (weather). As a result of that, we started our propaganda of 'we're building our team, it's cold up here, it's Packers weather.' Let's go with that. Suddenly we made that an issue. People say it doesn't make a difference, but it gets in your head.

"I remember when we played the Raiders, it was (December 26) 1993, their guys were going to be so tough they came out in T-shirts. That was stupid. They lost the game. Our guys came out in parkas, that's how cold it was. And their guys couldn't go back because that would be a sign of . . . I remember Al telling me that he didn't thaw out until halftime. He would always stand on the sidelines."

The Packers won that game, 28–0.

So, the mantra became height, weight, speed, and cold-weather guys.

"To take this further," Wolf said, "there was the year we took (defensive backs) Antuan Edwards, Freddie Vinson, and Mike McKenzie, '99 (in the first three rounds). I loved Dre' Bly (cornerback, University of North Carolina, taken by the Rams in the second round). I thought he was it. But he was 5–9. And I would beat our guys down. I don't want to hear about these guys, because our corners are going to 5–11½ or taller. I couldn't do it. I couldn't take the guy I really wanted.

"I mean, you can look at it as idiotic. The guy (Bly) played for (11) years. But it's like Parcells said: 'If you make an exception, pretty soon you'll have a team of exceptions.'"

After the Buckley draft, Wolf set a firm standard for the height of cornerbacks employed by the Packers: 5–11½. He wanted 6–0 even, but "there were so many small guys playing those positions."

The Buckley experience also reinforced what was an essential part of Wolf's makeup, anyway. Honesty is not only the best policy; it is the only policy.

"If I screwed up, I screwed up," Wolf said. "I'll never forget, I'm doing a radio interview with a young guy from Milwaukee and he is building this up, he is blasting me, he is blasting Terrell Buckley. He says: 'What would you say to the fans of the Green Bay Packers about Terrell Buckley' and he went on for what seemed like two minutes but was probably only 30 seconds. He said: 'What would you say to them?'

"I said: 'Well, the fans of the Green Bay Packers are correct.' He couldn't come back. They were right. It was a bad pick."

That gets us into another life lesson for the new general manager: Pay relatively little attention to outside comments, because in Wisconsin, everybody has a Packers opinion, and everybody is more than willing to publicly share that opinion.

"I learned that early with the media," Wolf said. "We had just finished our first mini-camp. I was exhausted; physically, mentally exhausted. I'm sitting out on a chair in the backyard in Green Bay, I turn the radio on, and there is somebody talking about our team and he's evaluating every player. Well shit, I couldn't evaluate every player. Here's Harry Fan, saying: 'This guy sucks, this guy can't do that.' So, I say: 'whoa, I don't need to hear this.' So, I learned that."

At a public appearance in Madison in December of 2018, the first question Wolf was asked was about drafting Terrell Buckley with his first Packers pick. Even at this distance, there apparently is still a need for perspective on this issue. Wolf acquired Brett Favre in a trade and hired Mike Holmgren as head coach before he drafted Buckley, so it wasn't as though he suffered from a slow start.

It ought to be noted that, after the pick of Buckley, Wolf selected three players who would be staples of the winning teams to come: Wide receiver Robert Brooks, drafted in the third round, who had 102 receptions in 1995; running back Edgar Bennett, drafted in the fourth round, who had 1,067 rushing yards that same season, along with another 648 yards on 61 receptions; and Mark Chmura, drafted in the sixth round, who became a top-shelf tight end, being named to the Pro Bowl three times.

Wolf, after spending roughly 30 minutes reliving the shortcomings of the Buckley selection, was asked about achieving that kind of impact with the rest of his 1992 picks. It was his chance to boast, to put a perspective around his initial Green Bay draft, to set the record straight.

"Not bad," Wolf said.

That may be the essential Ron Wolf, right there. The rest of the world could not possibly see it at that point, but the Packers were quietly on their way toward not just improvement, but a complete Titletown turnaround.

7

The Packers Get Better

IT WAS EASY to see the improvement on the field in the first year of Ron Wolf's administration. The Packers went from 4–12 in 1991 to 9–7 in 1992, narrowly missing the playoffs.

But behind the scenes, the changes were every bit as dramatic. Wolf remade the organization, demanding professionalism at all levels and bringing a sense of pride and purpose to the Lambeau Field workplace.

Wolf still defers credit for the winning record in the 1992 season to Mike Holmgren and his coaching staff. "To take that collection of players and win nine games? Unreal," Wolf says.

But Wolf's first major acquisition almost immediately gave indications of even greater improvement to come. Sure, Brett Favre would make decisions early in his career that were equal parts maddening and inexplicable, but there were also indisputable signs of extraordinary playmaking ability.

Before the '92 season began, Packerland was still abuzz with second-guessing about giving up a first-round draft choice for somebody whose 1991 season with Atlanta consisted of four passes, two of which were intercepted, and none of which were completed.

"The hate mail I got when he went after Favre was unbelievable," Packers president Bob Harlan said. "'Who is this Wolf guy you hired?

Giving up a Number 1 for a third-string quarterback?' Well, Ron proved them wrong as he did all along."

The first indication that Favre was something far above ordinary came in the third game of the 1992 season. The Packers were 0–2 when they came to a home game against the Cincinnati Bengals, who were 2–0. The outlook did not improve when starting quarterback Don Majkowski went down in the first quarter with what turned out to be torn ligaments in his left ankle. When Favre entered the Cincinnati game, as Majkowski's replacement, he had thrown 18 passes as a professional, completing eight of them, with three interceptions. One of those completions was to himself, a deflected pass attempt that he caught for a seven-yard loss. By the third quarter, the Bengals were up, 17–3. For the game, Favre would be sacked six times and charged with four fumbles.

But the Packers came back in the fourth quarter, spurred by a touchdown on a 58-yard punt return by Terrell Buckley, who looked very much like a first-round draft choice on that play. Favre threw a touchdown pass to his primary target, Sterling Sharpe, although Sharpe subsequently had to leave the game with an injury.

In the final minute of play, the Packers still trailed the Bengals by six points. With the ball on the Bengals 35, Favre pump-faked once and then threw long right, an on-target, in-stride strike to Kitrick Taylor, Sharpe's backup, for the tying touchdown with 13 seconds left on the clock. The Packers won, 24–23. This was a truly memorable moment, a turning point, a cause for celebration, a tangible signal that better days could be ahead.

Ted Thompson, who was later to become the Packers general manager, but in 1992 was in his first year in the team's player personnel operation, recalls: "We're playing Cincinnati in the third game of the season in 1992 and Brett throws a long touchdown pass and we win the game. Only we were tied at the time, and we had to kick the extra point. And Brett was our holder at the time and he wasn't a great holder. So there was a certain amount of tenseness if you get my drift. But we win the game and it was just as much fun as anything that you've ever been a part of. It just seemed like those kinds of games happened a lot. We started to win games and people couldn't believe it. People finally learned how to say Brett's name."

Andy Reid, later head coach of the Philadelphia Eagles and now the Kansas City Chiefs, was in his first year as a pro assistant, coaching the tight ends and assisting with the offensive line. He had coached against Favre when he was coaching at Texas El-Paso, but Favre as a professional was an untested notion—until the game-winning touchdown pass to Kitrick Taylor.

"The first year we discovered the Brett Favre thing," Reed says. "Ron brought him in, but he was raw. Majkowski, he was the guy, but he was banged up a little bit, and then he did get banged up in that game. Brett came in and, as much as he drove Mike crazy, they had this special relationship, and he was kind of able to take that huge risk that Ron took in bringing him to Green Bay, and we were going, 'Whoa, what's this?' and kind of mold him into what he ended up doing for his career, really, and still let him have enough freedom to do his thing.

"The Cincinnati game, where he made that one throw and we went: 'Whoa, this guy is something special.' I knew from college and high school, if you don't have a quarterback, you're in bad shape no matter what level football you're playing," Reid said with a chuckle. "I had played against Brett at the college level, coaching at El Paso, so I'd seen him when he was young in college, and he just kind of knew how to win and make the play and do these crazy things without any technique. But that Cincinnati game was it, he had done it at the highest level. I was going: 'Whoa, if he can do that here, we've got a chance.'"

The improbability of that play at that time cannot be overstated. Kitrick Taylor caught 47 passes in his NFL career, but only one, the pass from Favre, went for a touchdown. While Favre was Ron Wolf's hope for the future, to most people at that point he was a barely known commodity, who had next to no pro experience and had thrown one nice TD pass at crunch time. Despite the game-winning heroics of that pass, it took a bit longer for Favre to transform everyone into believers.

Harlan, asked when he thought the corner had been turned with Favre, responded: "Well, I'd like to say when he threw that first touchdown pass against Cincinnati, but I thought maybe that was just a stroke of luck. He threw it and somebody was there. But the longer he played the more you could see that there was just something there that we hadn't had.

"He was such a crowd-pleaser taking his chances. Sometimes they backfired, obviously. But he just brought a new element to the position for us, something we just had not had. The competitiveness and the daring, the 'I'll show you how to win the ballgame.' He thought he could win on every single play he made. You just had the feeling that we really do have something special here. We always talked about: 'Why can't we find a quarterback?' It's like other clubs complaining now: 'Why does Green Bay get these two guys (Favre and Aaron Rodgers)?'"

The Wolf/Holmgren pairing was operating on an increasingly effective level, even with constant roster churn and a season that started out 3–6.

"That was my first pro job, so I didn't have anything to compare it to, other than college," Reid said. "That's what I saw. Again, I'm just a little scrub-bucket in the big picture of things. (Assistant offensive coach Jon) Gruden and I and (quarterbacks coach Steve) Mariucci, we were like toilet cleaners. We were just young kids and we were able to sit back and see some things.

"Every day was a new day. Looking back, we're in Green Bay and here's Brett Favre. Ron Wolf goes off the deep end and brings this guy in for a first-round pick and people are going: 'Okay, he's crazy. What is he doing?'

"But I remember after like the first month of Mike Holmgren and Ron Wolf, I'm going: 'These two guys got their stuff together now.' There was just this incredible bond right there and I just felt like we were in good hands. I can't explain it, other than that, any different than that. I was a young guy, and this was a very secure feeling. It was about a month where I go: 'Really, this is good stuff, man.'

"I was impressed with Ron's leadership ability. He's quiet. He doesn't miss anything. He's got like, sniper eyes. He just sees everything. And when he asks questions to you, sitting in meetings, there were no wasted words and he was going right to the point. There was no beating around the bush at all."

Wolf was impressed by Holmgren's ability to get the most out of a constantly changing, work-in-progress sort of roster. Holmgren was impressed that Wolf could give him a dose of reality whenever that was essential.

"One time, he was in town and I came off the practice field, and I was just so mad at the special teams," Holmgren said. "I rarely did this, but I went in and said: 'We've got to change this, this guy's got to be out of here.' He listened, and he said: 'Okay' and then we walked to his office.

"And we always had a 'hot board' up there of players who were available on the street. He says: 'There are the kickers. Which one do you want?' The kickers are up there, and one guy is like 80 years old," Holmgren said with a smile. "There was no one up there. And so, he goes: 'Pick one. Which one do you want?' I said: 'Okay, okay, you got me.' "

Wolf was finding out everything else that went into being a GM, well beyond his proven expertise as a talent evaluator. The lessons weren't all pleasant.

"We're in the process of trying to hire a head coach, 1992," Wolf recalled. "The guy we want to hire is Mike Holmgren. And I get a call from a guy in the National Football League office saying that we have to settle with the San Francisco 49ers, give them compensation for Mike Holmgren. Not only did I get the call, Bob Harlan got the call. In other words, we have to give up a draft choice, that's what it was. And we gave a second. For which Al Davis called up and chewed my ass out, because they're across the Bay, right? It was good to get those calls—'I don't work for you no more,'" Wolf said with a chuckle.

"It turns out that Mike Holmgren did not have a signed contract, did not have a legitimate contract at all that he should have had. So, they didn't deserve anything. But we had been misled by the leading counsel in the National Football League, both Bob Harlan and myself. One thing I told Bob was, we've got to get that decal off the field. You know, they had that (NFL) shield (at midfield). We need to get that off there and put a 'G' there. And he agreed with that because they stuck it right up my rear. My seat wasn't even warm, you know what I'm saying, as general manager, and I just got stuck.

"People thought I had a hard-on for the league office, but I never did. We never got in any trouble with the league office, we never lost anything after that, but we weren't going to rely on them, because they weren't honest with us."

The Packers won six of their last seven games in 1992, including a 17–3 victory against the Bears in Chicago. The Bears, who had been the dominant team in the NFC Central in the '80s were one of Wolf's principal targets in measuring the progress his team would make. Beyond the Bears were the two dominant teams of the early 1990s—the Cowboys and the 49ers.

Reggie McKenzie, who later became the general manager of the Raiders, joined the Packers in 1994 as a pro personnel assistant, later becoming director of pro personnel. McKenzie had known Wolf since the Raiders had drafted him in 1985.

"He got the right players, not only to win the division, but to compete in the NFC," McKenzie said. "He saw that the 49ers and the Cowboys were the dominant ones and we had to match what they did. And that's how he built the team. And that's how he taught us—we're not going to get to the championship if we can't beat these guys. We've got to be physical enough to play with Dallas's offensive line and that running game. We've got to be big enough to play against Michael Irvin and the taller receivers.

"It was those type of things that player-wise we have to be able to compete. So, when we're scouting let's find the kind of players who can block the Cowboys and block the 49ers and cover Jerry Rice and stop Michael Irvin and get after Troy Aikman. We had to match what the championship contenders were doing. That's how we were able to quickly get into that championship group. Ron figured out a way to get that done."

Tangible signs of progress occurred during the 1993 season, but a play for the ages by Favre in the 1993 postseason was the most dramatic sign of improvement. The Packers were 9–7 for the second straight season, but it was a better 9–7 than the previous year and good enough to qualify the Packers for the playoffs for just the third time since 1967. This time the Packers were in Pontiac, Michigan, where they had just lost, 30–20 to the Lions in the final game of the regular season.

On this day, the incomparable Barry Sanders rushed for 169 yards in 27 attempts. Lions quarterback Erik Kramer completed 22 of 31 passes for 248 yards. For the game, the Packers were outgained, 410–293.

But after trailing, 17–7, they came back late, with a huge momentum swing provided by safety George Teague's 101-yard interception return late in the third quarter. (Teague was Wolf's second pick in the first round of the 1993 draft.)

With two minutes, 29 seconds remaining, the Packers, trailing 24–21, took over possession on their own 29. It was an imposing moment. Favre was in his first playoff game. The Packers were on the road. The last time they won a road playoff game was January 1, 1967, against the Cowboys. That was two generations ago in pro football terms. And to this point in this game, the Packers' biggest offensive play was a 23-yard gain. But four plays, three of them completed passes, moved the Packers to a second and four at the Detroit 40 with 1:23 to go. The clock was rolling, the Packers had two timeouts remaining. Another 10 yards and they would be in reasonable position for the tying field goal.

But Favre had larger ambitions. He had thrown four interceptions in this same building, the Silverdome, just six days before, but he was completely undaunted here.

The play call was for an out pattern that would get the Packers a first down. But Favre, seeing the Detroit corners roll up, scrambled to his left. And then, improbably, he turned back in the opposite direction and launched a throw not only across the width of the field, but into the end zone, that landed perfectly in the waiting arms of Sterling Sharpe for Sharpe's third touchdown of the game. Responsible estimates were that this precisely accurate pass traveled roughly 75 yards in the air. The Packers were 28–24 winners, advancing in the playoffs in Year II of the Wolf/Holmgren/Favre era.

"The fact of the matter was, I called a play that was a square-out for a first down," Mike Holmgren said. "I'm not watching Brett; the receiver is wide open. And the ball's not there. And I'm looking at Brett, yelling: 'No!' I did this a couple of times; he couldn't hear me, of course. And then he launched it and I'll be darned.

"He wasn't supposed to go over there. Instead, he's scrambling around. That's what I mean, every once in a while, he'd do something that not many guys could do, because he was strong, he had a great arm. And that one he made."

Looking back on that play, a quarter century later, Favre said: "I think some of my success early on, was more about my ability than my knowledge. The Sharpe play, I remember, it was red left, 25 double square out. That would have put Sterling on the left, because he was the flanker. Max protection, two guys basically are in the route and it's an out to the left and an out to the right. There was two deep coverage and they don't convert because there was a cornerback just sitting in the flat. Then they convert to go routes up the sideline. Sterling was just absolutely gassed, and I didn't realize that he was lined up on the wrong side. He just lined up on the side he was on, which was smart. He didn't have to go across the field. The routes were mirrored, so outs on both sides if he had off coverage.

"Twenty-five double square out. To be honest with you, I didn't recognize coverage until I started scrambling. And when you look at the play, I didn't really have to start scrambling, but that was kind of my deal. I didn't trust the protections, because I didn't understand them. If someone blitzed, I didn't think we could pick it up, so I was just going. I was just more comfortable on the move, buying time. I felt obviously that my arm strength could trump anything.

"So, when I started scrambling, I realized that it was not an out-route coverage and realized that Sterling was on the opposite side. I had made a living in college and high school playing that way; backyard, school-ball. If I rolled left, there was a good chance that the safety back left, the side I was rolling to, wouldn't play true to his defense. The human element becomes a factor. He's paying attention to where I'm going, there's no way I'll throw it back across the field, because who does? But yet, that's what I was banking on, that's what I was gambling on, that he would not play true cover-two. It was a gambler mentality. I trusted that I could make that throw, first of all, and he would be out of position and that Sterling would be where he was supposed to be. And all were true.

"I gave it a big heave-ho. I just threw it as hard as I could."

The sequence was weird, the whole idea was iffy, the odds against this play working were astronomical and then some. But the pass, the pass was pure perfection. This was precisely the kind of thing that set Favre apart from the rest of the quarterback population.

At various points in the season, the gambling, chance-taking, risk-welcoming Favre, had been much-maligned. This was particularly true of the week after the four-interception regular season finale.

After the Detroit victory, Favre said: "That was the hardest week I've ever had to go through. It was not me. Maybe I pressed too much. I studied hard this week, and not just on the plays, but on being conservative. I never thought that by being conservative I would throw three touchdown passes today."[1]

There can be some debate about whether the 75-yard, ad lib, perfect strike for the ages actually qualified as "conservative." But there was no doubt that this play put a new and improved perspective around Favre's potential.

But, after this game, Wolf, who believed from the beginning, said: "We've put our future in his hands. If that young quarterback read everything written about him, I don't know that he'd make an appearance, other than in disguise."[2]

Now, the memory of that play has not dimmed a bit. "I was listening to a replay of that game with Hank Stram and Jack Buck; they did the radio of the game," Wolf said. "They're talking about how the Packers are hanging in, but there was no way they were going to win the game. You know how Stram would talk. He would just say whatever he really felt. And all of a sudden, they call the play and suddenly the Packers win the game."

"He could do that. He's something with that ball now."

Ron Wolf has a habit of emphasizing the point he is making, by putting the word "now" at the end of his comment. So, even though "now" was in a previous century in this case, you knew exactly what he meant.

The 1993 season also saw a breakthrough in touchdown celebrations—"the Lambeau Leap" in which a Packer player scores a touchdown and then leaps into the arms of the grateful Packer fan base behind the end zone. The invention occurred on December 26, 1993, making it something of a delayed Christmas present for all parties.

Ironically or not, the inventor of the Lambeau Leap was a defensive

---

1 *Milwaukee Journal*, January 9, 1994.

2 Ibid.

player, safety LeRoy Butler. It was a good day for a celebration, because the Packers, with a 28–0 victory over the Los Angeles Raiders, were putting themselves in position for just their third postseason appearance since 1967.

The play in question occurred in the fourth quarter with the Packers holding a 14–0 lead. Butler caused a fumble that was recovered by Reggie White. White attempted to advance the ball, but while being tackled, alertly tossed it to Butler, who carried it 25 yards into the end zone.

Anybody who knew the effervescent Butler might not have been surprised by what happened next. He leaped into the crowd and was caught, lifted and hugged by adoring fans.

"I know people say: 'Well, act like you've been there before,'" Butler said. "I'm a defensive guy. I may not ever get back there again. So, I was going to make the most of it."[3]

Meanwhile, Wolf was doing everything he could to upgrade the roster. A series of extremely good decisions was going to be required for this task. Wolf was assembling a team that fit his philosophy and his Northern circumstances. Height, weight, speed, came along from his Raiders days, but this also needed to be a team that functioned without losing a step in the late-season, extreme cold of Lambeau Field. Favre could throw the ball in any conditions, but the situation also demanded big linemen who could impose their will on the opposition. And the running backs would be sizable, dependable, durable backs who would keep their footing and maintain their forward momentum in the worst circumstances the climate could offer. Wolf knew exactly what he wanted and exactly what he was doing.

"The key thing in sports is that you have to have a philosophy on personnel," Bill Parcells, a Hall of Fame coach and a close friend of Wolf, said. "It can't just be 'well, this guy's a good player, that guy's a good player.' You just can't be throwing darts. You have to know what you're looking for, specifically, and things that you can fit into the system that your coaches are employing. Everybody has to have an understanding of that.

"And that's what Ron did for Green Bay. I mean what kind of backs

3 ESPN.com, January 8, 2015.

Ron was going to have, I knew what kind of receivers he was looking for, I knew what he wanted his tight end to be, I knew what he wanted to be defensively at those positions. I mean, after a while, when you see people integrate people into their team and you see it repeatedly, like I could see it with Coach (Tom) Landry in Dallas, I knew what kind of players he was looking for. I played against them so much, that I knew, 'well, this is the prototypical Dallas Cowboy at this position. And this is the prototypical Cowboy at this other position.' That's kind of the way it was for me looking at Green Bay. Now I had a better knowledge, because Ron and I communicated. I wasn't in the inner sanctum, so to speak, but I certainly was on the periphery of understanding what kind of players he was looking for."

While the Packers were making some strides on the field, Wolf was assembling a young, but extremely astute, group of talent evaluators, who would learn to see the players through his tutelage. Five of these men became general managers in the National Football League—Thompson with the Packers, McKenzie with the Raiders, John Schneider with the Seattle Seahawks, John Dorsey with the Kansas City Chiefs, and Scot McCloughan with the San Francisco 49ers and later the Washington Redskins. Schneider, since becoming the Seahawks' GM in 2010, has had two Super Bowl teams and one Super Bowl champion. In 2018, which was supposed to be a rebuilding year for Seattle, the Seahawks went 10–6, qualifying as the first NFC Wild Card team.

Dorsey, from 2013–16, had a record of 43–21 with the Chiefs, who had gone 2–14 the year before he became general manager. His dismissal before the 2017 season was a shock to many throughout the league. But Dorsey returned to general manager status with one of the largest challenges in the game, taking over the football operations of the Cleveland Browns, winners of one game in the 2016–17 seasons. In a truly stunning turnaround, Dorsey and his assistant general manager, Ron Wolf's son, Eliot, remade the Cleveland roster as much as possible. Coming off a two-season record of 1–31, the 2018 Browns went 7–8–1, and were not only competitive, but entertaining.

Brian Gutekunst, named to succeed Thompson as the Packers GM after the 2017 season, arrived later in the Wolf administration, but was also a product of the Wolf scouting system. That makes six general managers who developed their skills under Wolf's tutelage. Some people call this a "general manager tree." At this point, it might be closer to a "general manager orchard."

Wolf gave his people basic instructions: Get the right information, get all of it, and focus on the positive.

"It's like everything else," Wolf says. "When you're in the business of evaluation, you want to know the plus factors. Tell me please, the plus factors. Don't give me the negatives. Everybody can see the negatives. Because what happens is, that negative stays up in there and you can't divorce that, no matter what you try to do."

Nearly a quarter-century later, this is exactly the way Reggie McKenzie did business with the Raiders. In 2012, McKenzie took over a team that was imprisoned in a terrible salary cap situation and had not had a winning season since 2002. In 2016, the Raiders went 12–4 and McKenzie was named NFL Executive of the Year by the Pro Football Writers of America. McKenzie's influence waned after the Raiders hired Jon Gruden as head coach for the 2018 season. Impact players McKenzie had drafted, such as dominant pass rusher Khalil Mack and prize wide receiver Amari Cooper, were traded and McKenzie was dismissed in December. Still, the job he had done with the Raiders was widely admired. In February 2019, McKenzie was hired as a senior personnel executive by the Miami Dolphins.

"If you ask any of these scouts for the Raiders," McKenzie says, "I passed it to them, I preached it to them. 'Hey, don't tell me what he can't do. Tell me what he can do.' That's scouting. The evaluation process, coaches get bogged down in what a guy can't do. No, he wants us to tell him what he can do. What can he do? That's where the true evaluation, the true scouting comes in. Find out what he can do. Then, we can figure it out from there. A true scout really understands what it's all about. He will be a better scout if he goes about the evaluation process like that. That's the way I tell it. Anybody can see faults. Everybody is going to have faults. But tell me what he can do. What can he do great? Then we can talk about how good a guy is. (Emphasizing the negative), you'll go nowhere fast. You don't want to tread water or go backwards, because that's what that will do for you."

And for Wolf there was the steady and certain emphasis on what a splendid calling it was—doing this work, scouting these players, watching this film, rating this field of potential NFL draftees—all on behalf of the Green Bay Packers.

"When we did the draft work in preparation for the draft," Wolf says, I would go: 'Gentlemen, we're in this room to pick the best player we can pick for the Green Bay Packers. It's not your pick. It's not his pick. It's not my pick. It's *our* pick, for the Packers. Now, let's sort all this out and get the right names up there where we would select them.' I think to this day the guys still do it that way."

Did these adult males buy into this Glorious Green and Gold stuff? Maybe not right away, but eventually, yes, indeed. Or else they departed for employment elsewhere.

"It kind of grows on you," Ted Thompson said. "It grew on you because Ron had the belief that he could turn things around and make it a good place. He has an uncanny knack of knowing and appreciating history, of the National Football League and of sports in general. And this was one of those places that he had always talked about and thought about."

So, over time, Wolf's vision of the Packers became reality.

"That, and the rest of us knuckleheads, took a little bit longer to figure it out but we got on the bandwagon with him," Thompson said with a chuckle.

John Dorsey, having played linebacker for the Packers for five years in the 1980s, has a unique perspective on the changes that occurred when Wolf took over for the Packers.

"Unfortunately, I played in the dark days," Dorsey said. "To watch it evolve, from the dark days, to the heights, is so unique and so special. It's just from my standpoint, okay, now I saw the dark side, I saw how not to do it, then you see how Ron transformed this organization back to its rightful place in the history of the game. That history component tends to stay within you as a person and you respect the game that much more. The one thing he did teach was to respect the history of the game.

"There was a sense of pride (after Wolf became general manager). There was a sense of recommitment. There was a sense of we were going to do this thing how championship teams do this thing. Now it was building blocks, and he'll tell you, it took two or three years to create that culture. And part of that culture-building was to get guys in that locker room who understood what winning was about. That was one of his foremost things that he did early on. That is, you have to have a very good locker room that drives this whole process. That's the whole key to have a culture of winning environment. I think the very first thing that Ron did, he goes and gets the quarterback that he identifies, and he turns the whole franchise around. He is wise enough to understand that you will go nowhere if you don't have a quarterback."

Reggie McKenzie had been scouted and drafted by Wolf for the Raiders. He had a personal belief in Wolf, which grew to become a belief in the Packers.

"No question that it was a calling, because there was no way I could have gotten there if it wasn't," McKenzie said. "Once you got there, you felt privileged to be there. The way Ron ran the football side of the organization, I felt like we were a pack, a team within the team. I felt like everything we did was for the team. There was great communication amongst each other and I thought he did a great job of fostering relationships between us all. We all came from different backgrounds but a lot of the guys that Ron brought in early had a connection. A Raider connection, really; Scot's father worked with Ron. Shaun Herock's father, Ken, drafted me as a Raider. It all connected. John Dorsey was there as a player. Ted Thompson through Mike Reinfeldt. That bonded us."

John Schneider grew up in nearby De Pere, went to Abbot Pennings High School, and was a running back who played in college at the University of St. Thomas (Minnesota). As a Packer fan, he was born too late for the Titletown, USA victory pageant of the Lombardi years.

But coming to work for the Packers, first as an intern, Schneider got a full dose of the Packers' historical importance from Wolf.

"That was the history part for him," Schneider says. "There were some Saturdays he'd be in there watching Mr. Inside and Mr. Outside (Doc Blanchard and Glenn Davis, great Army running backs of the 1940s), you know, in black and white. He just loved the history of the game and you could tell that it was an honor for him to be running the franchise.

"For me, as a kid growing up there when the Packers never ever had success, I was just so enamored with him: 'This guy is amazing.' He changed this franchise. I remember as a kid the biggest win we ever had in the playoffs was when I was working for Ron. It had been forever. It was a really, really big deal for me to watch him operate, and how he interacted with Coach Holmgren, and how he brought all the alumni back and really made them feel like they were such a big part of everything, you know? Naming the Hutson Center after Don Hutson, was a huge deal for him."

It was possible, in this atmosphere, to grow both personally and professionally.

"It was exciting," Schneider said. "You had to be on your toes. You had to be ready for anything. But as long as you had a good work ethic, you were all right. Everybody was striving for the same thing. In retrospect, when you look back at it, it was pretty cool. It was a really cool group of people. And he had a really strong influence on us, like a father figure. Even Ted (Thompson). Ted was done playing and he started five months before I did my internship. Shaun Herock, Scot (McCloughan), and myself were all the same age, and yet we were in a room with guys who had recently retired, like Ted Thompson, and John Dorsey, but yet, (Dave) Hawg Hanner (played defensive tackle for the Packers from 1952 to 1964, 16 seasons as an assistant coach, then scout from 1983 to 1996), Ray Wietecha (great center for the Giants, offensive line coach for the Lombardi teams that won Super Bowls), and Red Cochran (coached offensive backfield 1959–66 for Lombardi, later a scout for Packers for 30 years). And we're sitting in a room with these guys. They'd be talking about guys that Scot and Shaun and I would have no idea who they were even talking about. They would constantly be teaching, though. And John Math was in there, too. He was with the Rams when they drafted Kevin Greene, Eric Dickerson, and those guys. It was a great working environment, learning environment.

"I think all of us have tried to create that wherever we've gone. Ron never made it feel like it was just all about him. If you did your work, he'd listen to you. If you were just popping off about your opinions, and you hadn't done the work yourself, he wasn't real fired up about it."

The work was always checked, because the eye in the sky didn't lie. At the end of the travel, the 18-hour days and the scouting reports, there was the film. Wolf saw himself as a scout. He could empathize with his guys in the field. But at the end of the day, their assessments had to be spot on.

"The ultimate test is the eye," Wolf said. "The objective here is about the Packers and getting it right. It's not to bury somebody and say: 'You can't do it.'

"But you better show some positive form. If you're out there screwing around, it's going to come to light in that room. And it's coming to light in how you present yourself. And if you couldn't do it, I'd can your ass. We're talking serious now. One pick in 32. One pick in 28. I had my share of mistakes, don't get me wrong," Wolf said, managing a smile at the end of that statement.

"But we devised a system there to evaluate. Everybody thinks that when they retire they can evaluate. So, we devised a system to have them evaluate four or five of their players. You could have their reports and you could sit back in the room, and it's one of those things where you can either do it or you can't do it and there is no in-between. And that comes out when you write your report. Now some guys can't write, they can't express themselves, but when you sit and talk with them then you hear what they're saying is 'ah-ha,' then you can evaluate. It's not easy to do that."

The Packers' preparation for the draft was both extensive and intensive.

"We start preparation for the draft, the week before the Super Bowl, before we went to the combine," Wolf said. "We would start at 7:30 in the morning, finish 7:30 at night. We left from 12:30 to 2 to have a lunch to get the hell out of the building. That was a grind. People talk about being 'tough;' that might be where the toughness came from.

"I tried not to intimidate (the scouts) in any form or fashion. I wanted them to express their opinion. I wanted to hear that. What we would do is we would get in the room and we would start alphabetically by position. Centers—A through Z. The players that were in what we called the live books, the players that we were going to evaluate—we would start with Adams and a guy would say, 'I think he can play' and then he'd say why. Then we would get the film out and we would play three or four games of Adams. And you're on this big screen, we had a huge screen. You're sitting in the room, there's 10 guys in there, there's Adams on the big screen, and he's either good or bad. The eye in the sky isn't going to lie. That's how you did it. Like anything else, there were guys that were very good and there were guys that weren't very good. But the eye in the sky helped you."

This was work, necessary work, but Wolf was fortunate in the sense that it was also what he wanted to do and what he excelled at doing.

"It was all about being a scout," Ted Thompson said. "I never will forget Ron saying that he liked to be referred to as a scout. He said: 'Once a scout, always a scout,' or something to that effect, and I've always tried to model my thought process along those lines."

"Ron loved that scouting," Mike Holmgren said. "But in the offseason, he was in the room there every day, looking at film from morning to night. All the players, he was in there. And then three weeks previous to the draft, the board was taking shape and the coaches would come in there, because the coaches were all doing their work with the position groups. All the scouts, all the coaches—for three weeks we locked ourselves in there. He ran the projector and we just looked and talked. He was very inclusive that way. I said: 'This is really the right way to do this.' And guys were really in there a long time. He loved it, though. He loved that."

How was it for the people whose judgment was being publicly either applauded or condemned by Wolf and the eye in the sky? It was an experience that tended to reinforce the need for unbroken, absolute attention to the task at hand.

"It was great," Thompson said. "Most of us stayed in a dark room and watched film. With the draft meetings leading up to combine and obviously, the draft meetings leading up to the draft itself could be excruciating events, because if you got a guy wrong, and you just got through reading your report and telling people how good he is, and then all of a sudden, he misses six straight tackles, you were at the mercy of the room.

"It was a great learning platform though, and I think Ron did that intentionally to make sure people stayed on their Ps and Qs. And sometimes when you're out on the road and you're sitting in a hotel writing your reports in the middle of the night, it's easy to kind of get a little soft and forget what you're doing. But then you remember how those draft meetings go, and you kind of sit up and take notice and start writing your reports better."

The new generation of Packers personnel people were fortunate to work for the right man, at the right time, at the right place. They had the opportunity not only to learn from a top-shelf personnel man, but they also were in on the ground floor of a franchise revival. On the other hand, Wolf will be the first one to acknowledge that he benefited immensely from the people that he recruited for these jobs. The fact that six of them became NFL general managers is a tribute to their own abilities, but also to the foundation they received from Wolf.

"That is a source of real satisfaction for me, it is," Wolf said of the success of his former employees. "I mean, I was surrounded by really good people. These guys are really good at what they do in their profession. They like the game. They like and respect the game and to me that's so important.

"Ted started in the pro football end of scouting, which I thought was very, very important. We needed to have more people scouting in the pro game because people are going to cut guys and maybe we could find something there. . . . Thompson obviously was tough. He made it as a special teams player. Dorsey was tough. To me John Dorsey's biggest attribute was he was a player, a college Hall of Fame player. He became an accomplished evaluator. He was relentless in gathering information you needed about players. He was exceptional at that, exceptional."

"I think it's something that you grow into because you don't know the details of the personnel," Dorsey said. "I'm the classic overachiever, and I always thought if you did the little things you made yourself more valuable. That's like when I played, I knew all four linebacker positions. It's a little bit natural and learned traits. I always say if you have classic overachievers with great work ethics, you'll go to any lengths to get the job done. I, too, try to take some of the principles that Ron instilled in me and I try to teach people how to do it the right way. There is no shortcut to doing it the proper way."

Reggie McKenzie, when asked what he had learned from Ron Wolf, initially responded: "Whooee. I might have to do a dissertation. To put it in the simplest form, what he taught me was Number 1, do your work well. Whatever you do, give it your all."

There's a lesson learned. "Reggie McKenzie turned that whole (Raiders) franchise around," Wolf said. "Reggie was a rare bird. He was a 10th-round pick of the Los Angeles Raiders and comes in as a rookie, starts on a championship team as an inside linebacker, a position he never played. And he was tough, tough, tough. He was fast and tougher than hell. As a scout, he was good right out of the barrel.

"Some guys were very negative, but among the guys I had, John Schneider was very positive," Wolf said. "I mean, not afraid at all. Ted Thompson was reserved. Then he got his feet wet and he was really good. He was a steadying influence. Reggie McKenzie was good right out of the barrel.

"Scot McCloughan was a superb evaluator, superb. He goes to San Francisco, now they didn't get to the Super Bowl but those were his players under (head coach Jim) Harbaugh in a Super Bowl. Obviously, a strong foundation.

"John Schneider, like all those guys he's bright and he really likes football. Football is very important to him. He likes the game. He respects the game. He knows the history of the game. He works his tail off. The big thing about John Schneider is that he is not afraid to make his case. I think that's been borne out with the job he's done up there in Seattle. Very positive, he is that. Like all of us, that doesn't mean you're wrong.

"I'll give you a perfect example, he goes out and makes a trade for a quarterback (Charlie) Whitehurst, that doesn't work out. He goes out and gets the guy from LSU and the Packers (Matt Flynn), that doesn't work. He gets a guy from Minnesota (Tarvaris) Jackson, that doesn't work out, but he keeps on it and the next year he gets (Russell) Wilson. Tell you what, that worked. I was fortunate to have guys like that."

Schneider completed more than 270 transactions in his first season as Seahawks GM. He and Coach Pete Carroll were in agreement that this was the way to proceed. And they were right.

"We just thought that was a good fit in terms of trying to change the culture, providing competition, not letting people be complacent," Schneider said. "That was definitely a Ron Wolf philosophy. It helped create a culture of competitiveness. We talked about doing it better than anybody did before, and that's what we did. At every turn, if somebody got cut, we were evaluating everybody. If they were a tick better than the other person, we were going to do it."

With Wolf and the brain power he had assembled, the Packers became better in almost a linear way. Their drafts were never perfect, but they were certainly productive. Wolf had an astoundingly good record from the third round, through the seventh. All of the players here made a difference for what became a championship team:

1992: Wide receiver Robert Brooks in the third round. Running back Edgar Bennett in the fourth round. Tight end Mark Chmura in the sixth round.

1993: Linebacker Wayne Simmons in the first round. Tackle Earl Dotson in the third round. Cornerback Doug Evans in the sixth.

1994: Guard Aaron Taylor in the first. Running back Dorsey Levens in the fifth.

1995: Cornerback Craig Newsome in the first. Fullback William Henderson in the third. Linebacker Brian Williams in the third. Wide receiver Antonio Freeman in the third. Guard Adam Timmerman in the seventh.

1996: Guard Marco Rivera in the sixth.

Seven of the 11 players who started on offense for the Packers' Super Bowl XXXI winners were drafted by Wolf. And then there was Brett Favre, who Wolf saw as the future of the franchise when everyone else saw him as a deep backup for the Falcons. Four more Wolf draftees started for the Packers' defense in that game, although, as we shall see, his free-agent signings had a major impact on that side of the ball.

Yes, Wolf and company missed on some first-round selections. He still sometimes thinks about those on his morning four-mile walks. But on balance, the drafts worked for the Packers.

"We had more players in my time, a little over nine years, more drafted Pro Bowlers than anybody else, 18 Pro Bowlers out of the draft," Wolf said. "In that period, nobody had more than the Packers. I was proud of that, too, very proud of that."

Meanwhile, the rest of the world was forced to notice that the Packers were making strides. On Halloween night, 1994, the bad-weather team that Wolf was intent on creating, showed its mettle. In miserable conditions at Soldier Field, winds gusting up to 36 miles per hour at the lakefront stadium, rain falling in sheets, the Packers showed their resolve against the rival Bears.

In a 33–6 trouncing, the Packers forced five turnovers—three interceptions and two fumbles. Maybe the weather helped, but the Packers had no turnovers. This was no time for passing; Favre had just 15 attempts. But the dependable Edgar Bennett slogged through the mud for 105 yards and two touchdowns in 26 carries. Bennett also caught a touchdown pass. At this point in his career, the worse the weather became, the better Favre reacted. His 36-yard run in the second quarter gave the Packers a 14–0 lead. For the game, the Packers had 223 rushing yards to 94 for the Bears. The Packers came into this game ranked 26th in the league in rushing.

"Worst weather game I ever coached in," Holmgren said. "The wind was so bad the precipitation was coming straight across. They chose to give us the ball into the wind in the first quarter. Our punter, Craig Hentrich, kicks a beautiful spiral and it goes 20 yards. The next quarter, the Bears punter kicks one, and it blows back over his head and lands behind them.

"(Tight end) Ed West, remember Ed West? Great guy, had a speech impediment, stuttering. Early in that game, it was so windy, a little 10-yard pattern and the ball just goes," Holmgren said, making a jagged, twisting motion with his arm. "And he drops it, he couldn't get it. Great blocker, okay hands. He came over, he said: 'Coach Mike, Coach Mike, I don't have great hands. Don't throw it to me anymore. I can't catch it.' Edgar Bennett on bad tracks, he was remarkable. Everyone else is slipping and sliding, he just went."

Reaching the playoffs for the second straight year in 1994, again playing the Lions, the Green Bay defense staged a performance that was record-setting, startling, and unprecedented. The Packers held the previously unstoppable Barry Sanders to minus-one yard on 13 rushing attempts. Further, the Packers defense set a playoff record by holding the Lions to a grand total of minus-four yards in 15 rushing attempts.

The Packers won, 16–12, and it was widely thought in Packerland that defensive coordinator Fritz Shurmer should get an award for this performance. Unfortunately, Nobel Prizes are not awarded for "gap discipline."

"It's inconceivable to hold (Sanders) to negative yards," Reggie White said. "He does things that no other back does."

"Except for putting Reggie inside, we didn't do much different," Shurmur said. "It's really hard to use the word 'stop' with this guy and not smile a little bit."[4]

In fact, this "stop" had the Packers grinning from ear to ear. There it was, minus-one yard for the future Hall of Famer. Sanders had rushed for a league-leading 117.7 yards per game in the regular season, while averaging a league-leading 5.7 yards per carry. Sanders fashioned a Hall of Fame career making instantaneous, instinctive cutbacks. When he tried those in this game, there was always a Packer defender who had not strayed from his assignment, in Sanders' path.

"You have to give an awful lot of credit to Fritz Shurmur and his staff," Wolf said. "When you look at the greatest running backs in the history of the National Football League, you don't have to scroll down very far to find Barry Sanders's name. In my time in Green Bay he was the best (running back) we went against. To hold a player of that caliber to minus yardage, that's a magnificent achievement."

Maybe this was the sort of performance that could never be duplicated. But it opened the possibility that this Green Bay coaching staff would be capable of guiding this team to some truly lofty ground.

After three straight 9–7 seasons, the Packers moved to 11–5 in 1995, winning their first NFC Central Division title in 28 years. The Packers lost their 1995 opener to the then St. Louis Rams. It was a disheartening home loss in which Favre threw three interceptions. In the second game of the season at Soldier Field, Favre connected with Robert Brooks on a 99-yard touchdown pass in the second quarter and the Packers built a 24–7 lead by halftime. But in the second half, the Green Bay offense produced only a field goal and the Packers barely hung on for a 27–24 victory. On the surface, this was not a tremendously encouraging performance. Looked at from the other side, though, it became evidence that the corner had been turned.

---

4 *Los Angeles Times*, January 1, 1995.

"I remember it was another kind of a nutty deal," Andy Reid said. "We were playing the Bears and they were getting after us a little bit. Now, we're kind of climbing the ladder, we're supposed to be something, but we weren't playing very good. I remember going on the elevator with the Chicago Bears coaches, and one of them said to Sherman Lewis (Packers offensive coordinator), 'Man, that quarterback of yours is a hell of a player.' And we'd just got done going: 'Oh my gosh, this guy is not very good.'

"That was another time when I said: 'If that's how people perceive this guy,' and sometimes when you're in it, you're not seeing that. I felt like that gave me an opportunity to kind of step back and look at Brett from afar. And I thought: *Wow, we really have a chance to be champions. We can do this.* This guy was talking about Brett being the best guy in the league and being an MVP-type guy. I'm going: 'Are you kidding me? We were godawful in this game here.' That was the time when I knew we could go to that next level."

In fact, 1995 was pointing directly in the direction of "that next level." This would be the first of three consecutive MVP seasons for Favre. That loss to the Rams would be the Packers' only home loss of the season. And the Packers would climb a postseason mountain by defeating the 49ers, 27–17 in a Divisional playoff game at San Francisco, before losing to Dallas in the NFC Championship.

The San Francisco victory marked another height reached for the Packers, defeating the defending Super Bowl champions in the playoffs. On the Niners' first play from scrimmage, San Francisco fullback Adam Walker took a screen pass in the right flat and was drilled by Packers linebacker Wayne Simmons. Walker fumbled, and cornerback Craig Newsome picked up the ball and returned it 31 yards for a touchdown. That set a certain tone and the Packers roared to a 21–0 lead in the second quarter. Simmons, who starred at Clemson, was picked by Wolf in the first round of the 1993 draft.

"Truth be told, probably the best guy I ever drafted was Wayne Simmons, because he scared the shit out of everybody on the other side," Wolf said with a laugh. "Probably scared the shit out of people on his own team, too. He was a badass."

That victory made a big impression on people in Packerland. And those people, in turn, made a big impression on the members of the Packer organization.

"What I remember is we're coming home from San Francisco on the plane, and we found out that there were thousands of people at the airport," said Mark Schiefelbein, then assistant director of public relations for the Packers. "They were all jammed in there. Finally, they told people on the radio: 'Don't go out to the airport, there's no room out there.' They told people to turn on their porch lights to welcome the team home.

"We didn't know any of this, but they got word to the pilot. He says: 'Guys, there's a lot of people at the airport, they actually had to tell people not to come. They've told people to turn on their porch lights to welcome the Green Bay Packers home.'

"At that point, it's after midnight, we're over Green Bay, and everybody on the plane gets over to look out their windows. And, it still gives me goosebumps, the whole area was lit. To this day, I still get kind of choked up thinking about that. Then we land and there's thousands of people chanting: 'We want Dallas! We want Dallas!'"

The Packers got Dallas eight days later in Texas Stadium, for the NFC Championship. The Packers had been bounced out of the playoffs for the last two years by the Cowboys. This time, the Packers led, 27–24, after three quarters, but with the great Emmitt Smith running for two touchdowns in the fourth quarter, Dallas prevailed, 38–27, and the Cowboys were headed toward their third Super Bowl championship in four years.

It was a disappointing, but not demoralizing defeat for the Packers. An overall sense had developed under Ron Wolf's administration that better days were still ahead for this team.

"There was a different feeling in the building altogether," Bob Harlan said. "I remember the last time, after we had lost to Dallas three years in a row, and I'm walking up the tunnel in Dallas. Brett comes up, puts his arm around me and says: 'Bob, we're getting closer.' I said: 'I hope so.'"

The Packers were once again being noticed for football reasons, for reasons beyond "the frozen tundra" and thousands of people tailgating in blizzard conditions. The Packers, apart from their trips to Texas, were becoming a success story. Lambeau Field was becoming what it had been nearly 30 years before, a place of celebration.

"It gradually came into focus in 1995," Wolf recalled. "Suddenly, we're being visited by lots of people, national (media) people were showing up. We must be pretty good. Some magazines come out and say we're going to win the Super Bowl and all that stuff.

"I was fortunate, I never let that get in my way. I wasn't interested in all that stuff. I learned very early that there are three things you never do: You never listen to local radio, you never watch local TV, and you never read the local newspaper. I don't need somebody who doesn't know to tell me how stupid I am. I know when I make a mistake. I'm not perfect. But I don't need somebody who doesn't know to tell me how dumb I am."

Bud Selig was the Interim Commissioner of Baseball, owner of the Milwaukee Brewers, and a member of the Packer Board of Directors when Bob Harlan invited him to speak to a Green Bay civic group in 1992. Riding back from the event with Harlan driving and Wolf and Holmgren in the back seat, Selig recalls that Harlan had the car radio tuned to a sports talk show. Wolf chastised Harlan for listening to the program.

Selig responded that he also was a regular follower of sports talk shows. "Well, then, shame on you, too," Wolf said, to general laughter.

The Packers, though, were reaching a point where they would be beyond the normal range of criticism, a point at which all media references to the Packers general manager would require a definite degree of positivity.

8

The Packers Win It All

IN THE 1995 postseason, the Green Bay Packers played the Dallas Cowboys for a championship. This was real progress. The last time the Packers had been in a championship was also against Dallas—the storied Ice Bowl, December 31, 1967, for the NFL Championship and a trip to Super Bowl II.

After 28 years here were the Packers, in Dallas, playing for the NFC championship and a trip to Super Bowl XXX. The results were not as uplifting this time, although the Packers led, 27–24, after three quarters. At crunch time, they could not contain the great Emmitt Smith, who gained 150 yards and ran for three touchdowns in the Cowboys' 38–27 victory.

So near and yet so far. This was the third straight season in which the Packers were tossed out of the playoffs by the Cowboys, but in 1994, they had been beaten soundly, 35–9. It was another loss to the Cowboys, but for the Packers, signs of growth were everywhere evident.

On the flight from Dallas back to wintry Wisconsin, Ron Wolf approached safety LeRoy Butler, who typically would have something interesting to say.

"He said: 'What do you think, 36?'" Butler recalls. "I said: 'Next year, we're going to win it all. We just need one or two pieces. Not big pieces. Just one or two more pieces.'

"When you looked at Ron, you knew he was serious. I've never seen a guy more determined. Every loss pissed him off, because he could see a way for us to win. I said: 'We need a return guy. That's the difference between us, Dallas, and San Francisco. Not a receiver, a return guy.' That's all you're gonna do, Desmond, you're going to be best return guy in the world.' The next thing you know, Desmond Howard. Keith Jackson. Santana Dotson. Sean Jones. Andre Rison. We're just loading up."

This 1996 season was Ron Wolf's masterpiece, both in terms of all the team building he had done in the previous years, and the moves he made specifically for this campaign.

This was a team that went 13–3 and led the league in points scored and points scored against. The last team with that combination was the legendary 1972 Miami Dolphins, who went 17–0, becoming the only team with a perfect record in the Super Bowl era.

It was not as though the 1996 Packers had future Hall of Famers at every position. But they did have football players at every position, people fully committed to their craft, people who had both the mental and physical ability to go the distance. As good as the individual players were, joined together, the whole was even greater than the sum of the parts.

"'I think that's absolutely a fair description," head coach Mike Holmgren said. "Just take it by position for a second. At running back you've got Edgar Bennett, Dorsey Levens, (at fullback) William Henderson. They're good players, really good players, but unselfish players who would block. A lot of running backs can't block.

"Okay, at wide receiver, you've got (Robert) Brooks, (Antonio) Freeman, (Don) Beebe. They weren't first-round draft choices, but they bought into the system, they were precise. They worked hard.

"The offensive linemen—I think Ron would say this, our first-round picks over the years, they were just okay. His genius was, he brings in Bruce Wilkerson to play left tackle, near the end of the season. And Bruce had played a long time, he had a bad body, but what a great guy and he played great. (Wilkerson started the last game of the regular season and all of the postseason games.) Left tackle (was a problem).

"Now in the secondary, you had a Hall of Fame guy, in my opinion,

Where it all started: Wolf and Bob Harlan, on the day of Wolf's hiring by Harlan as a GM with real power. November, 1991. *Associated Press.*

Wolf meets the Wisconsin media on the day of his hiring as Packer general manager. *Jim Biever.*

Holmgren, Reggie White and Wolf happily announce that White will be coming to Green Bay. April, 1993. *Associated Press.*

Wolf and Holmgren face the media during their second draft together in 1993. *Jim Biever.*

Wolf and his mentor and long-time boss, Al Davis. August, 1997. *Associated Press.*

Edie and Ron Wolf, flying home from New Orleans with the Lombardi Trophy. January, 1997. *Associated Press.*

Terry Bradshaw Interviews Bob Harlan, Wolf, and Mike Holmgren as winners of Super Bowl XXXI. January, 1997. *Associated Press.*

Brett Favre, Wolf, and Mike Holmgren discuss another victory in the Packers' locker room.
Jim Biever

Wolf exuberantly points to the Lambeau Field crowd after the Packers defeat Carolina for the 1996 NFC championship. January 1997. *Associated Press.*

Wolf and his sons, Eliot and Jonathan, celebrate the Packers' championship (1997). *Jim Biever.*

Wolf and his quarterback, together as champions in the Superdome for Super Bowl XXXI. January, 1997. *Associated Press.*

Wolf was not given to long-winded dissertations, but he was candid and helpful with the media covering the Packers. *Associated Press.*

Wolf and Brett Favre, in retirement, but still at a Packers/Bears game. November, 2015. *Associated Press.*

Wolf gives a typically short, but typically effective speech at his Pro Football Hall of Fame induction. August, 2015. *Associated Press.*

Ron and Eliot Wolf and Ted Thompson check out a Packer practice. August, 2015. *Associated Press.*

Eliot and Ron Wolf pose with the elder Wolf's brand new Hall of Fame bust. August, 2015.
Associated Press.

Wolf is honored at Lambeau as Edie watches her Hall of Fame husband again speak publicly. November, 2015. *Associated Press.*

in LeRoy Butler. Eugene Robinson—got him in a trade. Our corners (Doug Evans, Craig Newsome, Tyrone Williams) were good. Our linebackers (Brian Williams, George Koonce, Wayne Simmons, Ron Cox) were good.

"But our big guys up front? *Wooo.* Those were the ones, that's where we had better than anybody. Sean Jones. Big Gilbert (Brown), Santana Dotson, Reggie, those four. Nolan Cromwell was the special teams coach. Desmond Howard was the return guy. Our special teams were good.

"But it was the team. They were functioning and that's what made that season great. There was no clash of egos. You had larger than life guys in Favre and White. Reggie was literally larger than life . . . I told them: 'You know what? When you win, there's enough credit for everybody. Everybody. You're all involved in this.' So, they bought in. They all did."

Look for a moment at that defensive line where the Packers were as good, or better, than anybody. Three free agents—White, Dotson, Jones—and one waiver claim from the Minnesota Vikings in 1993—Brown. These acquisitions were the result of deep knowledge, due diligence and Wolf's connections. And in the case of White, God telling him to go to Green Bay and/or the Packers outbidding the rest of football with $17 million.

"I was involved with drafting Sean Jones when I was with the Raiders," Wolf said. "We were able to engineer that with Earl Leggett, the defensive line coach, we were able to convince him and then Sean had a stellar career. He was an exceptional player and I don't think he truly got the recognition that he was due.

"But the guy that kind of made that thing go was Santana Dotson, from the inside, because he was a penetrating player. And again, this goes back into my connection with the Raiders. His dad, Alphonse (a defensive lineman), played with the Raiders when I was there. That was the connection there.

"Santana, as big as he was and as quick and as athletically talented as he was—which they all were—every one of those guys were exceptional athletes. Even taking it a step further, they were all in their way, exceptional athletes, I mean, Gilbert Brown ran the 100-yard dash in high school, to give you an idea of just how gifted he was.

"Jones and Dotson were tremendous foot athletes. They played with leverage and strength. They were exceptional at their positions in their own right. They were all those things—intelligent, well-spoken, good citizens. Football was very, very important to them. And they had a hell of a year. They kind of jelled at the right time."

And the Al Davis mantra—height, weight, speed—worked with this group. Jones, at defensive end, signed with the Packers in 1994, was listed at 6 feet, 7 inches and 270 pounds. Dotson, at defensive tackle, signed with the Packers in 1996. He was 6–5 and 285. White was listed at 6–5 and 300 pounds, but there were no suitable measurements for his presence, which was immense.

Gilbert Brown's days as a sprinter were gone by the time he became a Packers employee, clocking in at 6–2 and 350 pounds. He was a project when he came to the Packers as a mere waiver claim from the Vikings in 1993. But by the 1996 season he was entrenched as a starter at defensive tackle and he was a full-fledged run-stuffer.

"(Defensive coordinator) Fritz Shurmur really liked him," Wolf said. "And I think the fact that he could plug up the middle the way he did and the fact that he could also play on the other side of the line of scrimmage was very, very beneficial. He grew into the position. He became a fan favorite, 'the Grave Digger.'"

Wolf also brought in Desmond Howard, who would have a splendid season and postseason as a return man. Keith Jackson was added at tight end, teaming with the already established Mark Chmura to give the Packers an imposing duo at that position. Eugene Robinson, a savvy veteran free safety, was added in a trade with Seattle for Matt LaBounty, a defensive lineman, who, over the next six seasons, started a total of 10 games for the Seahawks.

"The guy who really helped put this whole thing together was Eugene Robinson," Wolf said. "We were able to get that guy in a deal with Seattle that kind of made that defense from the back side."

Each and every one of these moves worked and worked extraordinarily well. But there was one 1996 personnel decision that Wolf whiffed on, meaning that, even at this distance he will speak about it at much greater length than he will about any of his numerous triumphs for that championship season.

"That's one of the things, when you retire, you keep playing things back," Wolf says. "I remember the 1996 draft vividly. That's the draft we took (tackle) John Michels (from USC, in the first round). We were in the process we thought, with 20 seconds to go; we had a linebacker, Ray Lewis. We thought we had him. We were talking to Ray Lewis, talking to Ray Lewis' agent, and we're excited. All of a sudden, with 20 seconds to go, Baltimore says, 'We're going to take Ray Lewis.'

"I completely fell apart. That was not my finest hour. People were calling, asking if we could trade the pick. I should have done that, should have traded the pick. We would have had a guy named Tony Brackens, (defensive end, drafted by Jacksonville, All-Pro in 1999) would have been a hell of a lot better than Michels. Plus, I would have had more picks, I might have stumbled into one or two more.

"I think about that, but okay. I had that happen to me twice in my career, where guys who were really tough guys, suddenly were not tough. Both at the same position, offensive tackle. You know, take this young guy, he's really a stud, tough, played at the University of Southern California, really a terrific football program, he was tough, tough, tough. He wasn't tough, tough, tough."

Left tackle was a problem for the Packers for much of the 1996 season. Ken Ruettgers, so good for so long with the Packers, was battling a knee injury, tried to come back, made one start, and then retired. Michels was frequently nicked up, made nine starts, but was not performing at anything like the level the Packers would have expected from a first-round pick. Michels lasted two years with the Packers, before knee injuries ended his career.

But all was not lost at left tackle because Wolf had signed veteran tackle Bruce Wilkerson, 32, who was coming off a season in which he made no starts for Jacksonville. How important was that?

"He's the reason we won the Super Bowl," Ted Thompson said. "Quite frankly, you do that a lot and sometimes it doesn't work. Ron didn't get nervous about something not working. He was looking for something that was going to work. So, he'd just keep going. And some of us are not brave enough to keep going."

Wilkerson was signed as a backup tackle and in midseason started one game at right tackle when the starter, Earl Dotson, was injured. Wilkerson was given a start at left tackle in the final regular season game of 1996. Through that game, the playoffs and the Super Bowl, Wilkerson was solid, dependable, admirable—just what the situation demanded.

"Again, there's the Raiders connection," Wolf said. "I had drafted him when I was with the Raiders (second round, 52nd overall, 1987). "He was what he was. You hate to use this term, but he was what you would call a football player. He wouldn't mess up, he was a pro's pro, in that sense. Football was very, very important to him. And he played his tail off. We kind of lucked out there."

Luck had very little to do with it. The usual knowledge, diligence, and willingness to do the unexpected, and the unconventional worked for Wolf.

Wilkerson was a respected figure in the locker room. And he also supplied one of the most lasting anecdotes of the championship season.

Andy Reid, who was a tight ends and assistant offensive line coach, remembers: "Bruce had a speech impediment, a stutter. And we have a 'cow' call on the offensive line. He's playing left tackle for us and he's supposed to make this call. Well, his stutter kicks in right when we're lined up and ready to go. He starts going 'kuh, kuh, kuh, kuh', and then he goes, 'Mooooo! Moooooo!' He got it out. Great guy. That was an under-rated move."

The Packers approached the 1996 season with the sort of soaring confidence that had not been a regular part of the franchise's mental makeup for nearly three decades. Bob McGinn, at that time a *Milwaukee Journal Sentinel* staffer, whose award-winning career as a Packer beat reporter was to cover 40 years, approached Butler with a question about perfection. Most players, asked about an undefeated season before the season began, would say something like: "I don't know anything about that. We have to play them one game at a time." This is why McGinn asked Butler the question, because Butler was known to say exactly what was on his mind.

"That '96 season, I remember Bob McGinn asked me: 'You think you guys can go undefeated?'" Butler recalled. "I said: 'Hell, yeah.' So, that was the headline: 'LeRoy Butler Thinks Packers Can Go Undefeated.'

Mike Holmgren called me. He was like: 'You can't be saying that.' I said: 'But Coach, that's what I believe.' He said: 'Yeah, I know, but people read that and it's bulletin board material.' I said: 'It doesn't matter. We've still got to play the games.' Ron's about 20 feet away from me at practice. His hands are in his pockets. His glasses would turn dark outside, and inside they'd be clear. He looked at me like: 'I know what you're saying. It's okay. If my player says that, I'm down with it.' It was everywhere, all the newspapers, USA Today."

The Packers did not go 19–0 in 1996. But their 16–3 made them Super Bowl champions.

September 1, at Tampa Bay. Packers 34, Buccaneers 3.

This was bigger than it looked. The Packers won six of their last seven games in the 1995 regular season. The one loss was at Tampa. But this was a dominant performance by the Packers, outgaining the Bucs, 406–176. Offense, defense, it was all there. Favre threw for four touchdowns and a quarterback rating of 141.5. Keith Jackson caught three touchdown passes. The defense intercepted four passes. Butler had two picks, which he returned for 59 total yards. And it wasn't exactly "Packer weather." The game time temperature in Tampa was 81 degrees, which wasn't terrible, but the relative humidity was 82 percent.

"Going down there in the opener, first games for me were always flip a coin, because you didn't really have the film study base that you have later in the season," Holmgren said. "You don't really know what the other team is doing. So, first games, crazy stuff happens sometimes. And in Tampa, it's hotter than blazes. How are we going to react to this?

"And I remember Keith Jackson, they just could not stop him. Their defense, with what they were running, and then Brett found him, and it was just great, a great way to start the season. In '92, when we went down there, Tampa killed us (31–3). So, it was good."

September 9, Philadelphia at Green Bay. Packers 39, Eagles 13.

Another performance in the dominant category. The Packers led, 30–7, at halftime. Favre threw three touchdown passes, as the offense rolled up 432 yards. The Green Bay defense intercepted three passes. Robert Brooks caught five passes for two touchdowns and 130 yards. And as a measure of national recognition, Monday Night Football returned to Lambeau Field for the first time in 10 years.

"Three interceptions off Rodney Peete," Holmgren said. "Brooks had a big day, two TD catches. 'It's your turn.' That's how I used to teach the red zone. I'd get the team in there and I'd say: 'Look, you're going to score a touchdown on this play and the rest of you guys are going to help him. The next time, he's going to help you.' And I'd have fun with it that way. But yeah, those are my fondest memories of that, because they rooted for each other."

September 15, San Diego at Green Bay. Packers 42, Chargers 10.

All right, maybe they are going to be unbeaten. This was the third straight romp. The Chargers managed just 141 total yards. Favre threw three more touchdown passes. Brooks was in top form again with eight receptions for 108 yards. Butler had two more interceptions, turning one of them into a 90-yard touchdown return. And in what would become a sign of things to come, Desmond Howard returned a punt 65 yards for a TD.

"Butler, two interceptions, (Sean) Jones, two sacks, Favre, three TD passes, Brooks, another big day," Holmgren recalled. "We're rolling and we're scoring points and we're playing good defense."

September 22, at Minnesota. Vikings 30, Packers 21.

So they won't be the '72 Dolphins. This was one of the mountains the Wolf/Holmgren team had not yet climbed. This was their fifth straight defeat in the Metrodome, the Northern version of the Packers' chamber of horrors. The Packers were 1-for-11 on third down conversions; the Vikes were 9-for-19. The Packers were outgained, 351–217 and lost three fumbles. Still, the Packers led this at the end of the third quarter, 21–17. The game turned for keeps in the fourth quarter when Minnesota defensive end John Randle forced a Favre fumble on a sack in Green Bay territory. The Vikings couldn't move, but Scott Sisson could kick a 44-yard field goal for a 27–21 Minnesota lead.

"That was a tough place for us to play," Holmgren said. "They were fast, they were a different team there. We'd get them at home, we were better. Weird things would happen when we played up there. I'm not too superstitious, but those games up there were difficult. We lost games that we should have won. Didn't play our best football, typically, up there. It was frustrating."

September 29, at Seattle. Packers 31, Seahawks 10.

All it took was leaving the Metrodome. The Packers were dominant again. Favre threw four touchdown passes. Seattle's Rick Mirer threw four interceptions. Favre had a quarterback rating of 115.9. Mirer had a quarterback rating of 11.9. Freeman had seven catches, including two touchdown receptions. The Green Bay defense had 148 yards in interception returns, including a 46-yard return by Reggie White late in the first quarter that was returned to the Seattle 21.

"And then you know, you could just see the film study the next day," Holmgren said with a smile. "He'd be lumbering, and they'd be ripping him for running so fast. They had fun with him. But Fritz (Shurmur) did a beautiful job with our defense."

October 6, at Chicago. Packers 37, Bears 6.

Nothing like a thumping of the traditional rivals to point this season in a championship direction. Favre threw four more TD passes. The Packers had three more interceptions. Antonio Freeman continued to emerge as a receiver of the first rank, with seven catches for 146 yards, including two for touchdowns, one for 50 yards that gave the Packers a commanding 20–3 lead in the second quarter. "It was Freeman's turn," Holmgren said. "Good player."

October 14, San Francisco at Green Bay. Packers 23, 49ers 20 (OT).

Chris Jacke kicked five field goals, with the winner being a 53-yarder in overtime. The Packers trailed, 17–6 at halftime, but climbed back into the game on a third-quarter, 59-yard TD pass from Favre to Don Beebe. Beebe had more playing time than usual because Robert Brooks suffered what turned out to be a season-ending knee injury on a non-contact play in the first quarter. Brooks suffered a torn anterior cruciate ligament (ACL), a torn medial cruciate ligament (MCL), and a torn patellar tendon. Here, Beebe compensated in a huge way, with 11 catches for 220 yards. Favre threw for 395 yards, with one TD, two interceptions.

"That was a huge game, a Monday night game," Holmgren said. "Beebe had a great game, he did. And the 49ers were good. Beebe was really fast, and a really good route-runner, perfect for our offense."

October 27, Tampa Bay at Green Bay. Packers 13, Buccaneers 7.

The Packers' offense lacked its usual dynamism in this game, but there were reasons. Still, the defense was very tough. The Bucs were limited to 196 total yards and did not score until the fourth quarter. With Tampa Bay in a last-ditch effort at a game-winning drive, Butler and linebacker Brian Williams sacked Trent Dilfer on fourth down to preserve the victory.

"Freeman broke his arm in that game," Holmgren said. "And now we're starting to get hurt at the receiver position."

November 3, Detroit at Green Bay. Packers 28, Lions 18.

Favre had a huge day, completing 24 of 35 passes for four touchdowns and 285 yards. Beebe was a factor again, catching four passes for 106 yards and a touchdown. But backup wide receiver Terry Mickens also had an impact, with seven receptions, including two for touchdowns. For the Lions, Barry Sanders was in full form, carrying 20 times for 152 yards, with one touchdown and a run of 35 yards.

"Terry had to play because we were hurt at that position," Holmgren said, then added with a smile: "Barry Sanders did gain 152 yards. (Lions coach) Wayne Fontes would lie like a rug. He'd list Barry Sanders as 'doubtful' all week long, even though he knew he was going to play. Then he'd run for 200."

November 10, at Kansas City. Chiefs 27, Packers 20.

The Packers were hurting and the Chiefs on this day were the more physical team. Favre passed for 314 yards with two touchdowns and one interception, but the Packers were outgained on the ground, 182–75. The Packers had two turnovers. The Chiefs had none. The Chiefs dominated the game early, holding a 27–6 lead in the third quarter. The

Packers were already without Brooks and Freeman, and in this game, tight end Mark Chmura suffered a back injury.

"We were hurt," Holmgren said. "We were down to almost no receivers. And then I remember (cornerback) Doug Evans, he got kicked out of the game in the first quarter. You know, Doug Evans was the nicest kid I ever coached. He wouldn't say 'Boo,' he was just a real gentleman. And there was a pass interference call, and the official had his back to Doug, and Doug went over and tapped him on the shoulder. And he just threw Doug out of the game. But again, a tough place to play, Kansas City was a good club."

Packers staffers, when sitting in a press box on game day, would seat Wolf in the middle, "just to protect Ron a little," as they put it.

"The thing I remember about the Kansas City game, Ron could get a little upset if he didn't like the officiating," said Mark Schiefelbein, then a member of the Packers public relations staff. "Doug Evans got thrown out of the game. Ron stands up in the press box and says: 'Where is the blankety-blank NFL observer?' The NFL observer at the time was usually an older coach from the area, maybe a retired high school coach, just kind of monitoring things. It's not going to change the outcome of the game. Ron goes over to this guy, points to the officials and says: 'Hey, do these guys recognize there's a blankety-blank game going on out there?' Ron was respectful to the guy, but he was upset and that's saying it nicely. We get beat and then that Monday there is a memo from the league office that goes out to all the teams: 'Please do not approach the NFL observer . . .'"

Linebacker Derrick Thomas, in the midst of a Hall of Fame career, had two sacks and was a force throughout the game. Andy Reid, now the Chiefs head coach, then the Packers tight ends and assistant line coach, recalls the physical nature of the Kansas City defense that day.

"I remember Thomas like jacking (Don) Beebe on a shallow crossing route back into Brett's feet," Reid said. "I was going: 'You know what? We've had a lot of injuries at wide receiver. This could be the turning point of the season.' That's what I remember, not because I'm a Chief now, but because I remember coming back here and Derrick Thomas just destroying us."

November 18, at Dallas. Cowboys 21, Packers 6.

Given the injuries and the result, this was the low point of the season. The Packers did not score until the fourth quarter. Tight end Keith Jackson was a reliable target for Favre, with seven receptions for 98 yards. But nothing else worked consistently. On the plus side, the Cowboys never reached the end zone. Then again, Chris Boniol kicked seven field goals for them. The last one, coming with just 20 seconds left in the game, led to some bitterness. The bitterness was immediately displayed.

"That ended in a brawl," Holmgren said. "When they kicked the seventh field goal, they didn't have to. I remember talking to (Dallas head coach) Barry Switzer after the game, and I said: 'You didn't have to do that.' One of the few times I was anything but gracious," Holmgren said with a smile. "Boy, I was mad. I was mad at the referee, I was frustrated because our receivers were hurt, and we couldn't do anything.

"I was talking to (Cowboys wide receiver) Michael Irvin, we did an interview at the Super Bowl. After the last field goal, the brawl starts. And I had told the referee: 'There is going to be trouble if you don't fix this.' The tackle from Dallas was grabbing Reggie by the face mask, every time; that was their technique. And you've got to call that. He wouldn't call it. So, the brawl starts and I'm out there trying to pull guys off. And all of a sudden, somebody grabs me from behind and it's Michael. He's a great player. And he says: 'Coach, you shouldn't be out here. You really shouldn't be out here. Come on, let's walk over here.' He was right."

We interrupt the narrative to bring you Ron Wolf making another major move.

"The Friday before, Jacksonville had waived Andre Rison," Wolf recalled. "Those were the days of the $100 waiver claims. So, after we play the Cowboys, I remember going down into the bowels of the Cowboys stadium, sitting there with Mike Holmgren and (offensive coordinator) Sherm Lewis was there. We talked about it. I said: 'We're going to have to claim Rison. How do you feel about that?' Sherm was a Michigan State alumnus (like Rison). Neither of them had a problem with it, because we needed a receiver. It really helped us."

Rison came with what could charitably be described as baggage. His talent was indisputable. But the Packers would be his fifth team in eight seasons. He had been booted out of Jacksonville because of disputes with head coach Tom Coughlin and quarterback Mark Brunell about running faulty pass patterns. His past was dotted with controversy. Just as a sampling, there was the time in Indiana when he was clocked by state troopers doing 128 miles per hour in a 55-mph zone. There was the time in Atlanta when Rison had repeated altercations with his then girlfriend Lisa "Left Eye" Lopes, of the R&B group TLC. Following one disagreement, Lopes started a fire that eventually burned Rison's mansion to the ground. Charges and counter-charges of abuse and infidelity filled the air, but the happy couple agreed that the mansion fire was an accident.

Nevertheless, Rison was 29, a five-time Pro Bowler, and healthy. With a team looking for a championship, Rison was a chance Wolf would take.

With the Packers, Rison's signing created exactly the impression Wolf wanted. Andy Reid, who thought the season might be slipping away due to injuries to receivers, was suitably impressed.

"The cupboard was bare, other than Beebe," Reid said. "And then Ron Wolf goes out and gets Andre Rison. That's another one of those moves that says: 'We don't care, we're going after it, man.'

"I didn't know what was going to happen, I thought we were going to go down the tubes. And then it was, it's crazy, but we're going to do this thing. We got Rison, and everybody says: 'Whoa, that was bold.' He had a little controversy behind him, but he was a player."

"Our line was makeshift, guys were getting hurt, he got Bruce Wilkerson," LeRoy Butler said. "Ron Cox, came from the Bears because George Koonce got hurt. He got Don Beebe. He got Andre Rison after Robert Brooks hurt his knee. I was saying: 'This man is a genius. How can he know this kind of stuff? How can he put this together? Everybody else was playing chess. He was playing checkers."

November 24, at St. Louis. Packers 24, Rams 9.

The doldrums didn't end immediately in this third straight road game. The Packers struggled mightily on offense in the first half. They trailed, 9–3, at halftime, with the Rams picking up a safety when Favre was charged with intentional grounding, while throwing from the end zone. Cornerback Doug Evans turned the game, and possibly saved the season, intercepting a pass in the third quarter and returning it 32 yards for a touchdown, giving the Packers their first lead.

"Doug Evans won the game in St. Louis for us," Wolf said.

That play ended a surplus supply of Green and Gold frustration. Rison showed he could help with five receptions for 44 yards.

"We got Andre Rison for that game," Holmgren said. "But I was so angry before the first half ended, I couldn't think. So, I told Sherm Lewis, I said: 'You call the game now. You call it.' I've never done that. I had to compose myself because I couldn't hardly think. And then we went in at halftime and he looks at me and I said: 'I'm okay. I'll take it back. I'll get it now.' At least I recognized the fact that I was a blithering idiot," Holmgren said with a laugh. "It was very, very frustrating, so that was a huge win for us."

December 1, Chicago at Green Bay. Packers 28, Bears 17.

This one wasn't easy, but the Packers at least were regaining their health. The game was tied, 7–7, at halftime, but Desmond Howard gave the Packers a lead they would not relinquish with a 75-yard punt return in the third quarter. The Packers benefited greatly from the return of Antonio Freeman, who caught 10 passes for 156 yards. Dorsey Levens gained 69 yards on just five carries.

"Now, we're starting to regain our mojo, so to speak," Holmgren said. "Things were working, but clearly, you need the players. We had a solid system, we knew what we had to do, we had players who knew what to do. You need your players. You don't need All-Pros all the time, but you need your players, your guys. Getting them back, it helped."

December 8, Denver at Green Bay. Packers 41, Broncos 6.

The Broncos were 12–1, but John Elway was out. Bill Musgrave was in at quarterback for Denver, and he could not get the Broncos into the end zone. Green Bay outgained Denver, 379–178. Favre threw four touchdown passes, three of them to Freeman, who had nine receptions for 175 yards. Levens continued his emergence as a dynamic running back, gaining 86 yards on 14 carries, scoring two touchdowns. And Doug Evans continued to check all the boxes on defense with two sacks and a forced fumble.

"Freeman was really rolling," Holmgren said. "In those two games after he came back he had 19 catches. Doug was a good player. Tall, good."

December 15, at Detroit. Packers 31, Lions 3.

At this point, the Packers already had the NFC Central title in hand and the only issue was home-field advantage throughout the playoffs. They took no chances here, as all phases of the game clicked for them. Howard scored on a 92-yard punt return in the second quarter. Favre completed 16 of 25 passes for 240 yards with one interception and one TD. Reggie White had two sacks. Barry Sanders was held to 78 yards on 21 carries.

"(The Silverdome) was always a tough place for us to play, as well," Holmgren said. "When they were good, it was loud and a tough place to play. But we had a good game that day."

December 22, Minnesota at Green Bay. Packers 38, Vikings 10.

If revenge is a dish best served cold, late December in Green Bay seems like an ideal time. The wind chill was a modest 20 degrees, and the Packers rose from a 10–10 tie to outscore the Vikes 28–0 in the second half. Total yards gained favored the Packers, 440–252. Illustrating how different these clubs were playing under the sky as opposed to playing under the dome, the Vikings rushed 17 times for 49 yards. The Packers ran 41 times for 233. The Packers pounded the ball at the Vikings. Bennett rushed 18 times for 109 yards and a touchdown. Levens ran 11 times for 73 yards and a touchdown. Favre threw three touchdown passes, had no interceptions, and in Wisconsin Winter Wonderland conditions, had a quarterback rating of 132.6. All was well at 13–3, the NFC's best record, heading into the playoffs, but staying at home.

"We've got the team back," Holmgren said.

January 4, 1997, Divisional Playoff. San Francisco at Green Bay. Packers 35, 49ers 14.

Rain and 17-mph winds made for lousy field conditions. But these Packers were built for exactly these sorts of circumstances. Desmond

Howard got the Packers on the board first with a twisting, turning 71-yard punt return for a touchdown. Later in the first quarter, a 46-yard punt return by Howard to the 49ers seven-yard line set up a second Packer TD. The Niners had to go without quarterback Steve Young, who left the game in the first quarter with a rib injury. The Packers went up 21–0 before two special teams mistakes set up San Francisco touchdowns. Late in the second quarter, a bouncing punt struck Green Bay's Chris Hayes in the back of the leg. The 49ers recovered at the Packer 26 and, with Elvis Grbac now at quarterback, converted this miscue into a touchdown.

Then Beebe muffed the second-half kickoff, the 49ers recovered at the Green Bay four-yard line, and subsequently scored what would be their final touchdown of the day.

Years later, this particular sequence was remembered with laughter. Desmond Howard had earlier scored on a 71-yard punt return. He was to return the second-half kickoff, but he wasn't quite available.

"Desmond was really explosive," Holmgren said. "I was joking with him when Favre went into the Hall of Fame, he had a party that Saturday—it was great fun. The players, I'm ripping them, they're ripping me, we're all laughing. Desmond Howard has this infectious smile and I reminded him, we're going to receive the second-half kickoff against the 49ers, and I'm getting my headset on, this was (special teams coach) Nolan Cromwell's deal, I look back, and there's no one there, nobody there (deep to return). How do you get a timeout when the game hasn't started?

"And Beebe runs out there at the last second, so we have 11. They kick the ball and they recover on the four-yard line. I go to Nolan, 'What the . . . ?' And here comes Desmond walking out of the thing, coming out, walking over. I go: 'Nice of you to show up. Where were you?' 'Well, my uniform was all dirty and wet.' I go: 'Well, that's good. You know what just happened?' And then I blistered him a little bit. I was telling this story at that party, these guys are dying and he's dying, too. It was so much fun."

The Packers came back with a 12-play drive, in which they ran the ball 10 times. Bennett and Levens carried the load. On a third-and-goal from the three, Bennett had an uncharacteristic fumble at the one, but

Freeman recovered in the end zone. The Packers were back in charge and they were never threatened again. The Green Bay defense had three interceptions, two by Eugene Robinson, and two fumble recoveries. It was an all-around outstanding effort against a team that not all that long ago had been a dominant force.

"There were a lot of questions where the Green Bay Packers belong in the hierarchy in the National Football Conference," Wolf said. "Certainly, I think those questions were answered."

For Holmgren, with a lifetime of Bay Area background, the performance against the Niners was especially rewarding.

"In fact, if you talked to the players, I think I was focused most of the time, but for that opponent, they knew it was a little bit extra there, like playing against your brother in the backyard," Holmgren said. "A little bit extra. It was a bad-weather day. But right now, you're peaking at the right time, you're getting into your rhythm."

January 12, 1997, NFC Championship game. Carolina at Green Bay. Packers 30, Panthers 13.

It wasn't the Ice Bowl, but it was the Packers winning the NFC championship and heading to the Super Bowl for the first time in 29 years. It was Packer weather—3 degrees Fahrenheit, with a wind chill of minus-17 at kickoff. The Packers shrugged off the cold—and two early turnovers that led to two early leads for Carolina. The Packers outgained the Panthers, 479–251, with a beautifully balanced attack that included 278 yards passing and 201 rushing. Favre threw for two touchdowns and had a quarterback rating of 107.3 in the Arctic conditions, while Kerry Collins put up a 55.6 for the Panthers. Levens had a huge day, with 10 carries for 88 yards, and five receptions for 117 yards and a touchdown. With the Packers down, 7–0, he gained 35 yards on the last play of the first quarter, then, on the first play of the second quarter, caught a 29-yard pass for the tying touchdown. In the third quarter, a 66-yard pass play to Levens set up a four-yard TD run by Bennett for a 27–13 Packers lead.

It was a complete triumph for the Packers, made all the more triumphant for the championship drought that had preceded it.

"I remember the feeling in the stadium," Holmgren said. "I knew it was cold. I was always astounded with the players' ability to play in that weather. It was cold, cold. I remember they put in a new field that week. It was weird, at night they had the dump trucks lined up, and the stadium lights were on.

"You know who had a great game was Dorsey Levens. He had a great game. And again, that game the offense and defense played off each other. It was a nice balance there. Someone brought this up to me when I was at the Super Bowl. We scored the most points and gave up the least points. And also, I talked about unselfishness, sometimes you can get a defense/offense thing that is unhealthy. But these guys, Brett had a lot to do with that. LeRoy Butler and Bennett were best friends. A lot of guys. We had a lot of that going. That was a good group."

For Ron Wolf, this was the best moment of the season, including the Super Bowl. This was a victory for the Packers, a championship won in Lambeau Field. In the intense cold, the Packers received their trophy and it did not appear that any of the capacity crowd of 61,126 had left for the comfort of their homes, or at least the comfort of their cars. The cold was forgotten in this moment of shared triumph. Wolf, whether he wanted credit or not, was the architect of this moment.

"When I took the job, everyone was telling me how stupid I was to go to Green Bay," he said 30 years later. "'You can't go up there. You can't win there. You won't have a chance at all.' And to go down on that field and experience that event was probably the ultimate moment in my professional football career. That was it. I can't adequately express what that meant. There was a feeling I had, I was pumping my fist. I was just overcome with joy, elation. All your frustrations are all erased. We did something that people said would never happen again. They're going to move the franchise, they're going to do this, they're going to do that. No way. Made it happen. It all happened. Of course, it wouldn't have happened without guys like Santana Dotson, Sean Jones. They had a lot to do with that.

"What a thrill that was. What's so funny was they stuck a microphone in my face and I was going to use that Mel Allen line: 'How about that?' And I completely forget what I was going to say. I completely blew that. (John) Madden said: 'What the hell were you saying?' I said: 'I was going to say: 'How about that?' but I forgot."

"I just remember being down there, while people expected us to win, there's still disbelief," Mark Schiefelbein recalled. "They're putting that stage together, after the game, they're handing out the NFC championship hats. And then Terry Bradshaw is interviewing Ron and Ron says: 'Hey, Green Bay, how about this? Guess where we're goin'?' And the place just went crazy. They had never seen Ron like that before. I remember Bob Harlan breaking down in the locker room. You knew how much it meant to Ron, but he knew how much it meant to the fans, and then to do it in Green Bay. You're the GM who built this team. Talk about the culmination of things. Very emotional."

LeRoy Butler was with Wolf as the ceremony unfolded on what by this time might have literally been the "frozen tundra."

"The fans are everything," Butler said. "They wouldn't let us leave the stadium after we beat Carolina. We had to go around and shake everybody's hand. And it was freezing.

"Ron valued the fans. It was so cold. Nobody left. They were setting up the stage and he was very emotional. When I hugged him, he was trembling. He said: 'I envisioned this happening, but who would have thought it would come true?' I said: 'You must have known it would come true, with everything you did. This ain't luck.' You controlled your narrative. He was like: 'I guess you're right, but still I just got a lot of great players.'"

That wasn't luck. That was Ron Wolf reviving a franchise, building a real winner.

January 26, 1997, Super Bowl XXXI.
At New Orleans. Packers 35, Patriots 21.

The Ron Wolf memory that stands out from this epic event comes direct from the Louisiana Superdome press box. The Patriots were coached by Bill Parcells, a very close friend of the Packers' general manager. Although the Packers were heavily favored, the Pats were more than making a game of it. Late in the third quarter, Curtis Martin's 18-yard run up the middle cut Green Bay's lead to 27–21. On the following kickoff, though, Desmond Howard went 99 yards for a game-breaking kickoff return touchdown. Howard was to amass 244 return yards in this game and was named Super Bowl MVP.

As Howard completed his touchdown return, Wolf could be heard shouting: 'Keep kicking it to him, Bill! Keep kicking it to him!" This kind of outburst in a highly public place was completely out of character for Wolf. But, after all, this was the Super Bowl.

"I said that," Wolf acknowledged. "In fact, Bill reminds me of that, every once in a while. I've never seen a returner do what Desmond did for us that year."

It was one of those days when every facet of the game worked for the Packers. And they all had to, because, until Howard's return, the Patriots were playing past adversity. The special teams' contributions were apparent. The Packers intercepted four of Drew Bledsoe's passes. Reggie White set a Super Bowl record with three sacks. And then there was, of course, Brett Favre.

It was a dream for Favre, playing in a Super Bowl, just an hour away from his hometown of Kiln, Mississippi. He wasted no time making his presence felt on a 54-yard touchdown to Andre Rison on a post pattern. Favre celebrated by running around the field like he was being chased.

"Rison, bless his heart, he did the right thing," Holmgren said. "When we got Rison, Ron came in one time, and our receivers were hurt, we lost those two games because we couldn't pass the ball at all. Ron comes in and says: 'What about Rison?' I said: 'He's good, but he's kind of a loose cannon, you know?' So, Ron didn't do it the first time, we had been thinking about getting him earlier, then we lost a couple of games. And then he said: 'Mike, we've got to.' And I said: 'Yeah, okay.'

"Andre comes in, but he didn't know the plays and he was not a great student of the game, anyway. So, I told Brett: 'You call the play, and then tell him what to do.' That's how we did that. So, in the Super Bowl, there were a couple of audibles that he did know.

"That (play) was early in the game, and after the play, Brett took off his helmet and went running around. He was just like he would get. Even when he got older, he had a little kid's joy of playing. It was fascinating. It was one of the things that made him great. So, he comes over to the sideline and he's just all over the place. I go: 'Man, we've got another three quarters and a half to play. Nice going, that's great, but we've got a lot of football left.' He goes: 'Okay, okay, I'm down.'"

For Favre, at least part of the excitement was the improbability of it all.

"We didn't practice that play a lot because defenses were changing," Favre said. "That play was made famous by Joe Montana in the Super Bowl, years before. And he hit Jerry Rice for a touchdown. 'Razor' was the audible. The X (split end) runs a shake. It's basically an all-out blitz, check. I sat there and watched the Super Bowl highlights all week, because you have plenty of time to sit in the room and you just see them over and over again. I thought to myself many times: *It would be so cool to do that.*

"And did I think that would happen? No, because New England had not shown all year a max blitz. They were more of a conservative, bend-but-don't-break defense. But lo and behold, the first play of the game they line up in a max blitz. I remember thinking: *There's no way, there's no way, they're doing this. They're just showing something to get us faked out right out of the box.*

"I had to go with my instincts and call that play. As I dropped back, I saw the safety step up, which is a sure sign that what they were showing was in fact true. Then it was about making a great throw. Given the fact that we hadn't practiced that and Andre hadn't been with us very long, just made it all the more amazing. Andre was new to our offense and it took me two years to master all the terminology. So, to check to a play that we never checked to, had only talked about from time to time, was a tossup. But with a guy like Andre, he was streetball at its best and he was good at it. There was no doubt that Andre had a tendency, you'd look for him at the post, but he was running to the corner. Maybe he was wide open, but you were expecting him to do something else.

"So again, the fact that they gave me that blitz, I made the right audible, Andre ran the right route and I made the perfect throw, in the first pass play of the game, honestly, when I ran off the field with my helmet off, everyone was: 'Oh my God, look at his excitement.' What they didn't know was that I was thinking: 'Are you shittin' me? Did this work? I've been looking at this all week and think how awesome would it be to check to Razor and get a touchdown in the Super Bowl. Are you shittin' me?'"

The Patriots came back to take a 14–10 lead, but then Favre struck again, this time with an 81-yard touchdown pass to Antonio Freeman, at that time a Super Bowl record. He also ran for a touchdown and threw no interceptions. Favre had a quarterback rating of 107.9 to 46.6 for Bledsoe. In the biggest game of his life, as near his hometown as the NFL could get, Favre was exactly the quarterback he needed to be.

"It was a wonderful feeling," he said. "The script could not have been written any better. It couldn't have gone any better. It had a little bit of everything in the game, it was a great game. I actually had to make a couple of audibles in the game and they worked, I had to make some difficult throws, they worked. Again, it couldn't have been written any better."

Somebody in the Wolf/Parcells friendship had to lose this one. Parcells, on his way to the Hall of Fame, had already won two Super Bowls with the Giants. The 1996 Patriots were 14-point underdogs in this one. Wolf and Parcells spoke frequently, but not leading up to this game.

"I don't think to the best of my recollection that we talked about it," Parcells said. "I had a very young team. We were fortunate, we played well enough to get there, but the Packers were a little bit further down the road than we were, just a little bit. The game was competitive for a while. We had a couple of opportunities late in the game—you know, everybody will say that—but we did have legitimate opportunities to make that game even closer than it was and we didn't take advantage of them. And then of course, there was the kickoff return (by Desmond Howard), just at the point where we had closed it down to several points and we had quite a bit of momentum there. But Desmond Howard managed to take that away very quickly.

"Our punter, Tom Tupa, did a marvelous job of pinning Howard on the sideline with directional kicks. But on the kickoffs, we were reluctant to concede field position, because they were pretty dynamic offensively. You know, it only takes one of those to make a difference. They hit it, and they took advantage of it. But, hey, when you're in that game, it (inexperience) doesn't make a lot of difference. You have to take advantage of those opportunities."

Days later, Parcells left to become head coach of the New York Jets.

Wolf, meanwhile, had announced that, even with his current contract expiring, he intended to remain with the Packers. He was thinking of a championship run. After what had happened in the five seasons since he took over, any lofty expectation did not seem unreasonable. A franchise had been brought back to its previous level. The Pack was back. There was more than enough credit to go around, but the driving force behind this revival was Ron Wolf.

He had made the right choice with the quarterback, the head coach, the dominant defensive end, and then he had filled in with a group of players that had scored 456 points and had given up 210. But along with the tangible talents, this was a remarkably cohesive group.

"The other part of that that gets overlooked—and I don't think this is too Pollyannaish—is that was the most unselfish group of players I've ever been around," Holmgren said. "Really. You know, when you think of receivers, take the receiver group on any team. Now it's nuts, because of social media, but they want the ball, they want to contribute, and that means catching passes. Brooks, Freeman, Desmond Howard, those guys, Chmura at tight end; of course, they wanted the ball, but they never showed that. They were happy when other guys made the play. And it was just right. Just right. That had a lot to do with our success, in my opinion."

Ron Wolf, in the moment of ultimate success, as the Vince Lombardi trophy was being presented to the Packers on the Super Dome field, did not forget to extend thanks in the appropriate direction. "Green Bay, this is yours as much as it is ours," Wolf said. "And we thank you very much for that."

This magnificent team, put together by Wolf, had done exactly what it was designed to do. The Pack was actually back. The Vince Lombardi trophy was coming home.

9

Ron Wolf—A Man for All Seasons, but Football Season First

WITH RON WOLF, the distance between the public image and the private individual is substantial. But that distance occurs, not by way of a plan, but out of professional necessity.

This is not everyman. The public Wolf during his time with the Packers was a hard-bitten, driven individual, a guy who made difficult decisions; jettisoning popular players, firing long-term employees, and not particularly caring about the whims of public opinion.

This was the man who responded to Mike Reinfeldt's comment that firings of Packers staffers were creating a morale problem with the timeless: "What about my morale? Don't I count?"

At first, this was shocking for followers of the Green and Gold. Then, as success arrived, appreciation for Wolf's laser-focused management style increased. His approach couldn't have much to do with hurt feelings or mass approval. He was a victory of substance over form.

"It was hard for me to be somebody else," Wolf says, looking back. "I couldn't be Al Davis. I couldn't be somebody else. What I tried to do—and I'm sure there are a lot of people who worked in the office in Green Bay would say you're full of shit—but what I tried to do was to treat people like I would want to be treated.

"But what really ticked me off with a lot of people in there was it was just a job. To me, it wasn't just a job, you have a responsibility here. The responsibility is you're representing the Green Bay Packers and you must give the best you possibly can at that particular moment. Do the best that you can do. That's what you need to do."

Wolf was not much into masking his feelings for the sake of appearances. Mark Schiefelbein, who was a member of the public relations staff when Wolf arrived in Green Bay, recalls his first meeting with the new GM.

"When I first met him, I had been working for the Tampa Bay Buccaneers, after I interned for the Packers in 1989. Even though I was with the Buccaneers, I still followed the Packers. I'll never forget when they hired Ron Wolf, all the people at the Buccaneers said: 'That's a great hire, he's well-respected.' The owner of the Buccaneers at that time was Mr. (Hugh) Culverhouse. When I left to go to the Packers he said to me: 'Give Ron Wolf my regards.' I said: 'Sure.'

"So, I'm up in Green Bay and I met Ron right by his office. I said: 'Ron, by the way, Mr. Culverhouse sends his regards.' Ron just goes, 'ooooh' and turns and walks away. I thought: 'This guy is real friendly.' I didn't realize until later what had happened with Ron and Mr. Culverhouse (Wolf was fired by Culverhouse). We laugh about that now, but that was my first meeting with Ron."

Colleagues who became friends with Wolf had two sorts relationships with him. There were the public relationships, polite and deferential, and the private relationships, which were regular friendships. Schiefelbein became one of those people. Pepper Burruss, who Wolf brought from the New York Jets as head athletic trainer, was as well.

"I had a behind-the-door relationship with Ron, and another one in public with Ron," Burruss said. "I think most people were kind of 'afraid' of Ron. This is a guy who speaks softly and carries a big stick. And a general manager who had traded a first-round draft choice, had done that and done this. I used to get the sense that 'watch out, Mr. Wolf's on the prowl.' And he was bringing in a lot of people, too, tryouts and free agents and the like. People weren't running up and down the hall hugging Mr. Wolf and dancing a jig with him.

"There were a few of us, along with Schief, who had that behind-the-door relationship with him. You could go behind that door and there was a little ball-busting going on. But when the door opened, it was: 'Yes sir, Mr. Wolf, glad to do it, sir.'

"One time he addressed the team and the coaches, and we were all in the room. Afterward, we walked into his office, closed the door and he said: 'Did I sound tough? Was I a prick? How did I sound?'" Burruss recalled with a laugh.

"It's the understatement of the day to say that Ron never was a rah-rah guy. Ron was not Bob Harlan walking down the hall. Bob just exuded charisma walking down the hall. He was magnetic. Ron was a Raider, and a Jet, and he was a businessman on a business mission."

It was relatively easy to grasp how Wolf would be admired and respected by the people who worked with and for him. What wasn't widely known was how well these people *liked* him.

"There's a couple traits that Ron has that people really don't know," John Dorsey said. "He truly is a humble man. But he is so affable, you just like being around him. For some reason, you just know that it's going to be good, when it's all said and done at the end of the day, you're going to be in good hands. It's just the way he handles himself on a day-to-day basis. He's very approachable. He may not seem that way at times, but at the end of the day he is very approachable. And he's willing to listen to everything. He's no-nonsense when it comes to getting things done, but he's very approachable.

"He's a genuine man. To me, he's got internal strengths that some people may view differently, but he's got an internal strength about him that is really good. Now the other component, that scary component that kind of catches people, is his intellectual depth. He has unbelievable intellectual depth because he is so well-read. I mean he is well-read in every subject matter you could talk about. He's got depth on so many different levels and different subject matters."

Wolf's openness and his honesty were trademarks of his daily dealing. His willingness to be his own worst critic was also appreciated.

"There were so many things as I got to know Ron," Schiefelbein said. "I was very fortunate because he was so open to everything. Being in the public relations staff, it was just natural in that job, that I got to spend a lot of time with Ron. The more I got to know him, he really set the tone there. As a leader, someone who could make decisions and was not afraid to make the big decisions, and yet the thing I think few people saw was his personality. He's got a great sense of humor. He's funny. He's very reflective. He'll talk about the mistakes he made. Sometimes if you're listening to Ron, you'd have thought that he didn't accomplish anything, because he's very reflective and he admits his mistakes.

"My early impressions of him were that he was confident, but not cocky. And as I got to know him more, he was willing to answer a lot of questions. As I got to know him better I'd go up to his office and say: 'Ron, can I ask you something?' 'You can ask me anything.'

"But if Ron Wolf asked you a question, he already knew the answer, you know what I mean? And you learn to be prepared with him. There's a protocol in how you do things. I think Ron's experience in Tampa really shaped him. 'Okay, if this ever happens again, if I get a shot, I'm going to do it my way.'"

And there always was the common point of reference in Wolf's tenure in northeastern Wisconsin; the whole-hearted, sincere appreciation of what it meant to work for the Green Bay Packers.

"Ron used to stay in the office in the evening, he would watch highlights from the Packer films of the '40s and '50s and '60s," said Mike Reinfeldt, chief financial officer and later, vice-president of administration for the Packers. "He had such a feeling for what those teams were all about. The way he cherished the tradition, the legacy of the Packers, people did pick up on that. The way he was enamored of it. They picked up on that and all of a sudden, they fed off him, and he fed off the rest of the staff as to what the Packers were, or what the Packers could be or should be.

"If you didn't regard it that way, I'm not sure you should be with the Packers. It was an honor to work for the Packers.

"That was a big part of the success. He kind of set the table with both the focus and the embracing of the history. I think he also took it a step beyond that, by hiring really good people. Coach Holmgren, Ted Thompson, Reggie McKenzie, all of a sudden there were a lot of people that were being added. When you add the right people, good things generally happen."

Like Reinfeldt, Schiefelbein had grown up in Wisconsin. But there were still Packer lessons to be learned.

"I learned so many things from Ron, and one of them was an appreciation for the history of the Packers," Schiefelbein said. "And he always talked about that. Always do what's best for the Packers. He said: 'Always remember those who came before us. It was I think, 1993, Ron was the one who started the honorary captain program. There was a lot of talk that previous regimes didn't want the older guys around, that they wanted to distance themselves from the Packers of the '60s. Ron got in there and said: 'Hey, we need to embrace this. This history and tradition is second to none.' He had come from the Raiders and they were big on their history."

Wolf's appreciation for players was ever-present. Reinfeldt saw it from both sides, as a member of the Packers front office, but also someone who had a nine-year career as an NFL safety, including his 1979 All-Pro season when he led the league with 12 interceptions.

"Being a player and having a financial background gave me the ability to look at things through a player's eyes," Reinfeldt said. "You could make certain decisions and you could walk away and say: 'How would the players look at that?' And sometimes I think the players' view of the world is kind of a simplistic view, but they have great vision and they understand it. They have a great intuitive sense of what's right and what isn't right. And they pick up on all those little subtleties and nuances and as a player it did to me. I'm not sure what the magic percentage is, but a heck of a lot more times than not, the Packers did things the right way. They did it how you're supposed to do it. They did in a way that was conducive to winning, but they also did it the right way.

"Ron went out of his way to reach out to the former players and appreciated what they had done to put the franchise where it was. I think a lot of teams have followed in his footsteps, but he was one of the first. Having them come back and be captains and interact with the team. That goes to my earlier point about players picking up on things. The players pick up on that and it's kind of cool to know that one day you will be appreciated as a former player."

"I've always had a great admiration for those guys that played the game," Wolf said, "and particularly those guys who played the game back when there were only 33 players and they had to play special teams. It's remarkable to see how they approached it, because they're playing for $6,000; $7,000; $8,000; $9,000. They played 20 of those games. Twelve games and seven exhibition games. And then it went down to 12 and six, and then to 14 and six. But you had to play.

"And my first year with the Raiders, 1963, I'd go into the locker room in Santa Rosa, where we trained, and you have to understand where I came from, which was back in the woods. I'm watching guys shoot themselves up in their toes and not realizing what I'm watching, so they can practice, so they can make their $6,500 dollars a year. I see it, but I don't realize what I'm seeing. Afterwards, I would sit and talk to the trainer, because I roomed next to him, and he would tell me what they were doing. Those are the guys that paved the way.

"So, to have an opportunity—you look at those names when you walk into Lambeau Field and see those names. You know one thing and one thing only—they're Green Bay Packers. Nobody else. That's the uniqueness of Green Bay. Those are magical names. Just call them out. They're what this game is all about. And I was trying to get that into our young players, that this is a marvelous place to play. You have a chance to make your own history, a chance to make something new. Through the work of our coaching staff and our players, we got that. We got that.

"But we played on that. To me that is something that is so important to me; tradition, tradition, tradition. Where else where you can do it? You can go to Chicago and do it. You can go to the New York Giants and do it. I always thought there were four jewels in the crown and the fourth jewel was Washington. I'm not so sure I was right there. The fourth jewel might be the Cowboys now, but to me, they're an expansion team. To me."

Among the people who worked for him, Wolf opened some eyes, and later, opened some doors. He encouraged capable people to expand their capabilities and thus, their possibilities.

"I thought he was excellent to work for," Reggie McKenzie said. "One thing he did was, he gave you a job and held you accountable to do your job. He gave you every resource you needed, and he threw stuff at you to see if you could handle it. The way I looked at it, he already knew that I could handle it, you know? . . . He didn't hesitate, if he trusted you, he trusted you to the hilt.'

"With that being said, you make sure you're thorough in everything you do, you make sure you're right; right from the standpoint of you check it, you do it, you don't just half do something. You don't go into a meeting to talk about somebody when you've done no homework, you didn't research, you didn't watch enough film. You just don't do that. You do your work well, you do it right.

"And then just trust yourself. At some point, you've seen enough players, you've written enough reports, you've got to go with trusting your gut. That's what I thought he was really good at. He was extremely confident in what he believed. He didn't deviate. If he didn't like a certain type of player, if he didn't like that type of player, it was going to be put on the back burner. But he had a belief in the certain types of players that could help this team win, certain types of talents that were special, and hard to find."

It was the same thing with the coaching staff. With those people who demonstrated the work ethic, the accumulated knowledge, the curiosity, the potential for more, Wolf shared freely in what he believed, what he knew.

"Ron let me in his world," Andy Reid said. "That doesn't always happen. He trusted me on a couple things. He trusted me on (tight end Mark) Chmura that first year when we kind of red-shirted him. He saw something there that I didn't see, but he let me into that world. And taught me. I learned stuff from him about personnel, about how he saw things. And then, obviously Mike Holmgren had the biggest influence on me, but I took so much from Ron, I appreciate it to this day.

"That doesn't always happen. There can be walls built there. He allowed me in there, so when I went to Philadelphia, I did the personnel. I had the opportunity to do that and make the final decisions. He wasn't far down the road when he was in Annapolis there, so he came up often and we talked and so on. He was always a reference point. I learned about chemistry, I learned about a lot of things from that. And you're a pretty good coach, when you have good players, as long as you have a good system and you can teach, you're okay. A lot of lessons learned, but Ron gave us the opportunity to do those things."

Wolf shared his knowledge with people who asked, but they had to be people who exhibited the ability to understand and expand upon the precious information he was giving them.

John Schneider was a student at the University of St. Thomas in Minnesota when he applied for a scouting internship with the Packers and received "a standard rejection letter." With the kind of persistence that he was later to demonstrate as general manager of the Seattle Seahawks, Schneider wrote again, and Wolf responded by saying that Schneider should get back to him after the draft. Schneider did, by somehow getting Wolf's office number and calling him on the Sunday before Memorial Day. Wolf was, of course, watching film. Schneider had prepped extensively for his interview with Wolf and had shown determination in seeking this opportunity. Was Wolf impressed?

"I think so—he intimidated the shit out of me," Schneider said with a laugh.

But Schneider was to become an apt student of Wolf's in the school of football talent evaluation. The knowledge was there, for someone who put in the time and effort, because Wolf was eager to share that knowledge with those who demonstrated that they cared enough to learn more.

"That's the part that I thought was fascinating," Schneider said. "That was one of the reasons that I thought I had a chance with him initially, because I was a history major, and he was, too. I was like, 'Wow, okay.' I wanted to learn, like: Tell me what Hugh Green (All-Pro linebacker for Buccaneers in the early '80s) was like. How did you decide on Marcus Allen, take me through that process.' He was phenomenal that way.'"

Wolf was demanding, but he could be nothing less. His people respected him and liked him, but they were also motivated by the fear of coming up short of his expectations.

"You better not have any mistakes on your scouting paper when you file a report on a player," John Dorsey said. "He would take out a red pen and circle your mistakes. He wants everyone to understand the importance of grammar and sentence structure. That is how detailed and efficient he is. He will test you, which is good. He keeps you on your toes.

"Yet, Ron Wolf made the working environment very exciting. You didn't mind working the extra hours. Plus, with all the experience he had, he was always there to help you. He would show you how to understand why this way is better."

"The draft room," Dorsey said, "was like a three-phased thing: the beginning, the middle, and later. In the beginning, you had Ron who had set the tone of a very proud franchise. And he was very masterful at that in terms of allowing everybody ownership of the process. And then as they go along, you're taught the proper way to do things, and I think that as you go along, you had enough people in that room that were hungry enough to learn. You know, Ron has a very unique way of how he does things, but at the end of the day he's got very high standards, and he expects certain things, and he would never ask anybody to do anything that he wouldn't do, and I think that spoke volumes to all of us.

"And because he's so affable, you just wanted to please him."

The young scouts soaked up as much of Wolf's storehouse of knowledge as they could, if they qualified. And the qualification was not merely wanting to know, it was doing the precisely right thing with the knowledge.

"It was not just if you wanted to learn," Reggie McKenzie said. "If he felt that you were *capable*, he had to really know it in his gut that he could trust you to get the job done. I think that was the thing. He allowed you to do that, but he kind of pushed you to make sure you would do it right. He was really meticulous about certain things; that really made you check yourself before you said: 'Okay, this is my grade, this is how I see it. This is my report.' What he showed me was before you turn in anything, before you talk about a player, get all your ducks in a row. Know them, you know what I'm saying: Don't come in there half. That taught me a lot there. Be thorough. That's one of the things he taught me was how to be thorough.

Wolf said that McKenzie was on target with his player evaluations from the start. "Me and Ron would talk about these things a lot," McKenzie said. "And he would always say: 'Either a player can play, or he can't. Either you've got it, or you don't.' I think that's how he felt about me. He saw something right off the bat. When I went up there to interview, he hired me on the spot. He gave me four or five players to evaluate. He didn't explain how he wanted the evaluations to read. I just wrote them the way I did. (He was a graduate assistant at Tennessee at the time.) I wrote the reports, and I came in there and he read them, and then I sat with him and we talked about each player. I think the way I explained about each player, after not doing this ever, he probably thought: *Man.* I must have impressed him because he hired me on the spot. He felt I could do it. I had zero inkling that I was going to get into this line of work. My mindset when I was at the University of Tennessee as a grad student was to be a coach. We bumped into each other, while he was working, scouting, seemed like he was scouting for scouts, too. He kind of got word that he wanted to interview me. That was something he saw back then, in scouting me he already knew my background, the type of person I was, the type of work ethic I had. He had all that knowledge. He knew I was a smart player when I was playing for the Raiders. So, he wanted to give me a shot. He must have been very pleased with my interview because I got the job. And I kept it."

There was plenty of pressure on the Packers and everybody who worked for them. Wolf acted in ways that would put more of the pressure on himself. For instance, you might typically see a GM in the locker room after a victory, basking in the happy result, taking a share of the credit. Wolf, particularly on the road, made a point of going into the locker room after a Packer defeat. With the general manager available for comment, some of the pressure for reliving the loss with the media, and/or taking the blame, was taken off the coaching staff and the players. Mike Holmgren said that he appreciated Wolf doing that. The players also appreciated that. Even the writers appreciated that.

Wolf never gave away the store in dealing with the media, but he was available, and he was as candid and as quotable as anyone in his position could be. And he was relentlessly critical of his own performance.

"I guess I revered Ron Wolf as much as anybody I ever knew in any sport," Bud Lea, long-time reporter, editor, and columnist for the Milwaukee Sentinel, said. "He was always accessible to sportswriters. You always knew where you stood with him. You got no bullshit."

Wolf also set a tone with the executive committee and the board of directors that left no doubt about who was in charge.

Bud Selig, who later served as commissioner of baseball for 22 years, joined the Packers board of directors in 1990. He saw clearly and appreciated the difference that Wolf made.

"Could you notice the change when he took over? Oh, my God, could you ever," Selig said. "It was huge. In no-nonsense things, even in board meetings, he wouldn't tolerate any nonsense. And I liked that, I liked that a lot, because he was very professional, obviously very knowledgeable. He was good. I don't know how else to say it.

"I was there at the beginning, I was there in board meetings and this was not some happy little group any more—this was a guy who was going to win. It's a great story. It's a wonderful story."

"You learn an awful lot from your mistakes, not the other way around," Wolf said. "As you stay in this profession, the most important thing you have is selective memory. Don't dwell on your bad picks; in this particular case, just keep going on. I've always referred to this as a revolver. You've got six shells in a revolver, use them all. And if you've got two revolvers, use all 12."

And Wolf had remarkable insights into the people who worked for him. Their strengths were prized. Their shortcomings were worked on until they were no longer shortcomings.

"There are some guys that are information-gatherers," Wolf said. "You want to know what the coaches really think of a player, or how much trouble he is, there are guys that can get that for you. And if you're a young guy that formerly played, a young guy like Alonzo Highsmith, or Sammy Seale when they were young, they can talk to graduate assistants and you're going to find out what kind of personality we're dealing with here. (John) Dorsey was exceptional at that, exceptional."

In the end, the Green Bay organization that had struggled for a quarter century after the departure of Vince Lombardi, was transformed. It became precisely the kind of organization that it needed to be, exactly the kind of organization that Ron Wolf wanted it to be.

"Ron has a very unique way of how he does things, but at the end of the day he's got very high standards and he expects certain things and he would never ask anybody to do anything that he wouldn't do, and I think that spoke volumes to all of us," said John Dorsey.

"All of us who were in there, we just wanted to make sure we got it right, for the organization. At the end of the day, as Ron would say, it was the Packers' pick and not one individual; it was the Green Bay Packers' pick and that's kind of how we did this thing. He set the tone early and we all followed his lead. And we were all easily moldable back then.

"I'm talking everybody from the lowest level all the way up to the highest levels, he instilled pride in everybody, being part of a proud tradition. His whole objective was to get this organization back to its rightful place in the pecking order of the National Football League. And I think he said that early, and people began to jump on very early."

And it wasn't just his own people who trusted Wolf's judgment. Bill Parcells, twice a Super Bowl champion head coach, later a Hall of Famer, was the competition. But he and Wolf formed a lasting friendship, based on mutual respect and giving each other added perspective on the game that demanded their attention and gave them inspiration.

"He's a very honest guy, very forthright. If he knew the answer he would tell you, if he didn't know, he would tell you that he didn't know, or that he would have to think about it," Parcells said.

"I think in a lot of ways Ron has had a pretty strong influence on me, in my coaching. Most of the time, our conversations were about personnel and personnel acquisitions and trying to be relentless in never feeling that particular task was completed. As you go through the season, there were going to be opportunities, if you were vigilant, [and] continued to improve your team, as the season went on. I just was always conscious of, after the draft, and the preseason and the season gets under way, still trying to impart the philosophy to the organizations that I was working for, that there were still vehicles that we can use to improve our team. You know, they don't always work out and they're not always available, but you still have to keep flipping those rocks over and looking hard and trying to add something that maybe adds just a little aspect to what you already have.

"I was very fortunate, I could rely on Ron for the general manager's viewpoint and for a personnel man's view of things, not just in talent evaluation, but in the way that you try to integrate people into your team. He could act in a little bit of an advisory capacity to me on the personnel side and then on the other side, I think I could maybe give him a coach's point of view and try to call his attention to things that a coach might be thinking that aren't readily apparent to a GM. So, it was kind of a symbiotic relationship.

"But we also made some trades with one another, particularly when I was at New England and with the Jets, those two stops for me were ones that Ron was very helpful. We made some trades that were mutually beneficial, and we had a relationship that would allow each of us to some point in time to get the better end of the deal, knowing full well that that would come back around the other way some time. That happened several times with us, where we were kind of trying to help our own situation first, but when you have a relationship like Ron and I had, we could understand each other's point of view and try to act in a manner that might be mutually beneficial. After a while, the league passed a rule to kind of stop us from doing some of the things that we were doing—not illegally—but within the rules, but they kind of changed the rules on us."

On the lighter side of life with the Packers, the Wolf sense of humor was, and is, understated, droll; simultaneously expected, but surprising. In conversation, Wolf may be silent for a time, then, without turning his head or raising his voice, will make a remark that is completely hilarious.

Pepper Burruss found this early, when both he and Wolf were with the Jets.

"There was some issue when the Jets were at Hempstead at Hofstra University (Long Island), kind of sandwiched between the flight patterns of Kennedy and LaGuardia," Burruss said. "We had planes coming over all the time. The Concorde would come over and whatever. Somewhere along the line, it had to be camp of 1991, there had been a case where people had found chunks of blue ice in their backyard, because a plane—Lord knows how—had dropped frozen toilet water out of the plane and it had somehow landed in peoples' backyards. Blue ice.

"We were talking to him; Joe Patten, my co-worker, and assistant trainer were standing next to Ron, who was in those classic tight, white shorts he would wear. We were asking him questions: 'What do you think about this? What do you think about that?' We looked over at (three players) and we said: 'What do you think about that group?' Without him cracking a smile or turning his face, he said: 'If a chunk of blue ice fell out of the sky and hit the three of them, we wouldn't miss a beat.'"

The staff Wolf worked with developed a catalogue of "Ron-isms"—standard, humorous responses Wolf had to specific situations.

Reggie McKenzie recalls with a laugh the objections to a too short cornerback. "One time somebody had said something about a cornerback: 'He'd be good for us, he can play, he's this, that, and the other.' Ron looked under the table. He said: 'Look at that, they played a whole game right up under the table.' He was making the point that 'I'm not bringing any little midget, short corners in here.' He said: 'He can play right under this table and he won't even hit his head.' A backhand slap. 'Y'all know I'm not bringing a little corner in here.' He wasn't trying to be mean or anything, but he had his way of letting you know what he thought would work.

"I still repeated some of this to my draft room, to all my scouts. I'm sure they're going to pass down some Ron-isms."

"We always had a thing with running backs," said John Schneider. "I played running back so height didn't matter to me. But Ron was always a height-weight-speed guy. I remember I wanted to sign Erric Pegram from Atlanta, and Eric Metcalf from Atlanta, and he was like: 'Ah, those guys could run right under the table.'"

In his retirement, Wolf sometimes has made self-deprecatory remarks that were a form of humor, even if they were taken seriously by others. This makes Wolf smile. One of these remarks came during the later years of Favre's stay in Green Bay, when the question of his retirement became an issue that drove a wedge between the otherwise beloved quarterback and team management.

"I made a statement once when they were having a problem with Brett Favre after I had left," Wolf said. "I said: 'I wish I had done a better job of getting him receivers when I was up there.'

"He had receivers up the ass. (Mark) Chmura, and (Keith) Jackson, and (Sterling) Sharpe, (Robert) Brooks, (Antonio) Freeman. Just try to go play that team. You got (Don) Beebe coming in as your third receiver, Jackson and Chmura; who you gonna cover? Then you got (Dorsey) Levens coming out of the backfield. You got (Edgar) Bennett coming out of the backfield. That's a great group of receivers.

"But those young guys up there they just write that (the GM had not given Favre enough receivers)," Wolf said with a smile. "Okay, that's good."

Like the rest of us, Ron Wolf has some shortcomings. Wolf hired Pepper Burruss as head athletic trainer because he was looking for someone who could operate a state-of-the-art training facility. But, as Burruss, himself, will say: "It goes one step even beyond that.

"One day with the Jets, he walks back into the training room and I believe the segue was: 'I hear you know about swimming pools.' I said I knew about swimming pools and for a lot of years. He said: 'Good I have a swimming pool at the house and I have no idea how to run it.' I said: 'Okay, we'll take a look at it.' I said he should probably call a pool company, but I could do it."

Although Wolf wasn't handy around the house, "Then it transitioned into: 'I've got this switch that isn't working in the front of the house, I've got this cable TV that isn't working right, I've got these outlets in the dining room that only have two prongs and I want that third prong.' I said to him: 'I have tools and will travel, sir,' and fixed all of those things because as I've probably said 50 times: 'Ron Wolf doesn't know the difference between a Phillips Head screwdriver and a crescent wrench.' When I was coming out to Green Bay, I asked him if Edie wanted me to bring crescent wrenches and screwdrivers and he said: 'Absolutely.'"

Wolf wasn't fixing anything around the house, but there were important roles as he was a solid husband for Edie and father for their two sons, Jonathan and Eliot. Jonathan was adopted as an infant, but just two months later, Edie became pregnant. Their son Eliot was born when Jonathan was just 11 months old.

Ron Wolf was gone a lot, but this did not particularly bother Edie, even though she had the two boys to care for and her own profession as a clinical psychologist to manage.

"I don't think I necessarily understood the extent to which (Ron being absent) would happen," Edie Wolf says. "Although when I met Ron, he was in football and he traveled a lot, so I knew he would be gone.

"That's something people ask me: 'Wasn't it hard having him gone all the time?' That was an expectation I had since day one. Even when he was with Tampa he was traveling a lot. I'm an independent person and kind of like to be independent, so having him gone wasn't necessarily a problem," she added with a chuckle. "I missed him, but being able to run the house the way I wanted to run it, being able to run the family the way I wanted to run it, was okay with me. I mean, that fit. Maybe I didn't understand how much I would have to do that, but it was fine with me. I never saw that as a problem."

Jonathan is a professional pilot, currently based in Florida. Eliot, following directly in his father's footsteps, was the director of football operations for the Green Bay Packers. After Ted Thompson was removed as GM and made a consultant, Eliot interviewed for the general manager's job, but did not get the post. Subsequently, he took the position of assistant general manager of the Cleveland Browns, where he works for John Dorsey. The two sons, by their parents' estimations, were and are remarkably different.

"They're extraordinarily different from each other, which reinforces my belief, which I have not always held, but which I learned to hold, after they were born, that you are born with your personality and it doesn't have a whole lot to do with how you're raised," Edie Wolf said with a smile.

One thing that Jonathan and Eliot shared was admiration for their parents. The fact that their father was frequently on the road did not diminish their regard for him.

"He was someone I looked up to tremendously," Jonathan Wolf said. "I think every child, especially young boys, admire their father. But I always knew that there was something special about him and I was very eager to try to please him and to make him proud of me. That was, I think, partially maybe because he was on the road so much and when he did come home, I just wanted to be able to say: 'Hey, I did something really positive' to him. He was always incredibly supportive of both my brother and me, despite his professional obligations. To the extent possible, he made an effort to be active in our lives. You know, in the free moments he had, I don't think that was lost on either Eliot or me.

"I really looked up to him. He was this person, it's hard to describe, but I always had a sense of how intelligent he was, how wise he was, for some reason his approval seemed important. I think it was because as a child I just remember being in awe of how smart and clever my dad was. Just the things that he could recall at the snap of a finger. I always thought: 'He's so smart, he's so organized.' There was a certain master of his universe (quality), the kind of person, obviously you want to emulate as many of his qualities as you can.

"There's a little bit of nature vs. nurture between my brother and me. We're very different creatures. Growing up we had the same experiences, and I think we both took what we needed from our childhood and used it in the ways we needed to use it. We grew up to be very different people, but I think our childhoods were very similar.

"More than anything throughout my childhood, I remember my dad really making an effort to include me in everything that he included Eliot in, to the extent that I wanted to participate in it. Eliot was always into football. He was hanging around the office or in the draft room. He got that bug, that DNA, whatever it is. But I remember that the significant moments that we had, Packers in the Super Bowl in New Orleans, when the win was imminent, when my dad was going down on the field, he took my brother and myself with him. For him, it was never 'I'll ask Jon and see if he wants to go.' He made it very clear that both of his sons were going to be with him, not just the one that was into football. So that meant a lot to me. He always wanted to make sure that I was included in there with him and Eliot. That led to a lot of really cool experiences that I had as a kid."

The sons came to understand their father's place in the world, not only that he was a great big deal in Green Bay, but the standing he had with people who knew him. Wolf's public image didn't include this facet, but the vast majority of people who worked with him and for him, simply liked him. He was not only well-regarded. He was well-liked.

"I wondered about that, especially as I grew into a man, I wondered about some of the qualities my father possessed, because I realized that one of the reasons he is so well-liked is that he keeps his word about everything," Jonathan Wolf said.

"If he says he is going to do something, that's it. He is always the first person to send you a thank-you note, or let you know how much he appreciated what you did. And he's like that with everybody he knows. He makes an effort to remember peoples' names, to be kind and respectful, forthright with everybody he knows. He has that sort of consistency. I think the word for it is integrity. That sort of unwavering integrity really leaves an impression on people. The people that he's had interactions with over the course of his career, I think that's why they respect him and like him. I've never seen him doing anything other than that with people."

Eliot Wolf spent more time with his father, because he immersed himself in professional football from an early age. Eliot hung out at Lambeau Field whenever possible. And this was not done at his father's direction.

"I think the earliest documented thing was that for our fifth-grade graduation, we had to write what we wanted to be," Eliot Wolf said. "I wanted to be an NFL scout. It was cool, because my dad never pushed me in any definite direction, really never gave me a lot of pointers and still doesn't. He wants me to be my own man so much, that he almost takes it past the point of the fine line, you know?" he added with a smile. "Even when I had those interviews (for general manager jobs), I couldn't get two words out of him.

"But it was always something where I would go into the office with him. It was kind of an escape for me to get away from my academics and go into this other world, where, sure, it's their world, but it's a lot of fun, watching players. As I got older and got my driver's license, I would go there more often, after school, and sit in draft meetings, really just soak it all in."

Eliot loved being in the draft room and still does. He started attending the draft at age 11 in 1993. "My dad wanted me to be in the room after their first pick and they were 15 (linebacker Wayne Simmons from Clemson)," Eliot Wolf recalls. "My mom drove me in. It was cool because right when I got there they traded back into the first round and there was a lot of excitement about that and they ended up taking (safety) George Teague (at Number 29). But ever since then, I love it.

"I think, really, it's the anticipation and looking at it as it comes closer to your pick, the expectation builds up, the phone starts heating up, there's intensity in the room. And then drafting guys that your scouts really like and think that they can really contribute to the team.

"I've been lucky and I'm fully aware."

At home, at Lambeau Field, in the film room, on the road, people who know Ron Wolf well will consistently describe him as a man of few words. Perhaps the most cogent description of Ron Wolf's approach to the spoken word, was made by Jonathan Wolf.

"I would describe my father as a man of few words, but the words he says are significant and he thinks about what he says," Jonathan said. "He chooses his words carefully. And I think that leads to people who spend a lot of time around him, the things that he says carry more weight and are more significant when they are said."

Apart from the Packers' general manager being an extraordinarily high-profile position in Green Bay, the Wolfs do not lead a particularly public life. The fact that Ron converted to Judaism is not widely known, and even among some associates of Wolf is not known at all.

On the topic of his religious beliefs, Wolf says: "I was raised in New Freedom as a shouting Methodist. You know what a shouting Methodist is? 'Amen, preacher!'

"I converted because of Edie. The children were brought up Jewish."

Jonathan and Eliot attended a Catholic high school, Green Bay Notre Dame. Edie Wolf uses an example from that experience to illustrate a difference between her two sons.

"At Notre Dame, once a month, they have an all-school mass that everybody was required to attend and I said to the boys: 'When everyone gets up to take communion, what do you do?' This will illustrate the personality differences.

"My son Jonathan said: 'When everyone in a row gets up to take communion, I go with them.' I'm horrified, you understand. I said: 'What do you do?' He said: 'I take communion. I take the wafer.' I said: 'You're not supposed to do that. That's sacred. You're not supposed to do that, especially if you haven't gone to confession. I know you don't take confession.' He said: 'Everyone at the school knows I'm Jewish. The faculty says I'm Jewish. No one says anything to me. I do it. It's easier.'

"Eliot's response was: 'I stand up. I let everyone climb over me. And then I stay in my seat.' Personality difference. Eliot doesn't mind being who he is. Jonathan wants to blend in with the group. But I don't think it was hard for them being a minority religion in Green Bay."

Edie Wolf, who would know this better than anyone, says that success did not change her husband, that he retained a certain level of humility.

"The level of success he had here was sort of unbelievable to him," she said. "I've heard him have this conversation with Mike Holmgren and some of the others. It was like: 'Can you believe this?' Granted, they all worked really hard, but I think he always felt there was an element of luck to it. 'Gosh, we managed to get these players and everything jelled.' I think he always was, and still probably is, a little awed by how well everything went.

"Humility is one of his characteristics. And he is more ready to give credit to other people than maybe he should be. I think (focusing on mistakes) is part of his personality. Focusing on mistakes and, how can I learn from them, how can I make sure that I don't do something like that again. And I think that is something that is one of his good qualities. He will look at his mistakes and what didn't go well and try to make things better."

This is not a conventional football marriage. Edie was not particularly excited about football until arriving in Green Bay, where, as she points out, everyone else was excited about football. But with Ron running the Packers and the Packers winning, her extended family became excited about football. Still, theirs is not a marriage in which football is a dominant topic of conversation.

"Ron will confirm this," Edie said. "He thinks of me as a dumb fan. And the things that I ask are so far beneath him that he can't believe it. So, we hardly ever talk about it. We never talk about strategy. Never. Never. And he does not like to watch the Packers games with me. He would watch with Bob Harlan and whoever, definitely not me. We're just on such different planes. I don't really know anything. I know what I read in the newspapers, basically. However, I will say that he is more patient with other people who ask him questions than he is with me," she added with a laugh.

"And he will say that one of the things that he likes about our marriage is that he doesn't have to talk about football with me."

So in totality, it can safely be said that Ron Wolf's life, professional and personal, has been more notable for actions than words. Talking about trading a Number 1 draft choice for Brett Favre is a conversation many general managers could have had, but only one man made that deal. Turning over the team he was building to a coach with no previous professional head coaching experience was a concept other teams were contemplating, but it was Wolf who made the precisely correct choice with Mike Holmgren. Spending an unprecedented amount of money on Reggie White was not even a conversation for most teams, but Ron Wolf was the driving force behind White becoming a Packer.

Beyond that, Ron Wolf is the type of individual who is able to bring out the best in those around him—personally, professionally, consistently. In the end, all these qualities made him the man who saved the Green Bay franchise.

10

The Winning Combination Splits

BY MOST REASONABLE, objective measurements, the 1997 Green Bay Packers were every bit as good as the 1996 Green Bay Packers.

The Packers were once again 13–3 in the regular season. They reached some goals that even their Super Bowl champion predecessors could not attain.

They defeated the Dallas Cowboys, who had beaten the Packers seven times over the past four seasons, knocking the Packers out of the playoffs three times. All those defeats had occurred in Texas, whereas the 45–17 victory over the Cowboys on November 23, 1997, happened in Lambeau Field. The Cowboys were no longer among the elite teams in the NFC, but still, this was progress.

And the Packers managed to win one in the Hubert H. Humphrey Metrodome, beating the Vikings, 27–11, at Minnesota on December 1. As good as the Packers had become in the Wolf/Holmgren era, before this game they were 0–5 in Minnesota. So, again, tangible progress.

There was an inexplicable loss to Indianapolis on November 16, 41–38. The Colts came to this game 0–10, while the Packers were 8–2. But the Packers lost three turnovers and gave up 467 yards. The

Indianapolis defense scored twice; on a fumble return and an interception return. Brett Favre passed for 367 yards, but Paul Justin, whose name is otherwise not mentioned in the same hemisphere as Favre, completed 24 of 30 passes for 340 yards, one touchdown, no interceptions, and a passer rating of 125.0. The previously winless Colts had the football for 36 minutes, 54 seconds. There was a measure of revenge here for Colts head coach Lindy Infante, who had been dismissed by Wolf and replaced by Holmgren. But Infante was once again jettisoned when the Colts finished the 1997 campaign 3–13.

The Packers, on the other hand, could look at this game as merely an unhappy aberration. They closed the regular season with five straight victories, including the landmark wins over Dallas and at Minnesota, winning those five games by an average of more than 17 points.

And when the postseason arrived, the Packers once again appeared to be the class of the NFL. They beat Tampa Bay, 21–7, in the Divisional Playoff. Dorsey Levens rushed for 112 yards, a Packers playoff record, including 88 yards in the second half. The Packers blocked one Tampa Bay field goal attempt, and stuffed a fake field goal attempt for no gain.

The Packers encored with a 23–10 victory over the 49ers in San Francisco in the NFC championship game. Levens established another record with 114 yards rushing, and placekicker Ryan Longwell, who had been cut by the 49ers before the start of training camp, kicked three field goals on an afternoon filled with rain. Steve Young was sacked four times and intercepted once. The 49ers could only manage 33 rushing yards in 18 attempts. They did not cross the goal line until Chuck Levy's 95-yard touchdown return with less than three minutes left in the game.

This was the third straight year in which the Packers had eliminated the 49ers from the playoffs. Clearly, Green Bay's status as the best of the best had been reaffirmed by another march through the NFC portion of the postseason.

So, it was no particular shock that the Packers came to Super Bowl XXXII against the Denver Broncos in San Diego's Qualcomm Stadium as 11.5-point favorites. They were the defending champions. They were on a seven-game winning streak. The NFC was on a 13-game Super Bowl winning streak.

Denver's John Elway had a brilliant career, but he was 37 and his Super Bowl record was 0–3. The Broncos had qualified for the playoffs not as a Division-winner, but as a wild-card team.

What emerged was a thrilling contest, but not one that the Packers expected. Denver won, 31–24, driving for a touchdown with one minute, 45 seconds left in the game. The Packers moved the ball, but could not answer, with their own drive ending at the Denver 31.

On offense, the Packers had persistent difficulty handling the Broncos' blitz packages. Dorsey Levens had 90 yards on 19 rushing attempts, but had only one carry in the last 23 minutes of the game. On defense, the Packers' usually formidable defensive line was beset by injuries and fatigue and gave up 157 yards and three touchdowns to running back Terrell Davis.

It was a stunning defeat. After the game in the Green Bay locker room, a bitterly disappointed Wolf produced an unforgettable summation of his team's status: "We're a one-year wonder, just a fart in the wind."

Six months later, Wolf's reaction had not noticeably softened. "They out-executed us," he said. "I never thought that would be possible. But let me say this. We were defeated. There wasn't anything flukish about it."[1]

As it turned out, losing to Denver in the Super Bowl was not an indictment of the Green Bay franchise. The Broncos won Super Bowl XXXIII even more handily, 34–15 over the Atlanta Falcons. Still, the loss rankled. More than two decades later, it still does.

"Oh, I was disappointed," Wolf says now. "I was partly pissed at myself. I let people talk me out of Sean Jones (defensive end who retired after the 1996 season). If Sean Jones had been there, those defensive linemen who were over there on the sidelines, they would have been playing. I didn't know anything about Denver. I was running around the country assisting in writing this book, *The Packer Way*, and I was really pissed at myself after that."

The feeling of disappointment was felt, is still felt, throughout the

---

1 *The Ultimate Super Bowl Book*, by Bob McGinn, (MVP Books, 2009), page 247.

Packers organization. Bob Harlan, then Packers president and CEO, recalls:

"People still say: 'What's the worst defeat?' That one, Super Bowl XXXII. We should have won that game. You don't get there that often. When you get there you better win it, because you don't know when you're going to get back," Harlan added with a rueful smile.

"I think Ron would say that team in 1997 was good enough, it could have won another Super Bowl, maybe two more. You look at that defensive line back then, and you think: 'My God, how would you like to have that foursome today?'

"We should have beaten Denver. I mean, hats off to Denver. I remember we flew out on a Sunday before Super Bowl XXXII. Ron and I had breakfast together and I said: 'What do you think of Denver?' He said: 'They're just like New England. We can beat them.' So that gave me a lot of confidence. All the odds were in our favor. I think we were the better team, but when it was one-and-out we didn't do it. There are no excuses. We didn't do it."

"We had a great year," Mike Holmgren said. "In fact, I thought our team in '97 was not as good, but there were areas I thought we even improved a little bit there. I remember after the '96 season, I got (the players) together and I said: 'A lot of times, teams that win the Super Bowl, a lot of times they'll fall off the cliff the next year, because, in the offseason, everyone's telling them how good they are they're writing books, they kind of forget what got them there.' I said: 'Don't do that. In fact, all the stuff they're having me do, I'm going to cancel, my radio and TV show.' I said: 'Just so you are aware, I want you to think about that.'

"They came back, and we had a good year. Then we played Denver, and I've thought about this when we played Denver. I tried everything. I tried to yell at them, I tried to be nice to them, I tried to kick them, I tried everything I could think of, it was hard for me to get the team to believe that Denver was really good, they were really good. We go down to San Diego and we had good practices, but I didn't do anything different. But a couple of my players said: 'Could we back off a little bit?' near the end. I'm going: 'Ahh, this is making me uneasy here, you know?' That was a hard one. I thought we were good enough to win another one."

Andy Reid, who had been tight ends and assistant offensive line coach, took over as quarterback coach in 1997. During the week leading up to Super Bowl XXXII, there were distractions, he recalls, such as reports that Holmgren might be leaving to take over as head coach and general manager in Seattle. Those reports turned out to be premature by one year, but they didn't help. Nor did the departure of Sean Jones.

"We were better in cold weather than we were in warm weather," Reid said. "When that thing got above 70 degrees, I thought: *What kind of shape are going to be in*? And that ended up being a little bit of a factor. Sean Jones left after the first Super Bowl. He was a big part of the leadership on that football team. His play probably declined a little bit, but he just had such great presence, leadership, a real smart guy. Those were my honest feelings going in.

"Maybe we didn't take it as serious. We were 13-point favorites going into that game. And we had heard that all week. Then the thing came in that coach (Holmgren) might possibly be leaving. That kind of came in the picture and so there were distractions, between the 13-point thing and Coach maybe leaving. He didn't say that. It was the media that said it. It was one of those deals. We started off like gangbusters, with a touchdown and then it kind of got us. The blitz game got us. The blitz game, which is probably the easiest thing to pick up now, was a tough one back then. They got us."

There was considerable second-guessing of every aspect of the organization after the Super Bowl loss, but the fact remained that the team Ron Wolf put together had completed a remarkable six-year run, culminating in two Super Bowl appearances and one Super Bowl championship.

"We were 13–3, back-to-back, we were favored (in the Super Bowl) by 14 points again," safety LeRoy Butler said. "We hurt ourselves in that game. It was on the players. That doesn't change the fact that we had a hell of a ride for those two years.

"We knew that success was going to break us up. Holmgren wanted to be a coach and a GM and there were teams ready to give it to him. If we'd have won that second Super Bowl, we'd have won it again. Everybody would have just said: I'm just going to stay here.'"

The 1998 Packers did not fall off the face of the planet. They were

11–5. But they were displaced at the top of the NFC Central Division, by the Minnesota Vikings and the phenomenal wide receiver Randy Moss. The Packers lost twice to the Vikings, who went 15–1, but then were beaten in the NFC Championship Game by the Falcons, who were, in turn, beaten by the Broncos in Super Bowl XXXIII.

Still, Favre led the league in passing yards (4,212, his second consecutive 4,000-yard season), passing attempts, completions, and completion percentage. Reggie White led the NFC with 16 sacks and won the Defensive Player of the Year Award. This was not a team in dramatic decline.

In the Wild Card Playoff Game against the 49ers in San Francisco, Favre led a late drive that gave the Packers a 27–23 lead with one minute, 55 seconds remaining in the game. On the ensuing 49ers drive, the great Jerry Rice caught his first pass of the game and then fumbled. He was ruled down by contact, even though replay seemed to show that his knee had not been down when the fumble occurred. Instant replay challenges were instituted the next year, perhaps in reaction to this call, but that was no help to the Packers in this moment. On what turned out to be the game-winning touchdown, Steve Young stumbled as he dropped back to pass, then found Terrell Owens in the end zone. Owens had earlier dropped four passes and lost a fumble, but he caught this pass, and the Packers' bid to eliminate the Niners from the playoffs for four straight years was over.

Even at this distance, Wolf is still upset with this entire sequence. It meant the end of the hope for a third straight Super Bowl appearance.

"And you know what, there's an official's missed call, against San Francisco that led to instant replay, or we had a chance to go again," Wolf said. "We would have been okay if we had got through there. And Terrell Owens finally caught a pass. That's the only time those fuckers ever beat us. Talking about those hotshot 49ers this and the great 49ers that, that's the only time they ever beat us in a game and we lost because a rookie official blew a call.

"This stuff stays with you. I get up every day and walk four miles and sometimes I walk without something in my ear, and think about things. I still think about that. Some of the things I did that I shouldn't have done. I think about that."

The loss to the 49ers turned out to be an end to a specific Green Bay era. Holmgren's departure, which had been rumored for a year, eventually did occur. He had stated that he would remain with the Packers as head coach, unless another team made him both head coach and head of football operations. The Seattle Seahawks came through with the complete package, making him executive vice-president, general manager, and head coach.

Holmgren did take a Seattle team to the Super Bowl, going 13–3 in 2005, losing to the Pittsburgh Steelers in the Super Bowl, but he had been relieved of the general manager duties after the 2002 season. His coaching credentials were not at all diminished. He became just the sixth man to coach more than one franchise in the Super Bowl. Still, he second-guesses his decision to leave Green Bay, where Brett Favre made plays and Ron Wolf found talent.

"The only thing I can say, is that every once in a while, it comes up when I'm with Brett or with Ron, we see each other once a year, and I think about had I stayed," Holmgren said. "People would question: 'Why in the world would you leave Favre? Why would you do that? You had it all.' And I've told you, it was good. But Ron was always real encouraging to me, to continue to grow. And the idea of taking what I had learned from him and being able to do it myself, there was an appeal there. So, but Brett says: 'If we had stuck together, we could have won a couple more.' I go: 'Well, maybe,'" Holmgren said with a smile.

Of Holmgren's departure, Wolf says: "It's wasn't a surprise. It was a disappointment. A lot of his contemporaries were getting those jobs and I'm sure he felt that he was more qualified than some of those guys that were getting those jobs (head coach/general manager). So, I knew it was coming and we tried our darnedest to keep him, but couldn't match what Seattle gave him."

The irony is that had Holmgren remained in Green Bay for another two years, he could have become the general manager upon Wolf's retirement. But nobody could have known that.

"If he had stayed around Green Bay he could have been the GM, but he didn't know that," Wolf said. "Even I didn't know that. I was still full of piss and vinegar."

"You know what?" Holmgren said. "I remember (longtime NFL

head coach) Chuck Knox telling me: 'Eight years is about enough, and then you want to go somewhere else. The players have all heard the stories. The press has all heard the stories.' That was his philosophy. And he did that. I didn't necessarily believe that, but I do now believe that there is a shelf life. I had so much fun coaching, I don't want to be angry all the time. And now, with some of the stuff coaches have to deal with all the time, bless their hearts, it's just different."

But there was a sense among those who knew best, that, after Holmgren's departure, the Packers, for better or worse, certainly could not remain the same.

"I'll be honest," Brett Favre said, "When Mike stood before the team, and he got choked up as he told the team that he was leaving for Seattle, I may have been the only player who was crying along with him. I've got no problem admitting that. At that point, we were past that point, it's like when your kids are in the 'terrible twos' and you can't wait for them to get past the 'terrible twos' and you can actually enjoy them. We were past the terrible twos. And I really thought, you know, we had lost a Super Bowl, but we still were good. And I knew that he would be basically, he's not replaceable. That connection that we had that we had formed through a lot of blood, sweat, and tears, was gone. He was leaving. I didn't mind how tough he was on me because I demanded that of myself and I understood then why. I just knew it wouldn't be the same and it never was."

And it wasn't just Holmgren who departed. Some of Wolf's most trusted lieutenants went along to Seattle. Wolf didn't want to see any of them leave, but he also refused to stand in the way of the advancement of their careers.

"Every time somebody would leave, he would say, 'That's my best man,'" Bob Harlan recalled. "Well, why do you let him go then? He says: 'You've got to give people a chance. There's only 32 of these jobs.' I admire that about him. The first guy Holmgren wanted when he went to Seattle was Ted Thompson. Ron said: 'That's my best guy.' But he said: 'Give him a chance, give him a chance.' And that's a great quality for a person to have. He could say selfishly: 'No I'm keeping him,' but he never did that."

"Your feelings get a little hurt, everybody wants to go to Seattle," Wolf said. "So, go. Ted Thompson went there with him. Scot McCloughan went with him. John Dorsey went originally, but he didn't like it and came back."

Thompson, as the Vice President of Football Operations with the Seahawks, headed their scouting department, ran their draft operation, and thus played a major role in putting together Seattle's 13–3 Super Bowl season of 2005. Asked about Wolf's reaction to his departure, Thompson responded:

"Some of the things that were personal, I'm not going to get into, the things that were his and my business, some things are not. But he was encouraging, as best I recall. He came down and kind of matter-of-factly said the Seahawks had called, they were interested in talking to me, there had been a change in their organization. And it was kind of quirky, but he was sort of getting up to leave and he said: 'You probably ought to take that,' or 'you might want to consider that,' something like that. It was a very short conversation but there was no meanness on his part. Because sometimes you can kind of paint people into a corner, but he didn't try to do that."

Part of running a successful organization is losing key people to advancement in other organizations. But that, as Thompson suggests, is easier said than done.

"It's easy to say that, and talk about it in theory, but when all your people are walking out the door, it's a different thing," Thompson said. "He was very strong in that regard. He'd stick his chin out and say: 'Okay, whatever you're going to do, do, and we'll move on.' That's my perception of his attitude. He never told me that, but I think he was the kind of a guy, who would say: 'I'll do this a different way now.'"

Mike Reinfeldt, Packers chief financial officer and vice president of administration, was another important member of the Green Bay management team, who went to Seattle as vice president of Football Administration. He had a wide range of responsibilities with the Seahawks, including being in charge of contract negotiations and salary cap management. This was another man Wolf would have liked to retain.

"He very much wanted me to stay," Reinfeldt said. "He liked where we were. Ron and I had a very good interaction together. I think we had the ability to, not totally agree on something, but sit and talk for a long period of time and come to a conclusion that was probably the right decision. And it could be related to salary caps, what we paid players, all that sort of thing. Our relationship was very good and helped us overcome a lot of tough things. He wanted me to stay, I just don't think he was in a position to make that happen at that time. I think it was frustrating for him.

"Honestly, I think he was very angry with me. When we came back the next year, I think we beat the Packers, and he was still angry. But that's a normal reaction."

Holmgren's departure set up one of Wolf's rare mistakes. He hired Ray Rhodes as head coach. Rhodes did retain a reputation for being able to motivate his players and his record as a defensive coordinator, with San Francisco and Green Bay, was admirable. His record as a head coach had been distinctly mixed.

Rhodes, after being defensive coordinator for the Packers, had been the head coach of the Philadelphia Eagles for four seasons. In 1995, Rhodes's first season with the Eagles, the team went 10–6, qualified for the playoffs and advanced to the Division Playoff Game before being eliminated by the Dallas Cowboys. Rhodes was named NFL Coach of the Year.

The Eagles finished 10–6 again in 1996, but were eliminated by the 49ers in the first round of the playoffs. They slipped to 6–9–1 in 1997, and slipped much further in 1998, going 3–13 to set a franchise record for losses. Rhodes was fired at the end of that season.

Wolf said that he thought Rhodes was genuinely tough and he knew from Rhodes's earlier work as defensive coordinator of the Packers that he could be an exceptional motivator. Wolf was also fixed on the notion that the next coach should have NFL head coaching experience. This was a change of direction for a man who had just enjoyed seven seasons of success with Mike Holmgren, a man who had no previous NFL head coaching experience. Why make that previous experience a prerequisite for the job now?

"That's really an interesting question," Wolf says. "I'm wondering how I came to that myself. I've had ample opportunity to think about that and explore that, and I honestly don't know. Because Holmgren was leaving, I think I was looking for somebody to just come in and run it. For some reason, I put that parameter on there, that he had to have that head coaching experience. And for the life of me, I don't know why I did that. I've examined that time after time, myself and whenever I speak to anybody about hiring people, I tell them, interview everybody you possibly can. And you'll find your guy—which I did the second time, with (Mike) Sherman. Just having the opportunity to interview so many guys, you can find out who can and who can't in your own mind."

The Packers went 8–8 under Rhodes in 1999. There was at least one extenuating circumstance—Favre played through an injury to the thumb on his throwing hand. The Packers never had a losing record between 1992 and 2004. This was the only season that was not a winning season. And for the first time since 1992, they did not qualify for the playoffs. With a playoff berth in the balance, they lost three straight December games, including a defeat at home against Carolina.

Wolf fired Rhodes after the 1999 season. Rhodes became just the second Packers coach to be fired after one year. The other one was Ray (Scooter) McLean, but he had gone 1–10–1 in 1958.

"It was not an easy decision," Wolf said. "I just had to make that change. The team was too good to be floundering around like that."

When Rhodes was hired as head coach, the Packers planned to promote Andy Reid from quarterback coach to offensive coordinator. But Reid left when the Eagles offered him a head coaching job. In the end, Wolf says that not keeping Reid in Green Bay was one of the biggest mistakes he made.

Andy Reid left the Packers to become head coach of the Eagles in 1999, and he went on to have a highly successful head coaching career with Philadelphia and Kansas City. Reid took the 2004 Eagles to the Super Bowl. His 2018 Chiefs team went 12–4, regularly torched defenses with young Patrick Mahomes at quarterback, and advanced to the AFC Championship Game before losing to New England. In 20 years as an NFL head coach, Reid has a regular season record of 195–124–1.

"Part of the thing people don't know, we were in the process of paying him an awful lot of money, at that time, to be offensive coordinator," Wolf said. "I was really comfortable with that, having Rhodes as a head coach, and Andy Reid as an offensive coordinator. It never came to that, because Philadelphia came in and that was that. But Andy Reid is sitting right there, if I had hired him, I'd have been a genius."

"That's kind of him," Reid says. "Listen, I loved it there. I would have loved working for him, too, as a head coach. I know that. But listen, life's crazy and football's just a microcosm of that deal, right?"

In the search for the next head coach, Wolf didn't set any arbitrary boundaries regarding previous experience. Mike Sherman aced his interview and placed himself above the rest of the field.

"He was so prepared," Wolf said. "His interview was incredible. He dotted every 'i' and crossed every 't.' He knew exactly what he wanted to do, what he was going to do. He had it all down."

Sherman, who had been an assistant coach for the Packers for two seasons, and then Seattle's offensive coordinator in 1999, took over as head coach and stabilized the situation. Sherman's teams had winning records for five straight seasons, and for four straight years, beginning in 2001, qualified for the playoffs. For those four years the Packers were 44–20 in the regular season, with rosters, of course, that featured talent that Wolf had acquired.

The next major personnel decision Wolf made was a personal decision. His retirement prior to the 2001 season, came as a shock to many. He had years left on his contract and he was merely 62; to all indications, as vital as ever.

"I had told Bob Harlan (that 2000) was going to be my last year," Wolf said. "I said: 'I'm done. I can't do this anymore.' There were several reasons. One was that it was not enjoyable anymore. The amount of time one has to put into this business, you better get some enjoyment out of it. There had been a reason other than the paycheck."

"In July of that last year, 2000, he said: 'You know, this might be my last year,'" Harlan said. "And I said: 'Why?' and he said: 'I might be hitting a wall. I miss the old-time football when if I needed a tackle I went and got one. Now I've got to go to the cap guy and see how much money we've got. I miss the old-time football.' I wanted to have him stay until the new stadium opened in 2003. He said: 'Let's keep it between you and me,' so I thought there was hope.

"But then he comes back after the season and when he comes in my door I knew what he was going to tell me. 'I'm ready to go.' I was surprised because we were doing well, and the future looked bright. But once his mind was made up . . . The only thing he ever told me was 'I miss the old football.'"

Wolf left money on the table with that decision. Another man, a lesser man, would have stayed for three more seasons, taken credit for a successful football team, shared the glory in the completely renovated and utterly impressive Lambeau Field, while going through the motions. That was not Ron Wolf.

"He wasn't the kind who was going to give you a half-effort," Harlan said. "He was either going to give us everything he had, or he was going to step aside. I've even asked him: 'Did you ever regret leaving when you did?' And he said: 'No, I did not.' So, his mind was made up and he was convinced.

"I've always thought that one of the things that bothered him was that he missed the 'old NFL.' He said: 'I don't enjoy it any more. I can't even go to practice and enjoy it anymore, because I'm scared to death somebody's not going to get up and I won't have the money to get another one.' It really affected him, it really did.

"When he came in the last time, he stood there, and I almost knew what he was going to tell me.' He just said: 'Bob, I've just hit the wall. I've had it. I'm ready to go.'"

For Wolf, this was not even a decision. He demanded a total commitment from everyone who worked for him, but more than that, he demanded a total commitment from himself.

"I felt that I had an obligation to the Green Bay Packers and I felt that I could no longer conduct business the way it was necessary to be conducted, to keep the Packers where they belonged," he said. "So, I walked away from that, rather than take the money."

And there was the fact that the general manager of 2001 could not do the kind of wheeling and dealing that Wolf had done in the early years of his tenure in Green Bay, reviving a franchise in the process. With the salary cap and restrictions on trade, a GM's working life in the NFL had become more restricted.

"Yeah, you can't trade," Wolf said. "Boy, that kicked me in the fanny. I disliked that. I tried so many times to get new rules put in so that we could at least trade. Say I drafted a guy in the second round and you drafted a guy in the second round. My guy sucks and your guy sucks. Let's trade 'em. That way we'd have no cap issues. 'Well, we'd have to bargain that.' Why wouldn't the Players Association go for that? If you're going to cut the guy, I never understood that. Just to take the trade away, that played a big part in my getting out of there. Suddenly, you were being dealt 53 cards and you had to play all 53 cards. You couldn't do anything.

"You can't trade anymore because of that salary cap deal. You're going into a situation where a third of the roster changes because of the salary cap. So, you're looking at 17, 18 new players every year. Now you've only got seven draft choices. Somewhere else these players have to come. So, you have to use free agency? Well, what if you don't use free agency? Now, you've got to have 11 free agents make your team balance out. To me, that never made any sense because all of those seven players that you draft have to make your team. They have to make your team because of the salary cap. And we all know, when I was there, if you got three out of seven, you were doing a hell of a job. But you can't live doing that today. You've got to have four or five of those seven to be real players, to be successful. And I don't know anybody who can do that."

"And we were going through a transformation as an organization. I knew Bob was eventually going (to be retired)."

So, Wolf walked away with money left on the table. He had built a championship team in Green Bay, he had run an operation that never had a losing season during his tenure as general manager. He was not particularly old. His health was not in decline. He left because to do the job in the all-consuming manner in which he felt it had to be done, there had to be a measure of satisfaction and enjoyment in it. When it stopped being satisfying and enjoyable, when he felt himself slowing down, when he believed that he was losing even a little of his all-encompassing drive to compete, to win, he was honest enough with himself that he simply stopped doing it. Staying on board for the money was never a consideration. This was Ron Wolf acting not like a general manager, but acting like a human being.

On the surface, his retirement ended the Ron Wolf era in Green Bay. But in reality, his influence could still be seen in the success the

Packers had in the first 16 seasons after his departure. More than that, his influence can still be seen throughout the National Football League, in places where Ron Wolf disciples are running football teams and succeeding with lessons learned from him.

That influence will continue for many years to come—in Seattle, in Cleveland, and wherever his son, Eliot, is working. It might even be seen once again in Green Bay where, after a quarter-century run of success, two losing seasons have made the earlier success a memory. But even there, Brian Gutekunst, another Wolf hire as a scout, has taken over as general manager.

11

The Wolf Legacy

"'THE MOTHER SHIP,' that's what I call Green Bay because that's where it started for all of us," John Dorsey says.

"All of us" in this context are the Ron Wolf disciples who have gone on to successful careers running their own NFL operations. In this way, Wolf has helped to transform much more than the Green Bay franchise.

Six men who worked for Wolf with the Packers have gone on to serve as NFL general managers: John Schneider with the Seahawks, Reggie McKenzie with the Raiders, Ted Thompson and now, Brian Gutekunst with the Packers, John Dorsey with the Chiefs and now the Browns, and Scot McCloughan, formerly GM of the 49ers and the Redskins.

And in the category of direct Ron Wolf descendants, there is his son, Eliot Wolf, who spent 14 seasons with the Packers, joining them as a scout in 2004. He is now assistant general manager (under Dorsey) with the Browns. Dorsey also brought Alonzo Highsmith, who had been with the Green Bay organization since 1999, when he was hired by Ron Wolf as a college scout. Highsmith, who rose through the ranks to become senior personnel executive with the Packers, was hired to be vice president of player personnel for the Browns.

Ron Wolf takes great pride in the subsequent success of the men who have worked for him. But he doesn't take credit for their success.

They, on the other hand, give him plenty of credit. It is okay. There is more than enough credit to go around.

"They've done a heck of a job," Wolf said. "It is a (source of real satisfaction) for me, it is. I mean, I was surrounded by really good people. These guys are really good at what they do in their profession. They like the game. They like and respect the game and to me that's so important.

"Reggie McKenzie turned that whole (Raiders) franchise around. Reggie, the job he did just taking that franchise, they hadn't been above .500 since 2002. Finally, after serious (salary) cap malfunctions there, he was able to survive the first two years and then they were 12–4 (in 2016).

"I was fortunate to have guys like that. Reggie was a rare bird. He was a 10th-round pick of the Los Angeles Raiders and comes in as a rookie, starts on a championship team as an inside linebacker, a position he never played. And he was tough, tough, tough. He was fast and tougher than hell.

"To me one of John Dorsey's biggest attributes was he was a player, a college Hall of Fame player. He was relentless in gathering information you needed about players. Plus, he was an accomplished evaluator.

"Ted started in the pro football end of scouting, which I thought was very, very important. We needed to have more people scouting in the pro game because people are going to cut guys and maybe we could find something there. It never really worked the way I wanted it to work. Probably the biggest one that made a contribution was (defensive tackle) Gilbert Brown.

"But Ted became like a steadying factor. He was really good knowing when you make trades people wanted your third and your first was a 28. Well, what's that 28 worth? Is it worth a three and a four? He was really good at that. Plus, he was a really good evaluator. I mean, look at his career. His career, he goes to Seattle, builds a Super Bowl team. He leaves there, comes back to Green Bay builds a Super Bowl team. He can't be much better than that.

"Scot McCloughan is a superb evaluator. Goes to San Francisco (as general manager) those players were his players under (head coach Jim) Harbaugh, who went to a Super Bowl. Same thing—goes to Seattle (as a senior personnel executive) helps to build a Super Bowl team. Obviously, a strong foundation.

"Dorsey was tough. Thompson obviously was tough. He made it as a special teams player. Scot McCloughan was a baseball player. Second pick of the (Toronto) Blue Jays and blew out his knee. John Schneider was the leading rusher, wherever he was." (Schneider was one of the leading rushers in the history of his high school, Abbot Pennings in De Pere, Wisconsin. He also played college football at St. Thomas in Minnesota, before an injury ended his career.)

Dorsey inherited a Kansas City team that was 2–14 in 2012, the season before he took over as general manager. The next four seasons, the Chiefs went 43–21. Dorsey's dismissal after the 2016 season was surprising, to say the least, but new challenges came his way when he was named Cleveland general manager after the 2017 season. The Browns had won one game over the previous two seasons combined, but they went 7–8–1 in 2018.

With the addition of Eliot Wolf and Alonzo Highsmith in positions of influence and importance in the Cleveland organization, Dorsey has demonstrated that this Green Bay as "the mother ship" notion was more than mere rhetoric with him.

Dorsey played for the Packers in some lean years—1984 through 1988—as a linebacker and a fierce competitor on special teams. A knee injury ended his playing career in 1989, and in 1991 he became a college scout for the Packers. He was promoted to director of college scouting in 1997.

In 1999, he made the move to Seattle, where he was director of player personnel on head coach/general manager Mike Holmgren's staff. But Dorsey returned to the Packers in 2000, again as director of college scouting. He served in that position until 2012, when he was named director of football operations. One year later, he was the general manager of the Kansas City Chiefs. All along the way, Dorsey says he has practiced the lessons he learned from Ron Wolf.

"Four GMs came up under Ron and have had big success," Dorsey said. "That's not coincidental. The best way I always say it, is we learned from Ron the key components of team-building. Now we all tweak them to our own strengths and weaknesses. We carve out our own nuances of how to go about the team-building exercise, but we all do it in a way of the model that we've been taught. At the end of the day, I still think that model will teach you how to be successful.

"If you keep to the core principles of the system, I think it's pretty good. There have been nine things that Ron's said that have always stuck with us: Identify what needs to be fixed. Hire the best. Develop a perception of winning. You have a certain devotion, dedication, work ethic, and results. And you make it work and you keep it going, be able to handle the unexpected, and stay on top. That's it in a nutshell. There are no quick fixes to this thing.

"I knew of one model. I know of many people within the industry that want to know the model. But we don't want to get it spread too far within the industry, selfishly."

There is a wide variety of Wolf's attributes that Dorsey found not only admirable but useful, all the way from a tireless work ethic to a sincere humility.

"Hard work, there is no other way: That's what I tell these guys on the personnel side, because I, too, try to take some of the principles that Ron instilled in me and I try to teach people how to do it the right way," Dorsey said. "There is no shortcut to doing it the proper way. And that holds true with the whole process that takes place today, as it took place when Ron first got to Green Bay. Now, technology has helped, but it's the same process.

"And Ron taught us to stay humble. Definitely stay humble. Be honest, be honest with yourself, be honest with the organization. Be honored to be a part of it. Be humble. Respect the history of the game. Honor that history.

"But at the end of the day, as Ron will tell you, you better pick the right player, too," Dorsey said with a chuckle. "Maybe that's just assumed because I've been in it so long, you have to see those traits that make great football players. That's part of the teaching mechanism that Ron has taught the group, I think; how to see those traits through the lenses of one of the greatest of all times. I think each and every one of us saw these traits for specific positions."

And Wolf clearly picked the right players, not only in the draft, but in one terrific trade and the onset of free agency.

"I think there were two critical moves early on that he did," Dorsey said. "Switching the draft pick out for Brett Favre, and acquiring the talents of Reggie White. That begins to set the mindset of everybody within the community and the organization that, you know what, we're going to do this thing the right way.

"Ron's got a strong enough belief and conviction in himself as a man that you've got to understand and he knows he's going to do it the right way. He knew deep down, intuitively, that this was the right thing for this organization. With his profound respect for the history of the game, I'm sure he's seen model-building in terms of establishing franchises, what you've got to do. Those where probably principles that he learned as he grew in the industry, probably from Al (Davis) and others around him with that Raiders thing."

Working for Ron Wolf's Packers created a bond, a kind of community, Dorsey indicated.

"We lived in the present moment. And we wanted to keep that thing going. All of us, we were all in this thing together, and we didn't know, we just wanted to keep this thing going. We'd come into work as early as we can, we'd stay as late as we could, and we loved the process, we loved being around each other. We loved the game of football. We loved to walk in every day and get schooled by Ron, who taught us the respect and love of the game. So, it was one of those environments where it was a lot of hard work, but you know what? It was a lot of fun, too. To me, that's the way it should be."

Coming up under Wolf's tutelage was a very good break for the 21st-century GMs in Wolf's general manager orchard. They know it. They stay in touch.

"It's one of those blessings that you look back on," Dorsey said. "All of us say that. All of us owe a great deal of our success to that man. I'll be the first to tell you that, you know what, as you go through life, it's those people you meet that mean everything. It's that theory that besides your parents, you meet five people who have an impact on your life, and he's definitely one of the most influential men in my life. In my case, I've met four of those people, three of those people happened to be in Green Bay, and Ron's one of them.

"It's a friendship now. I still consider Ron a very close friend and a mentor. I still seek his wisdom today. I'll always be close to him. I'll always bounce things off of him."

Wolf wishes all of his guys well, but he has an understandable fondness for the success that Ted Thompson had as Green Bay's general manager. Thompson, who had a 10-year playing career with the Houston Oilers as a special teams player and linebacker, came on board early in the Wolf administration, joining the Packers in 1992. He worked his way up the personnel ladder, from assistant director of pro personnel, to director of pro personnel, to director of player personnel. After the 1999 season he joined the migration from Green Bay to Seattle to work on Mike Holmgren's front office staff as vice president of football operations. Thompson was instrumental in putting together the 2005 Seahawks team that went 13–3 in the regular season and advanced to the Super Bowl.

The sustained excellence of Thompson's term in office, to Wolf, "Really feels good. It does. That Frank Sinatra song, you know? He's done it his way. And more power to him."

"I think he developed a lot on his own. I think (it was) the fact that he was the 53rd or 54th guy all the time and he had to ride that out. You develop a toughness. He made his mark as a special teams player, not as a regular position player. He had a toughness to him, but he also had a tremendous amount of intelligence to him. Very smart person. I was delighted when he went to Seattle and on his own, built a Super Bowl team up there. And then came back to Green Bay and built another Super Bowl team. And again, he did it his way. I know a lot of people aren't always in agreement, but for him it worked. His first big splash; he brings in two of the best free agents you could ever bring in, (Charles) Woodson and (Ryan) Pickett. He fixed two things there, the interior defensive line and the secondary. I mean, my goodness.

"You can't knock his success. It's right there. He's hired to do one thing and he was very successful at what he's done. I'm very proud of what he's done, because I played a part in that, but I mean just from the embryonic stage. I wouldn't do it that way, but there was a reason I did it another way. I was very impatient. If you can't play, get the hell out of here."

Back in Green Bay, Mike Sherman had stabilized the head

coaching position and, after Wolf's retirement following the 2000 season, Sherman had succeeded Wolf as general manager. Sherman could obviously coach, but over time he could not coach his way out of the personnel decisions he made as general manager. Sherman was removed as GM after the 2004 season but remained as head coach for the 2005 season. The Packers fell to 4–12 that year.

Team president Bob Harlan saw the need for a change. He knew there wasn't going to be another Ron Wolf available, but there could be someone who had learned his trade from Wolf. That would be Ted Thompson.

"When I wanted to hire Ted, I wanted one more confirmation that it was a good move," Harlan said. "I called, and I said: 'Ron, if I want somebody to come in here now and do what you did for me in 1991, would you have a suggestion?' 'Ted Thompson,' he said to me, right off the bat. He didn't hesitate. I said: 'Thanks. That's all I needed to know,' and we hung up."

"That's something that I will always appreciate," Thompson said of Wolf's recommendation. "That takes a lot to do that. Because you had his reputation here, and the recognition, and he was very close with Bob Harlan. And so, it was a big step for him to step out and recommend me."

Thompson, brought in as general manager, replaced Sherman with Mike McCarthy as head coach, and a new era of Packer success set in with a Super Bowl triumph after the 2010 season and eight straight years with postseason berths, tying a record. The 2017 Packers were on their way toward a record-setting ninth straight postseason berth with a 4–1 record when Rodgers suffered a broken right collarbone. The team finished 7–9 without him.

"Here's the thing about Ted Thompson," Wolf said. "He drafted Aaron Rodgers and Clay Matthews. Never in my life did I draft two players as good as those guys. Well, Lee Roy Selmon would have been, but that's pretty good picking right there."

Rodgers, the franchise quarterback, was taken by Thompson with the 24th pick of the 2005 draft. Matthews, a linebacker and the best Packer defensive player of the last decade, was taken by Thompson with the 26th pick of the 2009 draft. Wolf, working for Tampa Bay at the time, picked Selmon, who would become a Hall of Famer as a defensive end, with the first pick of the 1976 draft. On Wolf's side of the ledger, he was also instrumental in the Raiders drafting Hall of Fame quarterback Ken Stabler, who may not have been the pure passer Rodgers is, but played in five consecutive conference championship games.

In Thompson's 13 years as Packers GM, the team had only three losing seasons and the 2005 season could hardly be held against him. The Packers won six division titles, one Super Bowl, and advanced to the conference championship game four times. Thompson was moved into the role of senior advisor after the 2017 season.

Thompson was a draft-and-develop general manager first and foremost, not strictly in the let's-make-some-changes here approach of Wolf. But he was yet another man who had learned his craft from the master.

Thompson, like Wolf, may have climbed to the top of organizational flow chart, but he never stopped being a scout, at heart, or in reality.

"It was all about being a scout," Thompson said. "I never will forget Ron saying that he liked to be referred to as a scout. He said: 'Once a scout, always a scout,' or something to that effect, and I've always tried to model my thought process along those lines."

Another "Wolfism" was: "Tell me what this guy can do, not what he can't do."

"I think, certainly, he wanted to know what a guy could do as opposed to giving me all these reasons why we shouldn't be interested in him," Thompson said. "He had an interesting concept of college All-Star game practices. Like at the Senior Bowl, or the East-West, things like that. His theory was: If you're playing major college football and you go to the East-West Game, you can't hurt yourself. There's nothing you can do that can cause your grade to go lower, because you've already established what your grade is. If you're from a smaller school, and you're able to play very well, then you can raise yourself, but the point being, that a kid plays major college football for four years, or whatever time that you play, then you can't hurt yourself at an All-Star Game.

That seemed sensible. "That's the way Ron is," Thompson said. "You know, you listen to him and at first, you're wondering: *Where is he going with this conversation?* And it comes around and then you say: 'Boy, that makes a lot of sense.'"

The wall-to-wall effort was an essential part of Wolf's approach. The good ones who worked for him understood what that meant and that became an essential lesson learned for his people.

"I think it's mostly applying yourself," Thompson said. "Everybody will turn the tape machine on, get the projector going, and watch a little bit of film for a little while, but he immersed himself in it. In scouting, you're always after the unknown quantity, you're always after the fish that got away . . . Certainly, the good ones that have hope like Ron did he was going to find the one that nobody else could see. Because everybody knows who everybody is, sometimes they just can't see them.

"I think in the scouting business, not only do you have to have faith that you're seeing it the way you're supposed to be seeing it, you've got to have faith in yourself. Otherwise, 'you're too bashful to bring it up.'

"And if you do the work the way Ron set it up for us to do it, there are probably half-a-dozen guys around the league that are sitting in a general manager's chair that worked for Ron and are doing it the same way Ron always did it. So, we're all puppets of his," Thompson said with a laugh.

There are varied personalities, varied temperaments, varied views among GMs. What they share is common knowledge picked up from Wolf.

"I had a marvelous time working with all those men," Thompson said. "But we're all different and we all see things a little differently. But I think we all have a better appreciation for professional sports and the National Football League, and we have a better feeling for it and what we're doing in our contributions because Ron Wolf was our mentor.

"He loved to tell stories about guys from the '40s and the '50s. I don't know how much of this was made up or how much was true. But it was just marvelous the way his excitement level would go up when he started talking about the two running backs at Army in the late '40s—Blanchard and Davis—yeah, he can talk forever on those guys. And then guys from the '60s and guys from the '70s, and of course the vaunted Raider team. He just enjoyed the sport and enjoyed the chase so much."

As a 10-year player, Thompson had particular appreciation for Wolf's genuine affection and regard for the men who played football.

"He has that," Thompson said. "And sometimes you don't get that. I run into people from time to time—they're scouts and they're probably good scouts and that sort of thing—but they never played and they don't have what I perceive to be enough appreciation of how difficult it is to play and when you get to finally play, to do it well. But I think Ron, even though he wasn't a player by trade, I think he came to the table with an understanding and an appreciation for it."

Thompson was as close as anybody to being Wolf's right-hand man, but Thompson said that Wolf handled his departure for Seattle in a completely even-handed way.

There were several key departures then, which may be the nature of running a successful organization. But Wolf's response to that situation went beyond that.

"It's easy to say that, and talk about it in theory, but when all your people are walking out the door, it's a different thing," Thompson said. "He was very strong in that regard. He'd stick his chin out and say: 'Okay, whatever you're going to do, do, and we'll move on.' That's my perception of his attitude. He never told me that, but I think he was the kind of a guy, who would say 'I'll do this a different way now.'"

The indisputable part of all of this is that Wolf's success carried over in Green Bay, far beyond his nine years as general manager. You can say that Thompson was a Wolf disciple, although his approach to roster building was far more conservative than Wolf's. But if you listen to the general principles that Wolf espoused, they stayed in effect with the Packers.

Mike Reinfeldt was the vice-president of administration and chief financial officer during Wolf's tenure in Green Bay, an executive with the Seattle Seahawks, general manager of the Tennessee Titans for five years, with a 46–34 record, and then became senior advisor, to Troy Vincent, the NFL's executive vice president of football operations. But his Wisconsin connections remain in place.

"I grew up in Wisconsin, went to college in Milwaukee. I have a special place in my heart for the Packers and the Packer team and the way they have been able to keep it going," Reinfeldt said. "Sometimes people don't understand it's hard to win a Super Bowl, hard to get to the top. It's even harder to stay at the top. You watch all the teams that get there for a year or two and that's all they do. I mean, the Packers have been right in the fray for the last 25-odd years. That's a tribute to Ron and a lot of people working very hard to maintain that tradition that he helped to reignite.

"Ron was GM in Green Bay for nine years. And obviously he was very successful from the get-go. He was successful in that time. Somehow, something permeated within the organization that continued to function (just) as well after he left, or almost as well. Whatever he gave to the organization maintained itself and stayed there. Usually, that doesn't happen. That's the uniqueness."

John Schneider is another Wolf disciple with a glittering resume. As general manager of the Seattle Seahawks, he put together a team that went to two Super Bowls, winning one.

"John Schneider, probably of all the guys is the most successful," Wolf said. "Like all those guys he's bright and he really likes football. Football is very important to him. He respects the game. He knows the history of the game. He works his tail off. The big thing about John Schneider is that he is not afraid to make his case. I think that's been borne out with the job he's done up there in Seattle.

"I'll give you a perfect example: he goes out and makes a trade for a quarterback, (Charlie) Whitehurst, that doesn't work out. He goes out and gets the guy from LSU and the Packers (Matt Flynn), that doesn't work. He gets a guy from Minnesota (Tarvaris) Jackson, that doesn't work out, but he keeps on it and the next year he gets (Russell) Wilson. Tell you what, that worked."

Schneider started with the Packers as an intern in 1992, after personally calling Wolf in his office to request a job. He then served as a pro personnel assistant with the Packers from 1993 through 1996. He moved to Kansas City as director of pro personnel in 1997, becoming a major NFL personnel executive at age 25. In 2000 he went to Seattle as director of player personnel, rejoining Ted Thompson and Mike Holmgren. He subsequently became vice president of play personnel for the Redskins in 2001.

He rejoined the Packers in 2002 as personnel analyst to the general manager, eventually becoming director of football operations in 2008. He became general manager of the Seahawks in 2010, with the title of executive vice-president added in 2013.

To the question of what he had learned from Wolf, Schneider initially responded, "Holy smokes." Then, he expanded. "First of all, work ethic. You, the evaluation process never stops. Aggressiveness, always looking for ways to get better, whether it was through trades, just in terms of acquisitions, whether it was waivers, practice squad, trade possibilities, Canadian Football League, Arena Football League, what have you. Obviously, the draft, free agency, reserve future signings. It just never stopped and you're never, ever, ever good enough, and once you think you are, you're looking for a job."

Schneider was steeped in the history of the Packers, having grown up in nearby De Pere. He was also entirely aware of the many recent shortcomings of the team. Wolf, he said, was exactly what the Packers needed.

"I think I can say this in retrospect now, as a leader who came into a culture that needed a change here in Seattle, I think he came in with a very strong personality into a culture that had been a little more of a country club, and he came in and changed that culture. I think that toughness, the sternness, he kept everybody on their toes."

"That was also a time when top-down leadership completely existed and now it really doesn't. Now you have to have everybody 'buy in.' He could tell me, 'Hey, John, go make me 20 copies of this,' and I'd do it as fast as I could. Nowadays, it's kind of like: 'You know what? I think you're a heck of a copier. Would you mind going to make 20 copies?'

Working for Wolf on a day-to-day basis was strenuous and challenging, but at the same time, enjoyable. Everybody was pulling in the same direction, which was Wolf's direction, but even more than that, the Green Bay Packers' direction.

"It was exciting," Schneider said. "You had to be on your toes. You had to be ready for anything. But as long as you had a good work ethic, you were all right. Everybody was striving for the same thing. In retrospect, when you look back at it, it was pretty cool. It was a really cool group of people. And he had a really strong influence on us, like a father figure."

Not surprisingly, the Wolf pupils, once they have their own shops to run, have tried to achieve the same shared sense of the workplace.

"I think all of us have tried to create that wherever we've gone," Schneider said. "Ron never made it feel like it was all about him. If you did your work, he'd listen to you. If you were just popping off about your opinions, and you hadn't done the work yourself, he wasn't real fired up about it.

"We all understood that it took a work ethic and the attitude that whatever you can do to improve your team, you're going to do. I think times have changed a little bit. Now it's a little bit more stretched; we have more staff than he had back then. The coaching staffs are a lot bigger now; we have a sports sciences department, a nutritionist, our chefs. That stuff has changed a little bit, but at the same time, it was so awesome because he could just concentrate on being a great leader and a great communicator with the head coach and doing whatever it took to fix the team. And strategize, project whatever issues we were going to have coming."

Schneider has epitomized the Wolf attitude toward personnel moves: "If you're not getting better, you're getting worse." In the first season as Seattle GM, he completed more than 270 roster transactions. That was definitely a page out of Ron Wolf's book.

"(Seahawks head coach) Pete Carroll and I didn't know each other, but we both had a very aggressive mentality," Schneider said. "We just thought that was a good fit in terms of trying to change the culture, providing competition, not letting people be complacent. That was definitely a Ron Wolf philosophy, having like 275 transactions or whatever. It definitely helped create a culture of competitiveness. We talked about doing it better than anybody did before, and that's what we did. At every turn, if somebody got cut, we were evaluating everybody. If they were a tick better than the other person, we were going to do it.

Small moments with Wolf make up his protégés. "He thinks Seattle is Moscow, so he never comes here," Schneider said. "But we met Ron and Edie in St. Louis before one of his games, he came over with Tony La Russa (then Cardinals manager and a close friend of Wolf) before a Rams game. I remember being super proud, because he was saying: "That's what a fucking defensive backfield looks like.' He was telling his buddy that."

Reggie McKenzie was a Wolf guy from day one. He was drafted by the Los Angeles Raiders in 1985 in the 10th round and played linebacker for the Raiders for four years. He had returned to his alma mater, the University of Tennessee, as an assistant coach, but Wolf hired McKenzie as a scout in 1994. McKenzie became director of player personnel and eventually director of football operations for the Packers under Wolf, and then, Ted Thompson.

McKenzie was hired by the Raiders as general manager in 2012. He inherited an operation that had too much overpriced, under-performing talent, with serious salary cap issues. McKenzie turned what was a 4–12 team in 2012 and 2013 into a 12–4 team in 2016, and was named NFL Executive of the Year.

McKenzie had every intention of pursuing a career in coaching when Wolf, out scouting for player talent, ran into him at Tennessee and suggested that he might want to join the Packers as a scout.

So what did McKenzie learn from Wolf?

"Whooee," McKenzie said with a chuckle. "I might have to do a dissertation. To put it in the simplest form, what he taught me was do your work well. Whatever you do, give it your all. With that being said, you make sure you're thorough in everything you do, you make sure you're right. . . . you do it, you don't just half do something. You don't go into a meeting to talk about somebody when you've done no homework, you didn't research, you didn't watch enough film. You just don't do that. You do your work well, you do it right.

"But as far as what he taught me, I still repeated some of this to my draft room, to all my scouts—I'm sure they're going to pass down some Ron-isms. We get together with Schneider and Dorsey and even Scot McCloughlan from time to time, and we talk about some of the same stuff. We talk about it and joke about certain things that he always said."

Through some difficult times in Oakland, McKenzie kept in mind the serious lessons he had learned from Ron Wolf.

"From the beginning, you need to have a system in place," McKenzie said. "We didn't really have a system in place with the Raiders, of how I wanted to build a draft board, to have a draft room, to get guys together to evaluate the draft process and how we could get a constant movement of bringing in players to work out to see what was out there. He was big into that. We always brought players in for tryouts. The Raiders weren't used to that in the numbers that I wanted to do it. But we were looking to find players, we were struggling to find players, I had to let so many of them go to get those salary cap numbers down.

"Even in negotiations, I thought Ron was really good at communicating with agents, at having agents relate to him. Whether it was just information or helping to do a deal, I thought Ron was really good at working with agents and having that respect there. If we needed to get a player, you could feel confident that he could get it done. I think that agents and players trusted him. That was big for me, because that's what I've built my thing on, is loyalty and trust. I thought Ron was extremely loyal to us all as long as we did the work, he trusted us. And we, in turn, really trusted him."

In one case, Ron Wolf trusted Reggie McKenzie enough to put his son in McKenzie's hands. It was an important moment for everyone involved.

"With his son, Eliot, in high school, he was always around the draft room," McKenzie remembers. "I remember Ron came to me and said: 'This guy is bothering me, talking about how good he is. Why don't you put him through this and see if he's any good at this?'

"I put him through it, gave him guys to evaluate, and he's just like his Daddy, he's a doggone machine. He wrote up guys and I put so much red ink on all his stuff, but I remember telling Ron: 'He's going to be all right. He's going to be good. He's going to be good.'

"I brought him in for an internship when he was at the University of Miami. That was after Ron had retired. But he was good enough to be a scout. I think that right there was Ron saying that he wanted to step away and not just be Eliot's only teacher. He trusted me that I could teach him the right way and that was cool. I knew after the fact that he trusted me not only to see if he was any good, but to teach him how to be good. That was a good moment for me. I thought it was special. He cared about his boy and he knew that his boy had passion for it, and he respected Eliot's passion."

And in setting up that encounter, Ron Wolf simultaneously had done something for both his son and McKenzie. Eliot received valuable evaluation and advice from a professional source other than his father. And McKenzie was given the knowledge that Ron Wolf trusted him with the well-being and potentially, the future, of his son.

Eliot Wolf rose up through the ranks with the Packers, from pro personnel assistant to assistant director of pro personnel, to assistant director of player personnel, to director of pro personnel, to director of player personnel, to director of football operations, a position he held in 2016–17. The younger Wolf was a candidate as a successor to Ted Thompson as general manager. When that job went to Gutekunst, the Packers asked Eliot Wolf to stay on, but he went to Cleveland as assistant general manager, the number two man in the organization, under Dorsey.

"Obviously, as a father I'm very proud that what he's been able to accomplish in the game has been totally on his own," Ron Wolf said. "Because I was out of the game by the time he came in. He's risen right up the ladder, and all of my guys tell me that he's ready to be a general manager. And they know. I don't know, I've never been in a room with him when he evaluates somebody. But I trust those people. They don't have to bullshit me.

"He got his toughness and intelligence from his mother, particularly the intelligence. Mom's really a sharp lady. He was in the room with me when he was in high school. He'd come in and watch us put the board together."

"He started when he was 12, going to camps. Ken Herock grilled him, put him in a room, made him write reports, watch tape. If the reports weren't any good, you had to redo it. He started picking up jocks, graduated to the next year, how to evaluate players, write reports.

"He doesn't ask for advice. Not really. I think it's because the game is different now. My game was essentially blocking and tackling. It's a different game now.

It is undeniable that, from a very early age, Eliot Wolf aspired to follow in his father's footsteps.

"For fifth-grade graduation, we had to write what we wanted to be—I wanted to be an NFL scout," he said. "It was cool, because my Dad never pushed me in any definite direction, really never gave me a lot of pointers and still doesn't.

"But it was always something where I would go into the office with him. It was kind of an escape for me to get away from my academics and go into this other world, where, sure, it's their world, but it's a lot of fun, watching players. As I got older and got my driver's license, I would go there more often, after school, and sit in draft meetings; really just soak it all in."

Ron Wolf tells a story, with suitable fatherly pride, about the 15-year-old Eliot. In the 1997 draft, the elder Wolf was the general manager of the defending Super Bowl champion Green Bay Packers. He decided to draft a placekicker, Brett Conway of Penn State, in the third round.

Ron says Eliot came to him afterwards and said: 'That was a dumb move."

"I'm sure I did that," Eliot said with a smile. "I thought I had all the answers. And it's not that I knew Brett Conway, it's that he's a kicker and you can get him later. Go look at it now. (Mason) Crosby's about the highest drafted kicker and he was a late six.

"He did the same thing a few years later with Josh Bidwell, the punter (taken in the fourth round of the 1999 draft). He said: 'I'm picking this guy in the third round.' I said: 'Don't do that.' He picked him in the fourth round. I'm pretty sure I said: 'Don't do that, either.' But he at least was good enough to be a guy."

There turned out to be valid reasons why the Conway anecdote suggested that Eliot Wolf was precocious, rather than just a wise-guy teenager. Conway was injured in training camp, Ryan Longwell was claimed off waivers from San Francisco, and he immediately looked a lot more like a placekicker that could have been drafted. Longwell went on to a stellar, 15-year NFL career, the first nine seasons of which were with the Packers. Conway kicked in 51 NFL games over a six-year span.

Apart from the occasional over-drafting of a kicker, football life was full of lessons that Eliot Wolf could learn from his father. Some were tangible, but some were the result of close and perceptive observation.

"I really think there was his passion for the job, just watching that," Eliot said. "Even with all the success he had late in his career, he still had that curiosity, and I think that's a great characteristic for people in all organizations, to have that curiosity. He kept that curiosity: 'New Orleans just signed this guy, I never heard of him, go take a look at him.' That, and his leadership. The guys that worked for him are still incredibly loyal. And it's real, it's not a lip service kind of thing. And really in terms of the team, to have a vision and stick with it and trust the process. It's a cliché that everyone says now, but it's true.

"Part of it was judging football talent, but part of it was learning how to deal with people in your organization. Probably number one is honesty. Something that still holds true today, is honesty. No BS. No sugar-coating, none of that stuff, because if you do that, you don't have a true sense of where you stand. He's even more honest now than he was, because he doesn't have to try to be polite. When it came to the Packers, honesty with players, with coaches, everyone knew where they stood. If you weren't pulling your weight, he would let you know, and that's a great thing in leadership. Fortunately, I don't think I'm all the way there yet, because I still sugar-coat things sometimes, but just hanging around him for just 15 minutes now, you can tell. If you're not honest, you're just cheating yourself. Because honesty with others is honesty with yourself. You've got to be able to have some self-awareness."

The Wolf legend was not built solely on constant, warm camaraderie with the staff.

"They still tell stories about him in the draft room," Eliot said. "If you brought up a player and you didn't know that he didn't play in a certain game or he didn't look good right away, there was a lot of pressure on you. Or, the one that they tell a lot, he used to have a flashlight in the draft room, it would be dark in there. If the scout brought him up, some player who had a second-round grade, if, the first few plays, he didn't look very good, my Dad would turn on the flashlight and hold it towards the bottom of the board and start shaking it. And they knew what that meant. It was like: 'Oh, shit, I was too high on this guy.'

"They still talk about Alonzo Highsmith, the first guy he brought up his first year as a scout, was the record for the least amount of plays watched because he was so bad. They watched like literally two plays and my Dad was like: 'All right. Next.' And Alonzo was like, 'Oh, no.'"

There was an emotional involvement in football for Eliot, not only because his father was the Packers' general manager, but because this was Green and Gold football and it was emotional for everybody.

"It was high," Eliot said. "And it really hadn't been that way with the Jets or the Raiders. When my Dad was with the Raiders, I was a

Houston Oilers fan because I really liked Warren Moon. But I wasn't into football at that point where I would watch every game. It was just that was my team.

"And then when he got to Green Bay, you'd hear all this stuff from your friends in New York when we were getting ready to move: 'Oh, the Packers, they've never really done anything.' You go to one game and you see the vibe in the parking lot, and the vibe in the stands, and you see how important it is to all these people and you really start to buy in. Going from 4–12, to 9–7, from that point on, it was really cool. You understand how hard it is. Now the fans here seem to be a little spoiled. Part of that is, with Favre, he'd throw a couple of interceptions, but he'd pull it out at the end, because he's tough and gritty. With Rodgers, sometimes he goes three games without making a mistake.

"It's definitely live or die. I've also inherited my Dad's temper on game day," Eliot said with a smile. "That's something I'm trying to work on, too.'

When Eliot Wolf began working for the Packers he was proud to be able to carry on a family tradition. But he didn't want to fall into the trap of comparing himself to his father.

"When I got out of college, I had several job offers around the league," he said. "And almost everyone, including some people who were close to me, said: 'Don't go to the Packers. There'll be too much pressure on you.' I've never really looked at it that way. I've never tried to compare myself to him. I think that sets you up for failure. I mean, the guy is in the Hall of Fame. What can you do to top that? I'm proud of being able to continue the name in the business, but I've never compared myself to him, or thought of it as carrying on a legacy."

At the same time, Eliot Wolf knew that he would hear charges of nepotism. It would not make a difference that his father was four years into retirement when Eliot was hired by the Packers. It would not make a difference that he had been doing NFL internships for eight years. It would not make a difference that he was receiving job offers from other teams.

"All the time, all the time, the nepotism thing," he said. "People picking on the fact that there is nepotism in sports. Well, go look at any business. How do you separate one intern candidate from another intern candidate? It's something I've had to deal with, and it's something my Dad pretty much ignores, which is something you should do.

"I'm used to it by now. I would say the only thing I was given was, when I interned for the Falcons I did some scouting. But I was more of an operations gopher, checking guys in at meals, field security during drills. I was a freshman in high school—who am I going to throw out of there, you know?" he said with a laugh. "But my first Packers internship, when I really started to hunker down and write reports. My first batch of reports were so bad that I knew if had to actually had to interview for this position I wouldn't have gotten it. And that's the only time I felt like I got something that I didn't deserve. But my second batch of reports, I started to get better and better and better. I paid my dues. I did internships; '96, '97, '98, '99, 2000, and 2001, 2002, 2003, Then I graduated from (the University of) Miami and got a job with the Packers.

"Graduated in three-and-a-half years with a degree in creative writing. One of the pro scouts in Green Bay wasn't working out. I had interviewed with the Packers at the Senior Bowl in January. And they offered me a job, shortly thereafter; fired the guy and hired me. And I started at the (scouting) combine in '04."

Eliot Wolf has not been subjected to intrusions in his professional life from his Hall-of-Fame father. He is following the same career path as his father, but his father is not hands-on in his son's career. And that turns out to be a very good thing for the son.

"He's really big into not wanting to help, because he's aware of the nepotism perception and that kind of stuff. If I ask him something specific, he's not like: 'No, you have to find that out for yourself.' In most cases," Eliot Wolf said with a smile.

"He did give me a piece of paper the day I started (with the Packers), and it said "How to Fail." It's from a book by Patrick Lencioni, *The Five Dysfunctions of a Team*. Absence of trust, fear of conflict, lack of commitment, avoidance of accountability, inattention to results. It turns out that just two years ago, I found out it was from a book. I thought it was his thing. It's the exact piece of paper that he gave to me is in my office, hanging above my desk, I look at it every day.

"That's been kind of the main thing. And the "be yourself" part of things is a constant. As far as the scouting aspect, just write what you see. He says that a lot: 'Write what you see on a player and if you're wrong, so be it.' Write what you see."

But Eliot Wolf picked up plenty of useful lessons in football scouting, football management, and life in general by closely observing his father.

"He really would challenge you, with meaningful challenges," Eliot Wolf said. "John Dorsey would do the same things when I started with the Packers. He'd really see if you could handle it right away and if you couldn't handle it right away, he wouldn't necessarily fire you, but he would make sure someone else, one of his veteran guys was going in behind you on the road to make sure we weren't missing anything. And we've had some instances of that since I've been with the Packers, where you can kind of tell on a guy who is struggling with his time management or something like that. And that's why I'm proud of the internship program that my Dad started. (The Packers) still do it almost exactly the same. Give you players, put you in a room. There are ways to cheat now; I mean you can Google a scouting report. But usually we'll be able to see through that pretty quickly if someone is trying to do that."

And Eliot Wolf saw first-hand the winning partnership between his father and Mike Holmgren. Here were two bright, intense, competitive and willful men, but they functioned almost as one, restoring an entire franchise.

"Really, being around the Wolf/Holmgren model, seeing how well they succeeded, how well they communicated, and then fast forwarding to some of the things you hear about today with some of the lack of communication, when a GM and a head coach aren't talking to each other," Eliot Wolf said. "I get maybe you don't like the other guy for some reason, but you're absolutely fucked—both of you are, there's not one guy who is going to win and one guy who is going to lose—so wouldn't you maybe stop being so stubborn and try to make it work? From watching Holmgren and my Dad the way it worked so well, even hearing something like that is mind-boggling to me, still.

"There was the mutual respect aspect. They're both pretty good at what they do, so for them to find each other was pretty special in itself. Their mutual respect and their ability to feel comfortable enough with themselves to stay out of each other's way. I'm sure they'd have a personnel meeting where my Dad would say: 'Hey, why aren't you playing this guy more than that guy?' But it wasn't like: 'You need to play this guy, that's what I drafted him for.' You hear about that. But they didn't do that; still, we don't do that. And vice versa, not strong-arming my Dad into signing or cutting anyone. I'm sure they both made compromises certain times, but for them to have the success that they had and still be like that was pretty impressive."

The Wolfs were understandably disappointed when Eliot did not get the general manager's job in Green Bay. He had spent 14 seasons with the Packers. He had interviewed for two GM jobs previously. The Packers, when Ted Thompson was running the football operation, refused to allow him to interview for the general manager's job with the Detroit Lions, sending an apparent message that there were bigger things in store for him with the Packers.

The disappointment was real, but Eliot Wolf also saw the other side of his experience with the Packers. "On the other hand, they brought me in, they gave me a chance, they promoted me however many times. They gave me a chance to grow and learn and be a part of something, which is a great winning organization, which I'm going to bring with me here or if I ever go someplace else," he said. "So, it cuts both ways."

As soon as word got out that Brian Gutekunst had the Packers general manager job, Eliot had offers from other clubs. Within two days he had taken the job of assistant general manager, Number 2 to John Dorsey, with the Browns.

Eliot left behind plenty of admirers in Green Bay.

Bob Harlan, who as Packers president, made the decision to turn the football operation over to Ron Wolf, has a similar high regard for Eliot's ability and his future.

"Eliot is highly intelligent," Harlan said. "Going back a couple of years, the Detroit Lions were very, very interested in Eliot (as general manager), but he didn't get the chance to interview. He's got a bright future, and now with John Dorsey (in Cleveland), with Eliot and Alonzo Highsmith, John picked up two quality individuals, two good football people. Eliot's going to be a general manager somewhere, someday. He's a very astute student of the game."

And in Cleveland, John Dorsey got exactly what he was looking for as assistant general manager.

"Eliot has been a fine executive in this league for some time now," Dorsey said. "It's been great to watch him grow up around this league when I was with him in Green Bay and from afar for the last five-plus years. He's been a big reason for the consistent success the Packers have experienced over the past decade."[1]

The Browns won only one game over the 2016–17 seasons. Prior to 2018, they had finished last in their division for seven straight seasons. Their best record during that stretch was 7–9. There is work to be done in Cleveland, loads of work. The word "challenging" tends to dominate any reasonable discussion of the Browns. But with Dorsey and the younger Wolf and Highsmith and all those hard-earned lessons from Ron Wolf, the next direction for this franchise will be upward. The 2018 season was a breakthrough in itself, as the Browns went 7–8–1.

One bonus for Eliot Wolf is that, in Cleveland, he is removed from the large and imposing shadow of his father's accomplishments and reputation.

"No one here cares," he said with a laugh. "No one here cares a darn for it. Here, they know my dad worked in the business, and they maybe know he's in the Hall of Fame. Other than that, it's just a name. In Green Bay, everyone knew him, and for the most part it seems like they admired him. And I knew that when I took the job in 2004. It was a great run. Who thought I would be there for 14 seasons?

"It's extremely liberating. I went to high school in Green Bay, some of my best friends live there, in fact my best friend lives there. It's been good to come here, try to branch out, learn something new. It's going to be fun, it's a nice challenge. I'm pretty fired up for it.

"From the scouting standpoint, we're using the same rating system that my dad designed. Little stuff like that makes it just a tad easier to kind of assimilate into it. This is a challenge, going from a team without an owner to a team with an owner who is hands-on, who wants to know what it going on, which is great. And then meeting people, the coaching

1 Cleveland.com, January 10, 2018.

staff. We kept a fair amount of people, there probably wasn't as much turnover here as people expected. And to teach them our system, get them up to speed, and at the same time, learn the way it was done here before, and maybe learn the pitfalls, the mistakes that they made, that you try to avoid."

Meanwhile, in Green Bay, the Packers chose as GM a man who was not a direct genetic descendant of Ron Wolf, but was still a product of the Ron Wolf general manager tree. Brian Gutekunst first worked for the Packers as a scouting intern in 1997, worked for the Kansas City Chiefs for a year, and then was hired by Wolf as a fulltime college scout in 1998.

Gutekunst has his full-fledged football heritage. His father, John, was a longtime college coach, who was the head football coach at the University of Minnesota from 1985 through 1991. Brian Gutekunst played college football for two years at the University of Wisconsin-La Crosse, before a shoulder injury ended his career. He later served as an assistant coach at La Crosse, coaching linebackers in 1995, when the team won the Division III national championship.

With the Packers, Gutekunst spent 13 years as a college scout, scouting the East Coast for two years, and then moving to the Southeast, which constituted a promotion given the talent level in the SEC. He was promoted to director of college scouting in 2012 and subsequently became director of player personnel in 2016. Gutekunst was highly regarded, interviewing with three NFL organizations for general manager jobs. At the time that the Packers GM post became open, Gutekunst was reportedly the top choice for the general manager's job with the Houston Texans.

While Eliot Wolf obviously wanted the Packers' job, he was gracious about the post going to Gutekunst.

"I was happy for Brian," he said. "Brian and I are friends. He's a no-nonsense guy. He's a true scout . . . a hard worker, a good leader. He'll have some adjustments to make with the front-office stuff, just because he's been primarily a road guy. And he's not afraid. So, with all those things, I think he'll do pretty well."

For Bob Harlan, Gutekunst had already passed the primary test. "I remember when he was hired," Harlan said. "I've always told people I always have a lot of respect for anybody Ron Wolf hired, because Ron will not accept mediocrity. So, I felt about Brian, if he passed Ron Wolf's test, he's got to be pretty good."

The record suggests that if Ron Wolf hired a scout, and that scout stayed with him, yes, he had to be pretty good. In fact, there was an excellent chance he would be notably better than that.

It was no accident that six men who were taught by Wolf became general managers in the National Football League. If one of his guys had the intelligence, the work ethic, the enthusiasm, the stamina, and the proper respect for the Green Bay Packers place in football history, Wolf would share all the knowledge he had with that individual.

And that's not all that he shared. He shared the credit for the successes. He took the blame upon himself for the mistakes. The eventual GMs were astute enough to watch, listen, and learn. Plus, there was always a surplus of information to be gathered, to be weighed, to be considered, to be debated, and inevitably, to be viewed on film, and later, on tape. The film study was never-ending, because the eye in the sky didn't lie.

Scouting was not just a reasonable profession for these persons. It was an honorable profession, particularly, at Wolf's constant insistence, when it was being done on behalf of the Green Bay Packers. In that regard, scouting became a way of life.

That's the concept of Green Bay as "the mother ship," in John Dorsey's term. Working for and with Ron Wolf, the crew learned how to conduct themselves as professionals. They learned that if you did the necessary preparation and you believed in your work and yourself, you could act boldly and unexpectedly, swimming against a tide of popular prejudice, and you could still be right. Wolf didn't deliver long-winded lectures on any topic, but these individuals also learned, through years of observing Wolf, how a leadership role can be filled by someone acting not like a hotshot, know-it-all boss, but instead like a regular, decent human being.

That is part of the essential legacy of Ron Wolf. There is also the genetic legacy in the person of his son, Eliot. In a more perfect world, one with a neater narrative, Eliot would have gotten the job as Packers general manager, and the legacy line would have been unbroken. But even in this world, Eliot went to Cleveland where John Dorsey and he are in the process of taking a team that once appeared hopeless, and putting it on a path that has already made the Browns more than competitive. Eliot will eventually get his chance to be a general manager somewhere. At that point, the number of GMs in the Ron Wolf orchard will be at least seven. That's another part of the living legacy.

The Wolfs have moved so frequently over the years that a lot of what might otherwise be considered keepsakes have been discarded. But Wolf found one from the very beginning of his journey from NFL neophyte job-seeker to NFL Hall of Famer.

"Every year I would write to all the teams," Wolf said. "I found a letter that Vince Lombardi sent back to me, telling me that he had no openings."

Lombardi, as all-knowing as he was, couldn't have known that this particular job-seeker was going to become a Hall of Fame general manager. Part of the Ron Wolf legacy is being legitimately mentioned in the same paragraph as St. Vincent, both restoring the Green Bay franchise to its former glory.

12

Ron in Retirement

IN RETIREMENT FOR Ron Wolf, there was always the film library he had acquired over the years, with enough titles to rival Netflix. True, these were all game films, but they filled a large room in the basement of the Wolf family home just outside Green Bay. And they were filed in typically total order and neatness. The Library of Congress wasn't any more orderly than Ron Wolf's collection of football films.

Wolf was a football scholar, and that designation didn't disappear with retirement. His natural inclinations and his inherent curiosity led him to develop considerable expertise in another sport. That was baseball. It became a convenient activity to explore when the St. Louis Cardinals and the then Florida Marlins moved their Spring Training base to the Roger Dean Stadium complex in Jupiter, Florida, not far from the Wolfs' winter home.

Tony La Russa was managing the Cardinals at the time, on his way to the Hall of Fame. He would finish his career with three World Series championships and the third-most victories for a manager in the history of the game. On this February morning in 1998, things were at their most basic. The Cardinals were opening their first Spring Training in Jupiter, and as far as spectators went, the complex was virtually deserted. La Russa did, however, notice the persistent presence of one individual sitting in the bleachers.

"He was there quite often. I figured he was some kind of scout from another organization, trying to steal whatever we were trying to put in," La Russa said with a chuckle." I can't remember if I asked him or I had security ask him: 'Who is that guy?'

"He turned out to be Ron Wolf. Well, I knew who Ron Wolf was because I had lived in the Bay Area and I was a Raider fan, and I had followed Ron as the general manager of the Packers. So, I went over there and introduced myself, and he explained that he lived there during the winter and he was curious to see what Spring Training looked like, because he knew what football training camp looked like and he wanted to see what Spring Training looked like. So, I told him: 'Get on the other side of the fence. You're invited to get as close as you probably want to.' He took advantage of that. He was there probably every day for the next 14 years," La Russa added with another chuckle.

Wolf had played baseball in high school and college, so he had considerable knowledge of the game. But he was fascinated by the game's parallels to football in both player development and evaluation of talent. So, he became, particularly after his retirement, a fixture at Cardinals camp. He was given total access and he got to a point where his opinion would be given a hearing.

"We would always get a big kick out of this," La Russa said. "He would invariably start the conversation by saying: 'You know, I don't really know a lot about your sport, or your team,' and then he would take about 10 minutes explaining what he saw on the team, what we should be doing, and he would proceed to give us his analysis. We would just laugh. I'd say: 'I thought you didn't know anything.'

"He got to know the Marlins, too. . . . The guys took him as a friend, he was, an unofficial member of the staff, probably an official member of the staff the way he was walking around there," La Russa said with a laugh. "Not all the time, but often enough, Bill Parcells was with him, and guys really enjoyed that, as well . . . Guys felt like Ron was part of the team."

As he had been with the Packers in his job, so Wolf was with this retirement activity: A details guy.

"That definitely describes him," La Russa said. "He's a technician.

I'm not sure that there are a whole lot of people who are successful who can ignore attention to detail.

"He was paying attention and he certainly learned. But now, he didn't learn as much as he thinks he learned," La Russa concluded with a sizable laugh. "I want to make sure I get that in."

Walt Jocketty was the Cardinals general manager from 1995 through 2007, and his career had some distinct parallels to that of Wolf. He brought in La Russa as manager, and he built teams that became perennial contenders. The 2004 Cardinals won 105 regular season games, but lost in the World Series. The 2005 Cardinals won 100 games, but lost in the NL Championship Series. The 2006 Cardinals won only 83 games, but had the ultimate success, winning the World Series. Jocketty was in an excellent position to appreciate who Wolf was in light of what he had accomplished.

"For a guy who's had the success that he's had, Ron's just very easy to talk to," Jocketty said. "He's a very humble guy. He was very interested in baseball and talking about baseball, and I think our personalities, we're both kind of low-key, background types of guys. Let the players and coaches shine—they're the ones that should get the attention. I think we both are of that same ilk. I think we both got our starts in Oakland, with owners that were a little 'different' than the others. He had Al Davis, and my first year in Oakland was with Charlie Finley," Jocketty added with a laugh.

"He's been very successful, but I would guarantee that most people didn't know who Ron Wolf was. They knew who his players and his coaches were, but they didn't necessarily know who the guy behind the scenes putting it all together was, the architect. And that's the way you want it. There are too many guys today, in both sports, in all sports, who feel that they have to be up-front, taking credit, making sure that everybody knows how smart they are. Ron and I didn't feel that way. We loved what we did, and it was all part of the work ethic.

"It's hard not to like the guy. He's very humble. A guy in his position, somebody who's had the success he's had, a Hall of Famer, could be an arrogant so-and-so, but he's just very down-to-earth.

"Ron is never trying to take advantage of you. He just wants to be your friend, talk about baseball or football, enjoy each other's company.

"I think that's something that's not very common any more. People are always looking for something from other people. Guys in our position, often people want something from other people. Ron is never that way. He recognizes you for who you are, what you are, and he's good with that.

"He's a unique guy. A great guy, in that, he does reach out and try to stay in touch with people. I really enjoy whenever we get a chance to be together."

At the same time, Jocketty was impressed with Wolf's attention to baseball, and his growing insight into the game.

"He would watch practice every day," Jocketty said. ". . . over the years, we got to be friends. I was amazed by his knowledge of baseball. He loved the game, so he followed it and studied it. He asked questions, and that's how you learn. I'm sure he did that throughout his football career."

La Russa retired from managing after winning his third World Series in 2011. He went on to executive positions with the Arizona Diamondbacks and then Boston Red Sox, becoming part of yet another world championship in 2018. Wolf continued to be a regular at Cardinals camp, and he and Parcells continue to be regulars at Grapefruit League games. Their baseball-watching lives have become richer with two clubs, the Houston Astros and the Washington Nationals, moving their Spring Training headquarters to nearby West Palm Beach.

Parcells indicates that Wolf's routine does not change. "He's a good baseball man, too." Parcells said. "As soon as we get in for our first time in Spring Training every year I've been with him, the first thing he does is pull out the roster and tries to figure out who is what. Is this guy our starter? Is this guy the shortstop? Is this guy our first baseman? It's just inherent in the species you know?" Parcells said with a laugh.

"No way those guys (the coaching staff) know what a credit to the game they are," Wolf said. "Dave Duncan, Bill Parcells and I would sit there, and Dave Duncan would show us a book, which shows the last 80 pitches. And then he shows you from a hitter's perspective. They're going to play Robert Clemente. This shows what gets him out. I mean, I never realized they did that stuff. And then to sit, to have an opportunity with La Russa to sit and watch the preparation for one game. The game starts at seven o'clock. And you see all that preparation beforehand. How they talk about the pitcher, the players. The pitchers are in one room and the hitters are in the other room and they talk about is there anything you know about this guy? They go through that, each individual guy. What about this pitcher? How can you get to him? It was mind-boggling to me how thorough everything was. Everything was detailed, and the interesting thing Tony told me was, 'I've got to be careful because I can only keep these guys' attention for about 45 minutes. I've got to break it up.'

"Then, playing the ball off the wall. And the guy hitting the fungo bat. We go on one hop, then we go two hops, then we go three hops, with the infielders. They're magicians. They never get their due, or the respect they deserve. I'm talking about these guys, these guys, they make the game what it is. I had a great opportunity to sit there with Red Schoendienst (Hall of Fame second baseman) and listen to Red talk about baseball. And I see a pitcher throw the ball and the batter hits it to the third baseman who throws him out. That's what I see. Red tells me what the pitch is, what the hitter did correctly or incorrectly, what the fielder did correctly or incorrectly, what the runner did correctly or incorrectly.

"A couple of times I was able to sit with La Russa during a game in Spring Training. The Dodgers were up here in Vero (Beach) and they've got this guy Edwin Jackson. He comes in and they've got the radar gun and it's 101, 102 (mph), and I'm thinking 'Holy smokes!' The Cardinals make three outs and I'm sitting there with (then Cardinals coach) Joe Pettini and I'm saying: 'That guy can really bring it.' He says: 'Ah, we've got him figured out. We're going to hit him.' And I'm: 'Oh, yeah, you're going to hit him.' Well, they did because the ball didn't have anything on it, it was just straight. Sure enough, wham, they knocked him out.

"But they're still trying to win those games and the games don't count. But that was (La Russa's) culture. So anyway, I spend a month-and-a-half with that."

While Wolf was scouting the Cardinals, La Russa was evaluating Wolf, in part as a potential dinner companion. Dinners for La Russa during Spring Training often included an impressive group of diners from throughout the world of sports.

"At the same time he was checking us out, I was checking him out," La Russa said. "You look at his background now, he's an NFL Hall of Famer. So probably during the practices and the games, you're talking, but you're working. I'd love to have a dollar for every time we went to dinner over those 14 years. As it turned out, my family was in California and so they would not be in Florida. So, four or five days a week I'd go out to dinner. So, two or three times a week for the six weeks of Spring Training times 14 years, we would have these dinners and it was one of the highlights of my life, just because of the people that would come to the dinners.

"You'd have Parcells, Bill Belichick, Ron Wolf, and then there would be somebody visiting, Coach Kirk Ferentz (head football coach at the University of Iowa), and they'd go to dinner. Basketball, John Havlicek would be there, Coach (Bobby) Knight would be there quite often. If it was a Spring Training game, you could have Red Schoendienst there. Maybe Bob Gibson would be there. Joe Torre. Jim Leyland, whoever visited. Whoever came to those dinners, it was fascinating. And then you'd have people who weren't in sports. Maybe you'd have (author) John Grisham there. And a good friend of ours, Dick Strong, brought Lt. Gen. (Hal) Moore, the famous general from "We Were Soldiers." (College basketball coach) Tom Crean came. . . ."

"If there's one trait that someone like he has, who has been involved, in a responsible way, with so much success, when you get to know the person and you can't find his ego. He's not pushing people aside to draw attention to himself. He could hold his own in any conversation—his knowledge, his info, just his savvy—but I think that one reason he's likable is that he just doesn't turn you off with 'look at me, look at what I've done.' He's just in the conversation. And he does the other thing that's critical: He listens to you. He pays attention. He's not always looking around, ignoring you, or if you've heard the expression, being a 'topper.' A guy says: 'I went to watch this,' and before you even digest it, he's giving you what he did that was even better. That's a 'topper.' Ron has none of that. He's a really good person. Very smart, had a great career, but it's never gone to his head.

"I would always kid him, I want to visit Green Bay, and I want to drive down the 'Ron Wolf Highway,' or visit the 'Ron Wolf Athletic Center.'

"Part of why he was always included in the invitations was he was not only informative, he was entertaining, he was funny. He laughed at things that were funny. And then he told stories that were funny. Think about his background, he has thousands of stories, whether it's Al Davis, or his time with the Packers, Brett Favre, it goes on and on and on. He's a charmer.

"If you get to where you really get to know him, the complete package as far as the professional and the personal, I mentioned his interest in what you're doing and his sincerity about looking you in the eye and paying attention, being honest with you, he's really a wonderful human being, I'm proud to say he's a friend."

Wolf's connections broadened. For several years, he and Edie were part of the commissioner of baseball's party at All-Star Games and then during the World Series. The commissioner, Bud Selig, had come to know and admire Wolf when Selig served as a member of the Packers Board of Directors.

"Ron is a (baseball) fan," Selig said and, coming from him, this amounts to extremely high praise. "When I knew he was a fan, he called me after he retired, and he needed a Spring Training pass for he and his friend Bill Parcells. I knew he was a baseball fan, and the more we talked, the more I liked him.

"So, I said to him one day: 'You know at our All-Star and World Series trips, I'd like you and your wife, Edie, to come with us.' And they did. And they were wonderful, I must say that. You know, there was a friendship forged there out of two people who had been in sports all their lives. There was a lot of common ground."

"It was a great time, a great time," Wolf said.

Ron and Edie still winter in Florida. Since retirement, their summer homes have been in Annapolis, then Green Bay, and now with Eliot's move to the Cleveland Browns and the birth of Eliot's two daughters, in the Cleveland area. In Annapolis, Ron Wolf immersed himself in two subjects—watching football films, which wasn't a change of pace, and studying American military history, which was.

"When I first retired, we moved to Annapolis, Maryland," Wolf said, "and Steve Belichick, Bill Belichick's father, was a bigshot at the Naval Academy and he was very helpful to me, helping to get us settled and getting me to meet the people at the Naval Academy. I spent a lot of time over there, watching football practice and getting to know people. Watching that, and then I would assign tasks to myself. I had a football library so I would watch old tapes, like the '48 Colts vs. the Browns. You know, I liked the '49 Eagles. Just to watch these guys. But I had this extensive library and I spent time doing that. Watching the '44, '45, '46, '47, '48, Army-Navy games.

"Watching these guys that I had watched on TV as a kid, or listened to on the radio and then having this opportunity to come back and forth now and really watch them, that was thrilling."

There were periodically rumors that one team or another was pursuing Wolf to resume his career as an NFL general manager. On the surface, these did not seem to be outrageous reports, given Wolf's long record of achievement, particularly in Green Bay. But they never did have any substance, because the only man who mattered in these discussions had determined for himself that a professional GM job was no longer a duty he felt he could fairly assume.

But Wolf was willing to accept a role as a short-term consultant, if the fit was right. Right after the 2012 season, the San Diego (now Los Angeles) Chargers were seeking both a general manager and a head coach. Chargers owner and president, Dean Spanos, had made the decision to take a new direction with these positions, but was judicious enough to believe that he could use assistance in the process of finding the right people for these jobs.

"I didn't know Ron well at the time," Spanos said. "I had met him a few times, but I didn't have a personal relationship with him. We had a common friend in Carmen Policy (president and CEO of the San Francisco 49ers during the glory years of that franchise). He and I had been friends, along with our families, for years. I was talking with him just in general terms about what I should be looking for, because I was looking for both a general manager and a coach. There are different ways of structuring your organization in terms of how you want to run it. I had always been someone who was in favor of having a general manager first, having a kind of separation first, and having the general manager and myself hire the coach. But, that being said, I'm open to anything at that time. And then Carmen basically said: 'I think you'd be impressed with Ron and he's somebody you might want to consider hiring as a consultant to come in and help you.' And I said: 'Great.'

"So, Carmen set up a meeting for us in San Francisco, Ron flew out, we had dinner, and I think we both liked each other immediately. I said: 'Look, I need some help on this, you've been around, you've been successful, and I know you know what it takes to put a winning organization together. Would you consider coming to work as a consultant for us?' He said: 'Yes.'"

Wolf made a decision to sign on with this enterprise based on two factors. This was obviously a process to which he could bring some knowledge and expertise, so that was no problem. The other component was frankly whether he thought the people involved were people he actually wanted to help.

In this case, "the more time you spent with Dean Spanos, the better you liked him," Wolf said. So, this job was two-for-two with him.

Spanos had the final hiring authority but included in this process were Wolf and Spanos' son, John, who at that time was Chargers president of football operations.

"We went out and basically hired Tom Telesco as our general manager," Dean Spanos said. "Then the four of us interviewed maybe four or five different people and we ended up hiring our head coach at the time, who was Mike McCoy.

"The GM hiring happened very quickly, probably within a couple of weeks. We were flying all over the country interviewing different candidates. When we interviewed Tom Telesco, (at that time, director of player personnel for the Indianapolis Colts) I believe he was the last person we interviewed. It was kind of interesting because, Ron has a keen eye. When we walked out of the meeting he looked at me and I looked at him, and we both said: 'I think he's the right guy.'"

Wolf, Spanos said, added not only expertise, but a likable sort of presence to the process.

"Sometimes when you meet people for the first time, you never know how it's going to be," Spanos said. "But Ron is fun, he's very easy to be with, he gets right to the point, he has a keen eye. I think his greatest talent—and I think it's something you sort of have to be born with is the way I would say it—he knows what it takes for an individual to be a winner. Even to this day, he's still attuned to what's going on in the league. He knows the coaches out there. He knows the players out there. He knows why they're good. He gets a good feeling within himself as to whether this player's going to be good, or this team's going to be good. I think it's a natural thing that he has. Some people have it, some people don't. Because I asked him to do some work for us with our roster, take a look at our roster. We're always right in the middle—9–7, 8–8, 7–9. We couldn't quite get to that next level; 10–6 or 11–5. I said: 'Ron, is our cup half full or half empty?' He kind of laughed and he said: 'I think you get it.'

"As an owner, you sit there and you're 8–8. That's not the dregs of the league. And you always try to convince yourself you're a player or two away, and that'll get you over the hump. But it doesn't always work that way. I said: 'I'm in that area right now and it's not where I want to be. I need another set of eyes to look at that.' And there were some players who I thought were better than they were, and in his opinion, they weren't. That really helped me and it really helped Tom, and my son John, both, to have a different set of eyes.

"That's the thing I really liked about him. He just has this ability and it's a feel thing, that I really think this is the right guy, I really think this thing is headed in the right direction or, it's not perfect, but I think he's right more often than not."

"He and Bill Parcells are very close. They stay in tune with the whole thing. During this process people would come out of the woodwork wanting to be general manager. He would say: 'No. Yes. I'll get back to you.' And within four or five hours he would say: 'That's a guy we should talk to' or, 'let's pass on this guy.' Then he'd tell me why and I'd say: 'Perfect.' That's also where he really helped us because he saved us a lot of time and cut right to the chase.

It was not that Wolf dominated the proceedings, Spanos said. "He doesn't talk a lot," Spanos said. "He surely doesn't pontificate. He listens, and he looks at you and he's really listening to what you're saying. And then at some point he'll say: 'This is what I think.' He's a man of few words. But they're very specific and to the point when he starts talking.

"But when you're in a group talking you always look at him, because he'll look at me and wink or smile. I know what some of that means. He's really listening, even though he's not talking."

McCoy was let go as coach after four seasons of uneven results, to be replaced by Anthony Lynn, who went 9–7 in 2017, his first season as Chargers coach. Telesco is still the Chargers' general manager and appears to have put together a team that should compete for a playoff berth on an annual basis. The Chargers qualified for the playoffs in 2018, as a Wild Card team, with a 12–4 record that was tied for the best in the American Football Conference. It was the Chargers' best record since 2009. In the playoffs they advanced to the divisional round, before being eliminated by the Patriots.

"I think Tom's done a great job," Spanos said. "I can sit back and say that we've had injuries every year that have just killed us. Two seasons that we were devastated. We all still like our roster. The players that we have, the rosters that he's put together, his drafts, the free-agent moves that he's made, and I think he's really done a good job. And it's a good working relationship. Tom comes across as a very nice guy, but he's very strong in his opinions, which I like, too. It's really worked out for us."

In any event, Spanos is happy on more than one level that he and Wolf were brought together.

"He cut right to the chase, got right to the point, we didn't waste a lot of time," Spanos said. "And he did his homework. He would do an evaluation on his own and I'm sure he was checking with other people around the league that he knew, about some of the people we were interviewing, whether it was for the GM or the head coach, and he would get back to me. These weren't long meetings. I hired him for his opinion and his judgment, so I surely didn't challenge him on anything. I did ask a lot of questions, but at the end of the day he was very helpful to me.

"But he's also a guy you enjoy spending time with, even if it's not on a business relationship, just going out socially. He has a very wide spectrum of knowledge about all sports. He loves baseball. He and Bill Parcells go to a lot of games. Just listening to him talk about other sports and other things is very fascinating, too.

"Every time I see Carmen Policy now, I say: 'Thanks. That was really helpful to us.' It probably wouldn't have happened if it weren't for Carmen. But it's something that I'll remember for the rest of my life, working with Ron. Just having a friendship with him means a lot to me."

It has been a particularly rewarding retirement for Wolf—watching baseball, adding to his circle of good friends, watching game film when that fit in the schedule, enjoying his grandchildren with Eliot and his wife, Regan, having two daughters, Daisy and Liza Marie. As good as all of that was, there was yet another element to be added to the Wolf biography—the Pro Football Hall of Fame.

13

Ron Wolf Enters the Hall of Fame—With Help

IT WAS JANUARY 31, 2015, a Saturday afternoon in Phoenix, Arizona, the day before Super Bowl XLIX, between the New England Patriots and the Seattle Seahawks. The biggest game of the year was on tap, but the nominees for the Pro Football Hall of Fame were playing only the waiting game. The Selection Committee for the Hall had been deliberating, and the tension was mounting. Which of the finalists were going to be immortalized in the Canton, Ohio, Hall of Fame, and which were merely going to be deeply disappointed?

One of those waiting was not particularly impressed by his own credentials. For nearly 40 years he was one of the shrewdest personnel men in the game, helping to maintain a semi-dynasty with the Raiders, and then, more recently and more remarkably, reviving an entire franchise as the general manager of the Green Bay Packers. Now, Ron Wolf waited for word. Waiting was never really one of his strong suits.

"I was in my hotel room in Phoenix, talking with Edie," Wolf recalled. "The whole time I'm sitting in the room waiting, the plan is, Kevin Greene (former All-Pro linebacker, elected to the Hall in 2016) told me this because he had been in the running so many times and had been sent home. If you don't get a call right away, if they say they're going to call you at 4 o'clock, then you're going to be on the morning flight out of there, Sunday morning before the game, because they don't want you around. So, I figure it's 4 o'clock, I don't have the call, so I'm talking to Edie about how we're going to have to fly home.

"In the meantime, (Bob) McGinn (award-winning Packers beat reporter for the *Milwaukee Journal-Sentinel*) is calling me, and McGinn is giving me "well, how do you feel that you haven't been picked, that you've been passed over?" He calls me two or three times, and you know how aggressive he can be. So, I've got him, and then here comes a knock on the door. I am so excited. I get up, open the door, and it's the maid asking me if want ice.

"Then I get another knock. This one wants to know if I wanted the bed turned down. By now I'm convinced that I'm not in. About 20 minutes later, the real knock comes and I'm in. It's David Baker, who is the president of the Hall of Fame. I open the door and there he is, David Baker, telling me I've been elected to the Hall of Fame."

Wolf was not overcome by gleeful hysteria at this point. He began thinking about people who he estimated had accomplished more than he had. He was deeply gratified, but his feelings were not unmixed.

"Believe me, I was really honored, thinking about all the people that are in, all the people that will never be in. I was Number 295 and survived a lot of stuff. I was delighted that I got in, I know that. I don't know how to describe it. I want to say it's a magical moment, but my magical moment happened in Lambeau Field when we beat Carolina (in the NFC championship game on Jan. 12, 1997). That was my magical moment."

There it was, the collective achievement rising above the individual recognition. That's exactly the kind of thing that governed Wolf's tenure as the boss of the Green Bay football operation. Personal accolades were nice, but what lasted was the team's triumph. How could an NFC championship be more of a "magical moment" than a Super Bowl victory? Here's how: It happened at Lambeau Field.

Next up on the agenda of everlasting recognition was Ron Wolf's enshrinement in the Pro Football Hall of Fame, on August 8, 2015. It was accompanied by the usual qualities: humility and a droll sense of humor.

"To think that Ronnie Wolf, from New Freedom, Pennsylvania, who graduated 101st in a class of 83 from Susquehannock High School, is being inducted into this fabled Hall, is truly remarkable," Wolf said in his induction speech.

He succinctly summarized the task he faced, of turning the Green Bay franchise, from something of a punishment gulag to a championship team.

"At that time, there was always a threat to players of other teams that if they didn't shape up, they would be traded to Green Bay," Wolf said. "We worked hard to eliminate that stigma. Suddenly, players wanted to come and be a part of football's most illustrious franchise and to play in pro football's most storied cathedral, Lambeau Field."

Wolf dropped his voice an octave on "Lambeau Field" for the necessary tone, reverence, and historical reference point. Apart from that, this was not a speech laden with oratorical flourishes.

Wolf, who genuinely does not like public speaking, had a remarkably brief acceptance speech—six minutes, 48 seconds—much of which was taken up with expressions of gratitude to all the appropriate people. He concluded:

"As my Dad would say: 'I love a good speaker. I truly do. Not one who is polished, but one who is through.' Thank you, thank you very much.

"Go Pack go!"

Fittingly, Wolf was presented for induction by his son, Eliot, who recalled coming home from school as a child, and sitting down to watch game film with his father. The elder Wolf, Eliot said, enjoyed having his son there with him, "But he wasn't there to babysit me. He was there to build championship teams."

Eliot also recalled, more recently, dropping in at his parents' house, and seeing his father, in retirement, getting ready to watch game films of, for instance, the 1948 Chicago Cardinals.

"I'm just thinking: 'What are you doing?' Eliot said. "But he loves the game so much. There is not a higher honor he could see in the whole world, to be enshrined in the Mecca that is the Pro Football Hall of Fame."

In a boyhood recollection not shared with the Hall of Fame audience, Eliot Wolf smiled at his father's refusal to let familial logistical problems take him away from his work.

"I remember one time in high school, I don't know what I was doing, but I got to school, I dropped something out of the car, shut the door, locked the door with the engine still running," Eliot said. "And it was during draft meetings. My Mom was somewhere else. And he was in draft meetings. He ended up sending Shaun Herock, one of the area scouts, over with a set of keys. Shaun goes: 'Thanks for getting me out.' But it was one of those things where my Dad wasn't about to babysit my dumb ass for doing that."

The topic of the senior Wolf's enshrinement had earlier been discussed, but not in a particularly serious vein.

"That was something we always joked about," Eliot said. "It was like: 'Hey, Dad, when you get inducted into the Hall of Fame, I'm going to (present) you.' And we'd laugh. To actually have that come to fruition, it was really unbelievable to be a part of it. Just knowing what it meant to him, that's the culmination. I mean, he's so into the history of the league, and the legacy of the league, and proud of the league. He saw where it started and where it is now. That was really cool, just to see how happy he was. Some of the coolest moments of the weekend were backstage with the other inductees when they were all telling each other stories. It was just unbelievable. Charles Haley, Bill Polian, Eddie DeBartolo. It was pretty cool to be a part of that."

The 2015 Hall of Fame class is, in alphabetical order, Jerome Bettis, Tim Brown, Charles Haley, Bill Polian, Junior Seau, Will Shields, Mick Tingelhoff, Ron Wolf.

Here is a telling anecdote from a moment just before Ron Wolf was presented as a Hall of Famer.

"This is a good one," Eliot says with a smile. "He did that while we were at the Hall of Fame. Tim Brown comes into the Hall of Fame in the same year. My Dad drafted Tim Brown. So apparently, the Raiders were at six and they were trying to get Paul Gruber, the tackle from Wisconsin. So, the night before the draft they thought they had a deal to get up to Number 2 to get Gruber. And something happened where it fell through, but they still thought they were okay. But then Tampa

Bay picks Paul Gruber. Al Davis has, I don't know if it's a panic attack, but he leaves the room. So, there's three receivers there: Tim Brown, Michael Irvin, Sterling Sharpe. Now my Dad is getting ready to give his Hall of Fame speech. He goes: 'Ah, Irvin, Sharpe, Brown. I probably picked the wrong guy.' I'm looking at him like: 'You're crazy. The guy is going into the Hall of Fame.' I know what he means, he was the third best guy, but still . . ."

That anecdote is the essential Ron Wolf. He's about to be enshrined in the Hall of Fame and he's second-guessing his draft pick from 27 years ago, a draft pick who, just like Wolf, is going into the Hall of Fame.

Ron Wolf belongs in the Hall of Fame, primarily as a representative of a franchise that has been at the core of professional football's success. Walking through the galleries of the Pro Football Hall of Fame in Canton, Ohio, it is impossible to escape the pervasive Packer presence. There are 27 Green Bay players enshrined there and three leaders of the franchise, each representing an era of greatness—Earl (Curly) Lambeau, Vince Lombardi, and Ron Wolf.

There is Packers greatness wherever you look at Canton, from John (Johnny Blood) McNally to Brett Favre. The Packers are even represented in the exceedingly rare mistake by a bubble bum card company. A 1957 Topps card had Howie Ferguson, a Packer fullback in the 1950s, as "Howie Furgeson." Ferguson was good enough to get into the Packers Hall of Fame, and it must be said that he is in the building at Canton.

Through 2018 there were 318 members of the Hall of Fame, which means that nearly 10 percent of those enshrined were Packers. This is not only a tribute to the franchise's longevity—2019 is its 100th anniversary—but to those three eras of greatness. Lambeau founded the franchise, nurtured it, kept it alive against heavy odds, and won six NFL titles in the process. Lombardi staged a remarkable revival and became a larger than life figure in American culture, as pro football's emergence as an essential portion of American television programming coincided with the dominance of Lombardi's Packers. No less than Lombardi, Wolf took a franchise that appeared to be completely stagnated and moved it to the top of the game.

"The only historical analogy I can give you for what Ron accomplished is Vince Lombardi," said Bud Selig, a member of the Packers Board of Directors when Wolf arrived, and, after 22 years as Commissioner of Baseball, himself a member of the National Baseball Hall of Fame. "Nobody deserved the Hall of Fame more than Ron Wolf did. I've known a lot of executives in all sports. There isn't anybody that I respect more than I respect Ron Wolf."

For friends and associates of Ron Wolf, his enshrinement was a time of joy. Wolf wasn't much on tooting his own horn. Here was the official word that his career had been nothing less than great.

"As soon as the announcement that he had been elected to the Hall of Fame ran across the bottom of the screen, I called him on his cell," Bob Harlan said. "I said, 'I couldn't be happier, and I don't know of anyone who deserves it more than you do for what you did for this franchise.' I was thrilled. He deserves it without a doubt. He saved a franchise. It's that simple."

"He is just so smart," LeRoy Butler said. "He is always ahead of the game. I was so glad he got to the Hall of Fame. That made me feel like I was getting in."

"I was honored to be invited to his induction," Walt Jocketty said. "The treatment and the hospitality we had was phenomenal. I was proud to be there, associated with Ron, and I had known a few of the guys who were up there—Dick Vermeil and Mike Holmgren I had met before—and just being there was a privilege. Probably one of the biggest thrills was when Brett Favre came in and he introduced us to Brett. That was pretty cool. I've known quality athletes, but that guy is something special. For Favre to come up there and be a part of that and for him to be there for Ron was something special."

The former Cardinals were also represented at the induction by Hall of Fame manager Tony La Russa, and former trainer Barry Weinberg. "We knew of him, and just that alone was enough as far as credentials," La Russa said. "But then when you get to know him personally, displaying the depth of his knowledge, and then you became aware of how many organizations still reach out to him when they're hiring a coach or a coordinator or something, because he's so respected by the entire industry. You know that's true and you're impressed. But when you get to know him, you understand it; just the depth of knowledge that he has and the goodness of him as a person."

Wolf's droll humor and tendency to relive his own mistakes, were fully present on even this auspicious occasion.

"It's funny because when he went into the Hall of Fame at Canton, we were staying at the same hotel and Ron really took care of me when we were there," said Mark Schiefelbein. "We got on the bus and there's no place to sit. So, Ron, as an inductee, had a driver and we get in his car. Ron's in the front, in the back is Eliot, his presenter, and Coach Holmgren, and me, we're all jammed in the back, as we're driving, I said: 'Hey, Ron, after we lost to Tampa Bay, 31–3, to go 0–2 in 1992, did you ever think you'd be here right now?' And he started laughing. He said: 'I went 0–14 with Tampa Bay. I thought: I'm going to go 0–16 here.'"

Mike Holmgren remembered all that he had learned from Wolf and relished the way their relationship had meshed.

"I was very fortunate to have, my first head coaching job in the league, to have Ron, because he kind of walked me through some things when I'd get a little sideways," Holmgren said. "I learned, I watched his work ethic, I watched how he was with people, I could even get him to laugh a little bit, I could tease him. He'd ride on my motorcycle sometimes. It was good.

"And the fact that there was no owner, and you had Bob Harlan over in that wing of the building, running the business, and the only times that Bob would come down into my office, all he would say to me was: 'Do you need anything? What can I do for you?' That's kind of what he did. And Ron said: 'My responsibility that I have here, it's almost like I'm the owner.' He wasn't the owner but when I'm talking to him, I'm talking to the man who has the juice. It was good. It was a good time."

"Oh, there's no doubt that Ron revived that franchise," said Wolf's close friend Bill Parcells, himself a Hall of Fame head coach. "But the key thing in these sports is that you have to have a philosophy on personnel. It can't just be 'well, this guy's a good player, that guy's a good player.' You just can't be throwing darts. You have to know what you're looking for, specifically, and things that you can fit into the system that your coaches are employing. Everybody has to have an understanding of that. And that's what he did for Green Bay. I mean what kind of backs Ron was going to have? I knew what kind of receivers he was looking for, I knew what he wanted his tight end to be, I knew what he wanted to be defensively at those positions. I mean, after a while, when you see people integrate people into their team and you see it repeatedly, like I could see it with Coach (Tom) Landry in Dallas, I knew what kind of players he was looking for."

Brett Favre may still be the best evidence and the strongest advocate for Wolf's place in football history.

"He sent me a message: 'Twenty-five years ago I made the trade, the greatest trade I ever made, it made my career, blah, blah,'" Favre said. "And I said back to him: 'No. No. Ron, without that trade, with that genius mind, seeing something that others didn't, including myself. I was confident, but I didn't have to stick my neck out there. He did . . . In all honesty, and we have to be honest, and Ron will never take the credit, you get players, but someone has to select them. To me, it's about the GM, his overall conception of what is good and getting the players, which is the ultimate thing.

". . . It's about the right ingredients. And that takes the right GM, and that's the most important part. And the coach, Ron hired Mike Holmgren. He orchestrated maybe the greatest free agent acquisition in the history of the NFL in Reggie White. So, what a mastermind. He's not going to take that credit, but I did what he envisioned me doing. I didn't do anything that he didn't think I could do. Looking back, did he think it was going to be as good as it was? I don't know. But he obviously stuck his neck out there, and that could have made him or broke him right away. But he saw something that others didn't see. But isn't that the mark of what makes him so great?"

In his 2016 Hall of Fame induction speech, Favre said:

"I stood right here on the back of the stage last year and I watched Ron Wolf being inducted into the Hall of Fame and I could not have been more proud. Ron Wolf is the single most important person to the Packers' rebirth than any person out there; player, coach, GM. It had been almost 25 years since the Packers had any success when Ron Wolf took over. And since then, we all know what the Packers have done.

"Without Ron Wolf, Mike Holmgren would not have coached in Green Bay. There would not have been a Brett Favre, there would not have been a Favre-to-(Sterling) Sharpe, (Donald) Driver, (Robert) Brooks, (Antonio) Freeman, (Mark) Chmura, Keith Jackson, Dorsey Levens, Edgar Bennett, Frank Winters, Santana Dotson, Andre Rison, the list goes on and on.

"The single biggest free agent acquisition in NFL history is Reggie White. And as I like to say: Ron Wolf made it cool to come to Green Bay. So, I thank you, Ron, for believing in me, seeing something in me that others didn't see, probably including myself. And sticking your neck out there for one of the riskiest and craziest trades in NFL history, when you decided to trade a first-round draft choice for me, to Atlanta. So, I say thank you, Ron. I love you. You mean more to me than anyone."

The Ron Wolf portion of Favre's speech drew resounding cheers. Then again, Favre's speech, a heartfelt, emotional, and compelling 36-minute oration encompassing the personal and the professional Brett Favre, was at the other end of the spectrum from Wolf's concise remarks. The Wolf speech was a more modest effort, but its aims were still achieved.

"It was a pretty good speech," Dean Spanos said of Wolf's enshrinement address. "He told me he was practicing and practicing and practicing. You know Ron, he's sort of a low-key guy. He doesn't look for the stage front like some people do. And that's why you like him, one of the reasons that you like him so much. It was a great thing for him, and I know he was very proud. His work product over the years has been incredible. So, it's richly deserved."

"That was a really special experience—I just felt intensely proud of him," Wolf's oldest son, Jonathan, said of the Hall of Fame induction. "He was so humbled about that, in keeping with his character, for someone who grew up seeing the sacrifices he made, seeing the thousands of hours he put into this, the dedication of his life to his work, it seemed like an appropriate accolade.

"Down in Florida with my father, I think it was just the two of us, when he got the call that he was (a finalist for the Hall of Fame). I remember how incredibly humbled he was at that moment. That was really significant for me to see, to see what a profound impact this had on him. And I think that it made me that much prouder of him, because I knew how important it was to him, how big of a deal he felt it was. And that made me realize how big of a deal it was to me."

"Just seeing him at the Hall of Fame, interacting with the greats of the game, to know that he's really a part of that now—that's just so special to my Dad," Eliot Wolf said. "When he got inducted into the Hall of Fame, I cried. I doubt that he did, but I just knew what it meant to him. Just his love of the game. His love of the history of it is really something."

Ron Wolf, never forgetting where he came from, shared the Hall of Fame experience with his lifetime friends.

"It gave a thrill to me as his friend," Neil Harvey said. "I was glad to get the special invitation to go out there, and be a part of that as a spectator, and to meet the other inductees and meet the other individuals at the Hall. Ron called me the night of the vote and he was happy. He'd made the final list and it was a final vote and he was quite happy. But he wasn't one to blow his horn about it. But with me he did say how happy he was.

"And he said: 'Can you believe that a guy from New Freedom got into the Football Hall of Fame?'

"Oh, my God, I thought, he deserved it," Larry Krebs said. "He knew what he was talking about when it came to scouting. He just knew. Of course, he put a lot of time into it, too.

"He would have succeeded in whatever he did. There's no doubt in my mind, absolutely. Work ethic—talk to Edie about that some time. And his boy is just like him, Eliot. He's walking in his old man's shoes. It's quite a family."

And that takes us directly to the topic of the Hall of Fame supporting cast, starring Edie Wolf. Time and time again, during the interviews for this book, Ron Wolf returned, without prompting, to a central theme of his success: Edie made it all possible. A lot of people thank everybody from their coach, to the training staff, to the entire agency that represents them. This is a man who fully comprehends that without his spouse, he could not have achieved what he wanted to achieve.

"She was wonderful to me because she let me do what I wanted to do," Wolf said. "She let me live my dream. That was a tremendous approach for her, because she has her own career (as a clinical psychologist) and her career was very important to her. It's a strange profession in that you have to get a license in each state you want to practice. She had to take the California boards and she had just taken the Florida boards. Then when we moved to New York, she had to do the New York thing. When we moved to Wisconsin, she had to do the Wisconsin thing."

Wolf's scouting report on his wife is: "She's very, very intelligent, and tough." Edie Wolf had her own career, but with her husband on the road scouting, or spending endless hours watching film, she also had a household full of responsibilities.

"She has a very strong personality, and in that way, she's tough," Ron Wolf said. "She raised our two boys, all by herself, I was never there. She did a heck of a job.

"She bought into it and she allowed all this to happen. This would not have happened without Edie, and without her commitment to raising a family, and to herself and to her profession, and to me. Family was always important to her and she made sure that everything was in order, that the boys were taken care of. The boys went to school, she drove them. When we were in LA, she took them to a school where it was going to benefit them. They were first."

On the topic of Ron giving all credit to her for taking care of the rest of the family, allowing him to do his job the way he wanted to do it, Edie Wolf says:

"I don't think I necessarily understood the extent to which it would happen. Although when I met Ron he was in football and he traveled a lot, so I knew he would be gone. That's something people ask me: 'Wasn't it hard having him gone all the time?' That was an expectation I had since day one. Even when he was with Tampa, he was traveling a lot. I'm an independent person and kind of like to be independent, so having him gone wasn't necessarily a problem," she said with a chuckle.

"I missed him, but being able to run the house the way I wanted to run it, being able to run the family the way I wanted to run it, was okay with me. I mean, that fit. Maybe I didn't understand how much I would have to do that, but it was fine with me. I never saw that as a problem. Part of watching my own parents, it was part of the era in which roles were clearly defined. The mother did the things in the house, the father did the things outside the house; work, yard work, everything outside. And the mother was essentially in charge of the children. That was the model that I grew up with and my parents had a great marriage and were not unhappy with their roles. So, I think that was part of my recognition, too, that even though I knew I wanted to have a career, I knew that in order to have the career, I would still play the role of the traditional mother in the family. And I would run the household. And it was never a problem for me. And, of course, my profession lent itself to that. I had a private practice which I could run any way I wanted. I didn't have a boss. I had no one setting my hours. So, if the kids needed me to take them to a Cub Scout meeting, or watch them play soccer or something, I just didn't schedule any patients that afternoon. So, it was ideal in that respect. And I always had an office in my home, always. So, again, I had no commute time, I didn't have to deal with an office staff. In between patients I could pop over and put a load of laundry in. It was perfect."

"My most favorite Mother's Day gift was when Ron and the boys bought me a riding mower, because I also did the lawn," Edie Wolf said with a hearty laugh. "That was my most favorite gift. I loved that mower."

Moving frequently was a challenge—Tampa to Oakland to Los Angeles to New York to Green Bay. But Edie Wolf had a mindset for every locale.

"I'm an adaptable person and I always looked at each move as more of an adventure," she said. "And also, I'm a very optimistic person, so I always looked at it as, 'Okay, I haven't ever lived in this part of the country, or I haven't been here, what can I learn, or what new people can I meet?' So, to me, lots of people say, 'it must be hard to move.' But really, it was not hard to move. I sort of developed a way of learning how to immediately get involved in a community. So even when we were moving, and the kids were small, I think I always looked at it as an adventure. 'Okay, this is a new place for me to sort of conquer.' And I really didn't find it that difficult."

Green Bay, of course, would be entirely different. It would be life under a microscope for a prominent Packer official and his family. Again, Edie Wolf found the positive aspects of this situation.

"People in Green Bay knew that we were moving here, so right away, I was contacted by a number of charitable boards, asking me if I wanted to serve," she said. "And it was solely because I was his wife. Of course, they wanted the Packers' connection. So right away I met a whole bunch of people that I wouldn't normally have met.

"The flip side of that, and to be honest with you, this is the part of my personality that Ron did not share. I kind of like being a big fish in a small pond. I kind of like the idea that we got some attention that we got just because of his position. He does not like that, but I kind of liked that. But the other side of it is that, people are very respectful. We could go out to dinner, even at the height of Ron's success, people would not bother us. They might walk by the table and say: 'Great game!' And/or 'Good luck this Sunday!' But they wouldn't stop because they recognized we were out to dinner with our family. I found that very endearing. People in Green Bay are impressed with Ron, but they're also respectful."

Ron Wolf was not an immediate hero in Green Bay, what with trading a Number 1 draft choice for a quarterback who almost never got off the Atlanta bench, or firing the occasional long-term employee of the Packers operation. Having a father who made decisions for the Packers, was a higher profile proposition.

"I remember playing in the neighborhood a little bit, and getting basically what they would call bullied now, about the Favre trade and coming home all upset," Eliot Wolf said. "And this was before he had played a game.

"Or we would be getting crap over someone who was fired or releasing a popular player. I talked to my mother about it and she definitely helped me figure out how to handle it."

"I think the boys were in third and fourth grade when we moved here," Edie Wolf said. "And we came here in the middle of the (school) year, in February. So, they were thrown immediately into unfamiliar school classes. And after a couple of weeks one of them came home very upset because some kids at school had bad-mouthed Ron for some firing. He had fired somebody, and I'm sure these kids had heard their parents at home talking about 'how could he come in and fire this person?' I don't even know who it was. And so, these kids had made derogatory comments about Ron to our kids. They were very upset. So, I sat them down and explained to them the nature of what they might hear, practiced with them how they might respond, and it never was an issue after that. Not that they didn't hear things. I'm sure that they heard things, but they weren't thrown by it any more. But by and large, everyone was very positive."

The topic of Ron entering the Hall of Fame was brought up periodically, by Edie, over the years, and routinely dismissed by Ron.

"For years I would say: 'One of these years, you'll get into the Hall of Fame," Edie said. "He would just say, 'No, it's not going to happen.' And he really believed because 'I'm in the kind of position that doesn't get elected to the Hall of Fame.' I just thought to myself: 'I hope that if it happens, it happens before he dies.' Because occasionally, they will put somebody in posthumously, and to me, that's an incredible waste. Why bother? For the family? I always thought to myself: 'If they don't do it while he's alive, don't bother. Don't do it because I'm going to feel good about it.'

"So, when it happened, when he was nominated, he really was dumbfounded. I know a lot of people will say that, but he really was dumbfounded. You could have knocked him over. He really did not expect it."

No, he did not expect it, but the record virtually shouts that he deserved it. Ron Wolf has had a number of other honors, among them having a street named after him in Ashwaubenon, Wisconsin, the municipality that borders Lambeau Field on three sides. Ron Wolf Way is near the new Titletown District, a commercial development in the area surrounding the stadium being undertaken by the Packers.

The street was officially made Ron Wolf Way in September 2017. The naming ceremony was well-attended by current and former Packers employees. "This is as much a part of you as it is of me," Wolf told them. "This is a tremendous honor."

Wolf was inducted into the Wisconsin Athletic Hall of Fame on January 24, 2019. Co-hosting this event was Donald Driver, three times a Pro Bowl selection for the Packers as a wide receiver, Driver had emerged from a truly difficult childhood in Houston, where he had been frequently homeless, to star at Alcorn State. While he played football there, Driver was much more noted for being a world-class high jumper. But in the 1999 NFL draft, Wolf selected Driver in the seventh round with the 213th overall pick. By the end of Driver's career, he was the Packers' all-time leader in receptions with 743 and receiving yards with 10,137. It was yet another case of Ron Wolf seeing possibilities that few others could see.

"This person here has something special, incredible in my heart," Driver said in the introduction of Wolf. "This guy gave me a chance . . . He is one of my closest, closest friends. I love him to death. He changed my life forever."

Wolf expressed his gratitude for the honor of induction and then said: "Let me introduce the person who made this award possible: My wife and best friend, Edie. She allowed me to live my dream and without her devotion to our family, I wouldn't be standing here today."

Wolf thanked Pepper Burruss, whom he had brought in as head athletic trainer, noting that Burruss was actually his first hire in Green Bay, even though he was not able to join the Packers until a year later. And he thanked Jeanne Bruette, his administrative assistant in Green Bay. "Jeanne was my sounding board," Wolf said, "and provided me with the necessary ingredients with her integrity and honesty that made a lot of my decisions easier."

Wolf subsequently referred to himself as "one of the most fortunate individuals in the United States of America." Wolf's remarks were, of course, much more concise than those of the typical inductee. He has made a virtue of being publicly terse, and it is apparent that he has done some research in order to bolster his case.

Wolf ended by thanking the fans for their undying support, and he concluded that he accepted this award on behalf of everyone who had worked with him on the restoration of the Green Bay franchise.

So, the awards have piled up for Wolf. He could without stretching a point, look upon himself as one of the all-time greats, although he probably won't seize that opportunity. He is thrilled to be able to hang out with the all-time greats. Since he watched the Baltimore Colts as a teenager, he has regarded Gino Marchetti as one of the greatest defensive ends in history. Marchetti died in April, but two years before that, Wolf sat with him at a Hall of Fame function and was elated. "I'm sitting with Gino Marchetti at a table and I'm this far off the ground," Wolf said. "And he was just a normal person."

The talk shifts to his son Eliot, taking over the Number 2 spot with the Browns. The rest of us think this is a golden opportunity because the Browns won one game over the 2016–17 seasons, and John Dorsey and Eliot will do much, much better than that. But Ron Wolf looks at Cleveland football with the long view and sees back to a time when the Browns were nothing short of great, such as the early '50s. Starting in 1950, the Browns played for six straight league championships and won three of them.

"You look at those guys the Browns had," Wolf says. "My goodness were they good. A guy like Marion Motley (a bruising fullback who became a Hall of Famer). Punter, Horace Gillom. Amazing. I know as a youngster I never saw a punt go that high. And they all wore high-tops. (Hall of Fame quarterback) Otto Graham. (Running back) Dub Jones, "Special Delivery Jones." (Placekicker/left tackle) Lou Groza. Frank Gatski was the center, big man then (6–3, 233)."

This is part of the football pageant that presents itself to Ron Wolf as the history of the game. Some of it, he saw in person. All of it, it seems, he has watched on film.

"All those things, I feel very fortunate to grow up and have an opportunity to watch those things," he said. "Even more fortunate to be able to live my dream, to be able to work in professional football. I'm forever grateful for that."

Wolf was fortunate to live out a dream by working in football. But it was a two-way street. The game was fortunate to have him.

In his Pro Football Hall of Fame speech, Wolf atypically but appropriately, dipped into another sport for a reference.

Wolf said: "To succeed in this game, you have to love it, respect its history and understand you have a responsibility to make it better. Michael Jordan said that, but the same applies to professional football. The ultimate team game."

That was what Wolf's guys would call the ultimate Ron-ism. It was a team game in Green Bay, for Wolf; from the players to the scouts, to the equipment manager, to the training room to the home front. All of it was working as he had hoped, because good people, the right people, were involved at every level.

Yes, at points he was lucky. Anyone who has a marriage that works as well for both partners as the Ron/Edie match must be considered fortunate.

But at work, Wolf was also intelligent, persistent, relentless, tireless and demanding, of himself as well as others. Beyond the qualities that he embodied that made success possible, he found an ideal in Green Bay. And that was the notion of the historic greatness of the Packer franchise. That was his Holy Grail; the revival, the restoration, the resurrection of this franchise.

For all the playing talent he brought in, for all the coaches he hired, for everybody who worked in the structure on Lombardi Ave., and/or worked on the practice facilities on the east side of Oneida St. for Brett Favre, and Mike Holmgren and Reggie White and Le Roy Butler and yes, Bruce Wilkerson, for all of that and all of them, the one central, indispensable part of this operation was Ron Wolf. He took the Green Bay franchise from the doorstep of oblivion to a Super Bowl championship, and he provided the structure that, even beyond that, allowed for another generation of Packers success.

That's the stuff of legendary achievement. That's Hall of Fame stuff. That's the story of Ronnie Wolf, from New Freedom, Pennsylvania.

ACKNOWLEDGMENTS

MY SONS, DAVID and Daniel Bauman, reminded me of how important the work on this book was, not only with the usual familial encouragement, but with the example of their devotion to the Green Bay Packers as a fundamental part of a Wisconsin heritage.

My son, Andrew Dunn-Bauman, read the draft versions of this book and made extremely helpful suggestions. His ability with the English language has my complete admiration.

During the writing of this book, my wife, Kathleen Dunn, put up with some prima donna behavior from her husband. But she consistently displayed her usual good humor and tolerance. It could be argued that she had practice tolerating that sort of conduct well before this book was written.

Every person who was interviewed for this book, provided knowledge, candor, insight, and a real enthusiasm for the project. To all of those people, sincere and lasting thanks for helping to turn an idea into a book.

Ronnie Alvarado of Skyhorse Publishing, edited this book with care, comprehension, and insight. Larry Baldassaro, an accomplished baseball author, supplied valuable assistance and invaluable friendship during this process

And to Ron Wolf, thanks for the golden opportunity to tell a story that was truly worth telling. The Packers' revival under your direction is a superb story, by any standard. Even with that, your willingness to critically examine your own work may be relatively rare at the Hall of Fame level, but it certainly is refreshing.